Get Hired!
How to Land the Ideal Federal Job and Negotiate a Top Salary

- **Leads to Hot Openings • Resumes & Cover Letters**
- **Application Essays (KSAs) • Interview Skills**
- **Salaries**

By
Lily Whiteman
Federal Career Coach

Published by:
FPMI • 101 Quality Circle
Huntsville, AL 35806
(256) 539-1850 • Fax: (256) 539-0911

Internet Address:
www.fpmi.com

ENDORSEMENTS FOR
INSIDER'S GUIDE TO LANDING FEDERAL JOBS

- This book will become an instant classic. It is chock-full of make-or-break advice — available nowhere else — about every step of the job-search process. Moreover, this is the only book to provide comprehensive guidance on fast-track federal hiring programs for women, students, minorities, veterans and applicants with disabilities.

  — **Kelly Paisley,** former Deputy Director of the Vice-President's National Partnership for Reinventing Government; Political Consultant

- Lily Whiteman's enlightening, entertaining book will teach you everything you need to know about how to put the right spin on your credentials on paper and in person.

  — **Ray Kurzweil,** Recipient of the National Medal of Technology, the nation's highest honor in technology/Best-selling author of *The Age of Spiritual Machines*

- In my former position as Chief Financial Officer of the US Mint, I hired and promoted many professionals of all levels. Based upon this experience, I enthusiastically endorse this book. It provides excellent advice on preparing succinct, informative and eye-catching applications, and on navigating the federal hiring process.

  — **Jay Weinstein,** former Chief Financial Officer of the US Mint

- Lily Whiteman has successfully combined classic job search strategies with a customized approach to the often confusing and mysterious federal job application process. With humor and an insider's credibility, she navigates the reader through the maze of creating powerful KSAs, readable and appropriately formatted federal resumes, cover letters **(and the biggest surprise of all: salary negotiation!)** She sheds brilliant, demystifying light on the hiring culture within the public sector. *Get Hired!* is an invaluable resource for job seekers and those who coach them.

  — **Renee Howatt,** Career Management Consultant, Result Strategies *(ResultStrategies.com)* in Washington DC

- This is the most complete federal career guide around. Whiteman provides valuable insights into how the federal application process works, how federal hiring managers think about applicants, how to find openings and how applicants can effectively present themselves in resumes, applications and interviews. She skillfully uses humor and provides real-life success stories to educate and cheer on readers who may otherwise find federal job searches exhausting and baffling.

  — **Robert Pernick, PhD,** Principal of The Amherst Group - Management & Organization Development Consultants/former Personnel Psychologist at the U.S. Office of Personnel Management

- In *Get Hired!*, an expert gives away her expertise. Peppered with humor, *Get Hired!* presents reader-friendly, easy-to-follow advice about the entire job search process — from finding openings and internships to writing applications, interviewing and negotiating salaries. With its creative style, real-life examples and thorough guidance, this book even makes the universally dreaded (but essential) task of writing application essays (KSAs) easy.

  — **Annetta Cheek,** Federal communications expert and leader of the federal plain language initiative

- *Get Hired!* will jump-start the careers of recent graduates and rev the careers of experienced professionals.

  — **Rick Cherwitz,** Associate Dean of the Graduate School (1995-2003)/Professor of Communication Studies and Rhetoric/Director of the Intellectual Entrepreneurship Program, University of Texas at Austin

PREFACE:
COMMON MYTHS ABOUT FEDERAL JOBS
fpmi

PREFACE
COMMON MYTHS ABOUT FEDERAL JOBS

1. **Federal salaries are low. No!** The average federal salary for new college grads is almost $40,000. The average federal white-collar salary in Washington DC tops $75,000, and the worldwide average approaches $60,000. Many feds earn more than their private sector counterparts. Also some new hires receive tens of thousands of dollars in signing bonuses. <u>This is the only career guide that gives the lowdown on federal salaries and bonuses.</u>

2. **Federal salaries are nonnegotiable. No!** Federal salaries and some benefits, such as student loan repayments worth up to $60,000, are usually negotiable. <u>This is the only career guide that instructs federal applicants on salary negotiations.</u>

"I had the dream about meaningful employment again last night."

3. **The best qualified applicant always gets the job. No!** The applicant who submits the most impressive application and gives the best interview usually gets the job. <u>This book provides the most comprehensive advice on preparing applications and interviewing for federal jobs that is available anywhere.</u>

4. **Federal internships do not pay. No!** Dozens of paying federal internship programs are open to college students, grad students, law students and recent grads. <u>This book provides the most comprehensive list of paying federal internships that is available anywhere.</u>

5. **The federal workforce is not diverse. No!** Forty-five percent of feds are women; 30 percent are minorities; and seven percent have disabilities. If you belong to one of these groups, you may be eligible to participate in fast-track hiring programs. <u>This book provides the most comprehensive explanations of federal diversity programs that is available anywhere.</u>

6. **The federal government is a single monolithic mass. No!** Federal agencies are as different from one another as are private organizations. Everything from pay scales to the level of formality within the office varies from agency to agency. <u>This book provides the most comprehensive advice on how to research federal agencies that is available anywhere.</u>

7. **It takes forever to get hired by the feds. No!** Job applicants are frequently interviewed within a couple of weeks of applying. New federal procedures are reducing the entire hiring process to 45 days.

8. **Government work is dull and unimaginative. No!** Government professionals use creativity and judgment to carry out public policies that impact millions of people. The job of making the world a better place is exhilarating.

9. **You have to pass a Civil Service test to become a fed. No!** The Civil Service test went the way of the Dodo bird; it doesn't exist anymore. Today, only a very few types of entry-level jobs require tests.

10. **Work schedules in the federal government are rigid. No!** Most federal agencies allow employees to, within reason, set their own daily arrival and departure times, work at home part of the week, and work longer hours on some days in exchange for taking off every other Friday.

11. **You must have inside connections to become a fed. No!** Federal agencies are literally bursting at the seams with employees — from entry-level to seasoned professionals — who got hired without inside connections.

12. **Most feds are lazy, dim-witted and nerdy. No!** Forget oddballs like Neuman on *Seinfeld* and Cliff Claven on *Cheers*. Most feds are tech-savvy, intelligent go-getters. Moreover, the federal workforce is steadily becoming younger and more educated.

13. **Most federal jobs are based in Washington DC. No!** About 85 percent of federal jobs are located outside of the Washington DC area.

14. **If you have previously been rejected for a federal job, it's not worthwhile to apply for another job. No!** Federal agencies advertise more than 15,000 openings every day and hire more than 250,000 new employees every year. Your standing in any particular job selection has no bearing on your standing in another selection.

15. **Large numbers of federal jobs are being privatized. No!** So far, only several thousand jobs have been privatized. Such losses are more than offset by a retirement wave that will likely open up half of the federal government's 2.7 million jobs during the next few years.

SECTION I:
GEARING UP TO APPLY

CHAPTER 1:
A GOOD TIME TO GO FEDERAL

The best way to predict your future is to create it.

— Unknown

The federal government has jobs that you won't find anywhere else. You can be a spy…a volcano watcher…a park ranger…a terrorist hunter…a disease detective…a curator of precious historical documents…a diplomat… The possibilities are practically infinite.

Federal employees work in every imaginable setting, from offices, laboratories, museums, libraries, hospitals, parks, forests and marine sanctuaries located throughout the United States to embassies located in far-flung countries. In fact, more than 80 percent of federal jobs are based outside of Washington DC.

And government salaries are nothing to sneeze at. Starting salaries for college graduates may exceed $50,000, and those for masters graduates may exceed $55,000. High-demand professionals, such as Information Technology Specialists, may command even higher starting salaries. Salaries of senior managers, with bonuses, may top a whopping $200,000.

> **The federal government is the nation's largest employer, employing about 2.7 million civilians. More than 200,000 new hires join the federal government each year.**

Moreover, the federal government is one of the few places where you can work an exciting job, earn a competitive salary and still have a life. Most federal employees stick to a 40-hour work week.

The federal government also offers these first-rate perks:

- **Steady Career Tracks:** Uncle Sam is hiring all the time for all types of jobs and internships — even when other organizations are laying off. And while non-governmental employees may be pink-slipped when the economy falters, federal employees are hardly ever laid off. Also, it is generally much harder to fire federal employees than employees in other sectors.

- **Advancement:** Federal employees are eligible for regularly scheduled promotions and receive annual cost-of-living salary increases that usually range from two to five percent. For more information about federal salaries, see Chapter 12.

- **Great Benies:** Full-time federal employees earn 10 paid holidays, and 13, 20 or 26 days of vacation each year, depending upon how long they have been employed by the federal government. They can take up to 12 weeks of unpaid leave to attend to a birth, adoption or seriously ill family member. In addition, federal employees are covered by top-notch health insurance, life insurance, retirement and investment programs.

- **Flexible Schedules:** The federal government's flexible work schedule programs and telecommuting programs are freeing many federal employees from the straight jacket

"True, the private sector has its benefits, but, then again, so does the public trough."

of nine-to-five work schedules. Such programs are, for example, enabling more and more federal employees to work at home several days per week. In addition, many federal employees can opt to work nine hours per day in exchange for taking off every other Friday.

- **Loose Academic Loans:** Some federal agencies will repay up to $60,000 of the student loans of a new hire who agrees to stay at the agency for at least three years.

- **Stay Close To The Kids:** Many federal agencies offer on-site childcare facilities.

- **Be a Do-Gooder:** The ultimate aim of most federal jobs is — in one way or another — to better the world. In the words of a Peace Corps staffer, "I am doing what I love to do, and it's all for a very good cause."

THE BRAIN DRAIN

Do you hear that giant sucking sound? It's the sound of the brain drain in the federal government. Indeed, the federal government, which currently employs more people in their 60s than in their 20s, is rapidly losing its most experienced professionals to retirement.

> **THE RIPPLE EFFECT OF THE RETIREMENT WAVE**
>
> For every retirement at top grades, human resource officers should deal with three or four staffing actions as lower level employees move up to fill the spots of outgoing managers and professionals.
>
> — *Government Executive* Magazine

The federal government predicts that by 2010, about 600,000 civil servants will retire, including up to 70 percent of the senior managers of some federal agencies. As the top brass bows out of the federal government, opportunities for swiftly climbing up the federal career ladder will only improve.

The federal job market probably will not be significantly impacted by a controversial "competitive sourcing" initiative that is designed to transfer some federal jobs to the private sector. So far, only several thousand jobs have been privatized through this initiative. Such losses are more than offset by the federal retirement wave.

NEW BLOOD

When you think of government employees, do you visualize school-marmish women and pocket protector-clad men toiling in musty offices? If so, your perceptions are overdue for an update.

Indeed, statistics show that the federal workforce is steadily becoming more skilled and more educated. And largely because of the approaching retirement wave and because of renewed interest in government service inspired by 9/11, "a potential for a quasi-youth movement in the government job sector" promises to infuse the federal government with new, revitalizing blood and fresh ideas, according to monster.com. In other words, the federal government is registering lower and lower on the stodgy-meter.

WHY YOU SHOULD READ THIS BOOK

Let's face it. We all know that — despite its changing face — the federal government is no stranger to bureaucracy. Partly because it must obey more regulations than other organizations, and partly because of its large size, the federal government's job application procedures are more complicated and time-consuming than those of other types of employers.

But a little red tape shouldn't stand between you and an interesting, well-paying, career-boosting job in the federal government. This book will help you cut through the red tape and enable you to churn out applications that will wow federal hiring managers.

Unlike any other how-to-get-a-government-job book, this book is the *only* federal career guide that:

✓ Is written by a federal career counselor — an experienced professional who dishes the dirt on how the system *really* works.

✓ Divulges little know strategies for finding jobs that are located in the US and overseas.

✓ Instructs you how to craft applications that will prove that you are a producer, and how to present yourself in interviews as the perfect employee. This instruction — which incorporates the advice of scores of hiring managers and reflects the experiences of hundreds of applicants for federal jobs — is applicable to everyone from entry-level applicants to executives.

✓ Thoroughly explains the federal selection process so that you can design your application to meet its special demands.

✓ Equips you with one-of-a-kind crib sheets and lists of dos and don'ts that will help you dazzle hiring managers.

✓ Is loaded with examples of resumes, application essays and cover letters that are specially designed to be eye-catching and brain-catching, and ensure that you STAND OUT FROM THE PACK!

✓ Explodes the myth, which is perpetuated by all other how-to-get-a-federal-job books, that federal salaries are not negotiable. This book gives you the skinny on how to negotiate a big fat federal salary.

✓ Warns of common fatal mistakes, and teaches sure-fire strategies for avoiding them.

✓ Directs you to the hottest internships and jobs for college students, graduate students, law students and recent graduates, and to dynamic fellowships for experienced professionals.

✓ Describes fast-track hiring programs for minorities, disabled professionals, veterans and women.

✓ Comes with a CD that provides beautifully formatted resumes that you can customize for yourself.

✓ Presents tips for mastering online applications.

✓ Features the latest federal jobs websites.

✓ Will keep you inspired through engaging writing, humorous asides and motivating real-life stories.

CHAPTER 2:
THE SEARCH IS ON: FINDING OPENINGS
fpmi

CHAPTER 2: THE SEARCH IS ON: FINDING OPENINGS

The first step toward success is taken when you refuse to be a captive of the environment in which you first find yourself.

— Mark Caine, Author of *The S-Man; A Grammar of Success*

You're at square one of your job search: Finding openings. But don't feel bad. Square one is way more comfy and serene than it used to be. Gone are the days when job-searchers had to race around town, trying to snatch up the latest published lists of job openings before other frenzied job-searchers beat them to the punch, or — dressed in their finest and most uncomfortable interview attire — stumbled blindly from door-to-door in search of openings.

Now, job-seekers like you can surf at home through cyber lists of job openings — dressed in your sweat pants and nursing your cappuccino. And instead of just dreaming at work about telling your boss to take that job and shove it, you can easily sneak peeks of cyber listings from your desk on your lunchbreak.

This chapter directs you to the best websites and other promising sources of announcements of federal job openings that suit your background and explains how to cultivate inside contacts who can pull for you from within the federal government.

WHAT CREDENTIALS DO YOU NEED?

Some federal jobs require college degrees and some require graduate degrees, but many federal jobs do not require college degrees at all. In addition, many jobs accept work experience as a substitute for degrees. In the words of the Office of Personnel Management, which is the federal government's human resources agency, "The nature of your specialized experience is what really counts."

The requirements for each job opening are spelled out in its announcement. For more information about federal salaries and what salary range you should aim for, see Chapter 12.

THE FEDERAL JOBS HOTLINE

USAJOBS (*usajobs.opm.gov*) is the official jobs website of the federal government. Clicking on USAJOBs is like hitting the mother lode of federal job openings; the site announces more than 15,000 jobs per day and is updated every business day.

Included among USAJOBS's listings are jobs located all over the world, and jobs that are at every level of almost every conceivable occupation. USAJOBS also announces some state, local and private sector job openings, and features links to the employment websites of many

H O T • T I P

DON'T WASTE YOUR MONEY
Several commercial websites charge members to access searchable lists of current federal job openings, and to receive customized lists of job openings by e-mail. USAJOBS provides these same services at no charge. Why pay for what you can get for free?

federal and state organizations. If you are unsure of which federal job titles best match your skills and interests, the resources posted at *http://career.usajobs.opm.gov* can help you identify them.

WHAT USAJOBS DOES NOT PROVIDE

Most jobs at federal agencies that are open to the public must be posted on USAJOBS. But some types of federal jobs are not required to be posted on USAJOBS. These jobs include jobs in the legislative and judicial branches, jobs that are only open to the hiring agency's current employees and jobs that are in the Excepted Service rather than the Competitive Service.

What is the difference between Competitive Service jobs and Excepted Service jobs? Competitive Service jobs — which account for the majority of federal jobs — must be advertised and filled through open competitions. By contrast, Excepted Service jobs can be filled through relatively flexible procedures designed by the hiring agency.

The Excepted Service includes the FBI, the CIA, the State Department and various other agencies. To access a list of Excepted Service agencies, go to *opm.gov.* Then click on the following sequence of links: "Career Opportunities"…"Job FAQs"…"Excepted Service Agencies." In addition, all federal attorneys, chaplains, doctors, dentists and nurses belong to the Excepted Service.

If you want to work for an Excepted Service agency or another federal organization that is not required to post its announcements on USAJOBS, look for its openings on the career section of its website. (Many Excepted Service jobs are advertised on USAJOBS even though they are not required to be.)

Also, note that most of the internships, recruitment programs and fellowships covered in Chapter 3 are not listed on USAJOBS.

VACANCY ANNOUNCEMENTS

Job announcements for federal jobs are called vacancy announcements. You can search USAJOBS's collection of vacancy announcements by various criteria, including keywords, salary, geographic location, job title and hiring agency. You can also instruct USAJOBS to automatically search for the types of jobs that you specify, and to regularly e-mail you vacancy announcements for jobs that meet your specifications. Access to USAJOBS and the site's services are provided for no charge.

THE WINDOW OF OPPORTUNITY

The window of opportunity for applying for federal job openings varies. Some jobs are advertised for several weeks or longer. But others are advertised for the minimum amount of time required by law: five business days for jobs that are open to all qualified applicants, and three business days for jobs that are open to current federal employees.

Agencies tend to keep the window of opportunity for applying short when they want to fill positions quickly, or when they expect to receive particularly large number of applications — either because they are posting particularly popular jobs or because high unemployment rates are boosting application numbers. Make sure that you don't miss out on juicy openings by surfing through USAJOBS's listings every few days.

OTHER SOURCES OF FEDERAL OPENINGS

You may also find vacancy announcements via:

➡ **Federal Websites:** It is a good idea to regularly check agency websites in addition to USAJOBS. Why? Because some agencies announce openings on their own websites before posting them to USAJOBS. In addition, although most federal agencies do post their openings on USAJOBS, they are not all required to do so. Further, many jobs in the legislative and judicial branches of government are not listed on USAJOBS. (You can access links to the websites of all federal agencies and links to organizations in the legislative and judicial branches of government on USAJOBS.)

➡ **Newspapers and Magazines:** The classified ads in the Sunday and online editions of newspapers list some federal openings. In addition, the hardcopy edition of *Government Executive* magazine features an executive recruitment section. Sign up for a free subscription to this publication at *governmentexecutive.com*. If you are looking for a job in Washington DC, also peruse these websites:

- The jobs section of the online version of *The Washington Post*. See *washingtonpost.com/wl/jobs/home*.

- The jobs section of the online version of *Roll Call*, a newspaper devoted to Capitol Hill. See *rollcall.com*.

- The "Hills Jobs" section of *Congressional Quarterly* magazine's website at *cq.com*.

➡ **Federal Jobs Telephone Hotlines:** An interactive telephone version of USAJOBS operates around the clock, 365 days per year. You can reach this hotline at 703-724-1850 or TDD at 978-461-8404. The headquarters offices and regional offices of some federal agencies also have their own jobs hotlines. You may find these phone numbers on agency websites, in the blue government pages of the telephone book or by calling information. Some federal jobs hotlines feature fax-on-demand functions.

➡ **Special Kiosks in Federal Agencies:** Touch screen computer kiosks that list federal job openings are located in many federal agencies throughout the nation, federal buildings and some colleges and universities.

➡ **Job Fairs:** See discussion of job fairs in this chapter.

➡ **The Human Resources Offices of Federal Agencies:** These offices can inform you of advertised openings as well as unadvertised openings that will be filled through special, streamlined procedures by special categories of applicants, including veterans, disabled applicants, displaced federal employees, returned Peace Corps Volunteers and Bilingual/Bicultural applicants. If you belong to one of these special categories of applicants, see "Ways That Federal Jobs Are Filled" on page 67, and Appendices 1 and 2.

➡ **The Senior Environmental Employment Program (SEEP):** This program hires retired and unemployed Americans who are at least 55 years old for clerical, administrative, writing, grant specialist, accounting, engineering, research and other jobs that support Environmental Protection Agency (EPA) programs. SEEP jobs are available in many cities, regional EPA offices and laboratories. (SEEP is funded by EPA, but SEEPers are not federal employers; instead, SEEPers are employed by SEEP.) See *epa.gov/rtp/retirement/see.htm*.

SEEP openings are not posted on USAJOBS. To find SEEP openings, check with the aging-related organizations that recruit for SEEP positions. These organizations are:

✓ The National Caucus & Center on Black Aged, Inc.
✓ The National Council on Aging
✓ The National Senior Citizens Education & Research Center
✓ The National Association for Hispanic Elderly
✓ The National Older Worker Career Center
✓ The National Asian Pacific Center on Aging

➡ **Post Offices:** The Postal Service hires from 85 district offices at the local level. Your local postal service is the best information source for postal jobs. The "Jobs" section of the Postal Services' website at *usps.gov* also lists openings.

➡ **The Senate Employment Office:** Go to *senate.gov;* then click on "Visitors."

➡ **The House of Representatives Employment Office:** Go to *house.gov/cao-hr.*

➠ **The National Academies of Science (NAS) Website:** NAS is a quasi-government organization that employs scientists, policy experts and administrative personnel. See *nas.edu;* then click on "Employment." (Because NAS is not a federal agency, NAS openings are not posted on USAJOBS.)

PROGRAMS FOR WOMEN, MINORITIES AND DISABLED JOB-SEEKERS

ATTENTION!

If you are a woman, a member of a minority or a disabled job-seeker, you may be eligible to participate in programs that are helping to increase the diversity of the federal workforce:

• Applicants who are fluent in Spanish or familiar with Hispanic culture should consider the Bilingual/Bicultural Program, which is discussed in Chapter 4.

• College students, graduate students and recent graduates should consider the internship and student jobs programs for minorities, disabled applicants and women that are highlighted in Chapter 3.

• Experienced professionals should consider the Office of Personnel Management's Senior Executive Service Candidate Development Program, which is discussed in Chapter 5.

In addition, special programs for veterans are discussed in Appendix 1, and special programs for people with disabilities are discussed in Appendix 2. Also, the SEEP Program for retired professionals is discussed on page 23.

Wonder which agencies are the best promoters of workforce diversity? According to an analysis conducted by the Partnership for Public Service, the top five federal promoters of workforce diversity are NASA, the Department of Energy, the Department of Commerce, the Department of Agriculture, and the General Services Administration. For more information about the rankings of federal agencies in workforce diversity, see *bestplacestowork.org.* In addition, the FBI is aggressively recruiting minorities and women for varied types of positions. As part of this effort, the agency regularly participates in career fairs that are announced at *fbijobs.com.*

RESEARCH...RESEARCH...RESEARCH

The federal government is not a single monolithic mass. Indeed, federal agencies are as different from one another as are private companies. Characteristics that vary from agency to agency include pay scales, management's willingness to reward high performers with bonuses and promotions, the average age of staffers, the agency's commitment to diversity, the level of office formality, how hierarchical offices are, and whether staffers tend to work cooperatively or compete against one another.

By researching federal agencies, you may identify agencies that:

➠ Are in the hiring mode.

➠ Are leading special recruitment drives that involve offers of recruitment bonuses or special fast-track hiring procedures.

➠ Offer particularly enticing pay scales. (For more information about federal pay scales and recruitment bonuses, see Chapter 12.)

➠ Promote an organizational culture that jives with your style.

What's more, the knowledge you gain about agency-specific priorities through your research will also help you gear your application to your target agency. Here are some free online resources that provide truckloads of information about federal agencies:

> **Many job-seekers believe that an outsider without inside contacts will never get hired by the federal government. Not so. The offices of federal agencies are bursting at the seams with employees who landed their jobs without any inside pull.**

➠ A frequently updated collection of articles of special interest to young feds and recent grads who are job searching is posted at *fendonline.com/youngfeds/index.htm.*

➠ The "Employment" sections of agency websites, explain salary and benefit policies, and may identify any ongoing recruitment drives and hiring bonuses. Links to agency websites are provided on *usajobs.opm.gov.*

➠ The "Government" section of *The Washington Post's* online edition, which features informative articles on federal hiring practices, trends, benefits, career strategies and what types of employees are in high demand. To access this site, go to *WashingtonPost.com;* click on the "Jobs" link on the upper right corner and then the "Government" link on the lower right corner. Also, sign up for *The Washington Post's* free daily e-mail newsletter, *The Federal Insider,* which provides updates on issues affecting federal workers. See *washingtonpost.com/ac2/wp-dyn/admin/email?referrer=email.*

➠ *FedNews™ OnLine,* a free daily newsletter published by FPMI Solutions for federal employees that often includes articles about hiring trends and other human resource issues that impact job-seekers. Subscribe to this newsletter at *fpmisolutions.com.*

➠ The website of the Partnership for Public Service, a non-profit that promotes federal careers. See *ourpublicservice.org.* Check out the site's daily and quarterly newsletters, which you can access by clicking on the site's "Press Room" tab. Also, review the Partnership for Public Service's annual survey of the best federal agencies to work, which is posted under "Rankings" at *bestplacestowork.org,* and blurbs describing the organizational culture and achievements of some federal agencies, which are posted under "Analysis and Profiles" at *bestplacestowork.org.*

➠ The website of *Washingtonian* magazine at *Washingtonian.com.* Every year (usually in October or November), *Washingtonian* ranks the best places to work in Washington DC, including the best federal agencies. The blurbs accompanying *Washingtonian's* rankings yield valuable insights about the organizational culture of various agencies. Rankings for several recent years are posted on the magazine's website at *washingtonian.com/etc/business/great_places_to_work/govt.html* and *washingtonian.com/etc/business/great_places_to_work/agencies.html*. Find other listings by accessing the online archive of back issues.

➡ The website of *Government Executive* at *GovernmentExecutive.com*. Pay special attention to this site's "Pay and Benefits" and "Jobs and Careers" sections. Also peruse monthly issues of *Government Executive*, which you can access by clicking on the magazine icon that appears on the upper right corner of the website's home page. And sign up for *Government Executive's* free daily e-mail newsletter at *governmentexecutive.com/email*.

➡ The website of *Federal Times* at *federaltimes.com*. Pay special attention to this site's "Top News", "Career Info" and "Management Issues" sections, which frequently post articles about hiring trends, federal recruitment drives and other personnel matters affecting job searchers.

➡ Monster.com's weekly newsletter on government/public service careers. You can sign up for this excellent newsletter at *http://my.monster.com/newsletters.asp*.

➡ Mike Causey's daily *Federal Report*, which is posted at *federalnewsradio.com*.

➡ The website of *Federal Computer Week* at *fcw.com*, and *The Washington Post's* Government IT website at *washingtonpost.com/wp-dyn/technology/govtit/review*. These sites describe trends in government IT practices and hiring that will interest computer professionals.

JOB FAIRS

The federal government frequently sponsors and co-sponsors job fairs throughout the nation. At a single event, you may meet directly with hiring managers from ten or more agencies that are recruiting for jobs at all levels. Some agencies use these events to fill high-priority jobs or internships through fast-track procedures or even on-the-spot offers.

Find job fairs that are attended exclusively by federal agencies by checking:

➡ USAJOBS for a list of federally sponsored career fairs.

➡ Local newspapers for advertisements for federal career fairs.

"I do intend to seek employment, but it will be at a time and place of my own choosing."

➠ The career sections of websites of federal agencies, which are more likely than USAJOBS to announce jobs fairs that are sponsored by a single federal agency than privately sponsored fairs that draw only a few federal agencies.

The federal government also occasionally sponsors virtual job fairs. During such events, which each usually last about one week, a one-stop website broadcasts announcements and accepts applications for high-priority job openings at various federal agencies. Hiring selections are usually made from these online applications via fast-track procedures. Virtual job fairs are announced on USAJOBS.

TEN TIPS FOR FARING WELL AT JOB FAIRS

1. Before the fair, check which agencies will attend. Then, troll through the websites of your target agencies so that you will be able to pepper each meet-and-greet conversation with evidence of your knowledge of the agency's goals and high-profile activities. Be sure to read the agency's recent press releases, which are probably posted on the agency's website.

2. Practice introducing yourself with a 30-second, punchy opener that highlights your key qualifications and how they would benefit the agency.

3. Present yourself as a decisive, goal-oriented job-seeker who knows what type of job you want. Recruiters are universally turned-off by job-seekers who expect career guidance from recruiters.

4. Prepare yourself for an on-the-spot job interview by reviewing Chapter 11.

5. Pack the following items in a professional brief case: 1) Twice as many resumes as you anticipate distributing. 2) Business or networking cards to distribute to potential employers and other networking contacts. (You can professionally print hundreds of business cards for less than $20.) 3) A portfolio of your work, including explanatory maps or charts, superior performance evaluations, awards, published articles, relevant papers, print-outs of web pages, artwork or samples of other work products. 4) A writing tablet for note-taking.

6. Dress as you would for a job interview. No eating or gum chewing.

7. Come to the fair alone. Don't bring significant others, parents or friends. By doing so, you will help prove that you are a sure-footed professional who doesn't lean on others or bring your personal baggage to the office.

8. Collect the business cards of contacts so that you will have the correct spellings of their names, titles and contact information.

9. If a recruiter does not have openings that are suitable for you, ask him/her for other leads.

10. Immediately after the fair, send thank you letters to helpful contacts, and follow up on promising leads.

FINDING OVERSEAS JOBS

FINDING AGENCY OPENINGS

Are you a globe-trotting adventurer? If so, you might be in the market for overseas federal jobs. More than 93,000 federal staffers are based overseas. Some of these staffers hold permanent positions and others hold temporary, contract positions known as personal service contracts.

Here are the major ways that the federal government recruits for overseas jobs:

➠ Permanent overseas jobs that are open to the public are usually announced on USAJOBS and/or agency websites. (Some permanent federal overseas jobs are only open to current agency employees and so are not advertised to the public.)

➠ Personal service contracts are announced on *Fedbizopps.gov.* To find openings for personal service contracts, go to *Fedbizopps.gov,* click on "Vendors" and then browse through agency listings. (Be aware that *Fedbizopps.gov* advertises for other types of contracts besides just personal service contracts.) Personal service contracts may also be announced on nongovernment jobs websites, such as *globalcorps.com.* (Openings for personal service contracts are rarely listed on USAJOBS.)

➠ The State Department advertises overseas Civil Service and Foreign Service jobs. For more information about these jobs, go to *state.gov* and then click on "Employment."

➠ Federal civilian jobs devoted to rebuilding Iraq and Afghanistan are advertised at *usajobs.opm.gov/sofia.asp* and on a website call SOFIA — short for Support Our Friends in Iraq and Afghanistan. See *http://cpolwapp.belvoir.army.mil/sofia.*

➠ The United States Agency for International Development recruits for its International Development Intern Program and its New Entry Professional Program. The World Bank and United Nations Population Fund also have recruitment programs that may lead to permanent overseas positions. In addition, the State Department's Fascell Fellowship Program places fellows overseas. Also, some Smithsonian Institution Internships are based overseas. See Chapter 3 for more information about these programs.

➠ Teaching positions in schools for the dependents of military personnel are announced by the Department of Defense Education Activity. Go to *odedodea.edu;* then click on "Human Resources" and "Employment." Contact information for other government organizations that recruit teachers for international positions is posted at *usajobs.opm.gov/ei26.asp, http:// exchanges.state.gov/education/engteaching/eal-jobs.htm#jobs* and *state.gov/m/a/os/c6776.htm.*

Remember to look for leads for overseas jobs in the news. As one overseas contractor observed, "I just read in the newspaper that the U.S. is opening a huge embassy in Iraq. So that is where I will target my job search."

AGENCIES THAT HAVE OVERSEAS JOBS

Agencies that may have openings for overseas jobs or for jobs that involve significant international travel include the African Development Foundation, Agency for International Development, Bureau of International Labor Affairs, the Air Force, Department of Agriculture, the Army, Department of Commerce, Department of Defense, Environmental Protection Agency, Fish and Wildlife Service, the Navy, International Trade Administration, Peace Corps, Overseas Private Investment Corporation, U.S. Geological Survey, U.S. Information Agency, and U.S. International Trade Commission. To access links to any of these agencies, go to *usajobsopm.gov*, and then click on "Explore Other Agencies" under "GOVERNMENT LINKS."

Agencies that belong to the intelligence community also have overseas jobs. *Intelligence.gov* is the intelligence community's website; it features links to all intelligence agencies.

INTERNATIONAL ORGANIZATIONS
For information about jobs with international organizations including the United Nations, go to *state.gov*, and then click on these links: 'Employment" ... "International Vacancy Announcements."

OVERSEAS FAMILIES
The dependents and spouses of overseas federal employees sometimes receive priority consideration for jobs at US overseas facilities.

ROLODEX STUFFING ACTIVITIES

You certainly don't *need* to have friends in the federal government in order to land a federal job. But it never hurts to have friends in high places. They can advance your job search by:

➠ Creating a job for you. Yes, under some circumstances, a federal hiring manager can tailor a job opening to the credentials of a particularly desirable applicant, and thereby ensure that the applicant will be a shoe-in for the position.

➠ Pulling strings for you with other hiring managers.

➠ Informing you of job openings as they develop.

➠ Referring you to other promising contacts.

MAKE A ROLODEX CONNECTION

Remember the rule about six degrees of separation? It says that every person on Earth is connected to any other person through six contacts or fewer. Well, you are probably connected to a juicy opening through only one or two degrees of separation. In fact, studies show that almost 40 percent of current federal employees were steered towards their current jobs by tips about openings from relatives or friends.

And I have heard many personal accounts that bear out this statistic. For example, I know a federal Writer who learned about her current position through a conversation with a stranger in the elevator of her apartment building; a Marketing Manager who was invited to apply for her current position after one of her clients, a government contractor, put in a good word for her at her current agency; and a Public Affairs Specialist who landed her position by submitting her resume to her current agency after the wheels had been greased for her by a family friend who was a former employee of that agency.

> # SALLY SMITH
>
> 10 Rose Avenue, NW Washington DC 20008   (202) 345-1111/SallySmith@email.com
>
> ## Executive Assistant
>
> **10 years of award-winning experience:**
> - **Managing the calendars of busy executives**
> - **Organizing all aspects of domestic and international travel**
> - **Managing high-traffic switchboards**
> - **Shepherding high-profile documents through the approval process**

What worked for current federal employees could work for you too. Increase your chances of hitting employment paydirt by working your Rolodex. Tell everyone you know about your job search. And ask everyone you know to tell everyone they know…And so on.

CREATE A NETWORKING CARD

Make it easy for your contacts to sing your praises by arming them with networking cards. These days, you can print business cards right on your own computer. Or better yet, you can professionally print hundreds of business cards for less than $20.

Hand out your networking cards to friends, family, colleagues, the parents of your childrens' friends, your spouse's colleagues, friends of your parents, neighbors and fellow residents of your apartment building. Don't hold back; shyness is the enemy of the job-seeker: Hand out your card with wild abandon. Give them to fellow travelers on trains, planes and buses. Pass them out at family gatherings and parties. Hawk yourself at meetings of:

- ✓ Professional organizations
- ✓ Religious groups
- ✓ Alumni organizations
- ✓ Community and PTA groups
- ✓ Political groups

BREAK OUT OF YOUR CUBICLE

If you are currently a federal employee, stuff your networking Rolodex by joining workgroups, committees and task forces, and by signing on to detail assignments that will expose you to colleagues from other offices within your agency or to professionals who work in other agencies. Enhance your chances of being appointed to such groups by informing your supervisor of your interest in them.

Also attend meetings of professional organizations in your field that are likely to be attended by other professionals who may offer promising leads. Stay in touch with new contacts by inviting them to lunch or other social outings.

If you want to branch out into a new field, look for opportunities within your current job that may provide pivotal experience. For example, I know a professional at a federal agency who wanted to land a job in Equal Employment Opportunities (EEO) management. How did she do it? She volunteered to help her agency's EEO office process EEO complaints as a collateral duty of her job. This experience helped her land a new job solely dedicated to EEO issues.

You may also gain pivotal experience by volunteering with organizations besides your employer. As Janet Hanson, the founder of a billion dollar investment firm and a networking guru, told *ELLE* magazine, "Volunteering is one thing you don't have to ask permission to do. You can go beyond your job description — there are no boundaries, roadblocks or glass ceilings."

COLD CALLING

Another method of making important contacts is by calling and sending your resume to federal agencies that do the type of work that interests you. But be aware that cold calling may be a more productive strategy for landing jobs in agencies that belong to the Excepted Service than those that belong to the Competitive Service. Why? Because the relatively flexible hiring procedures followed by Excepted Service agencies enable them to snatch up applicants on a spontaneous, ad hoc basis more easily than can agencies in the Competitive Service.

If you do cold calling or cold mailing, be sure to aim your efforts at a specific person. If, for example, you send your resume to a nameless recipient, such as "To Whom It May Concern," it is unlikely to concern anyone.

You may be able to obtain a copy of an agency's employee directory from its website or Public Affairs Office.

N E T W O R K I N G · S U C C E S S · S T O R Y

I GOT THE JOB!

BY KATHRYN BERNARDO, FINANCIAL MANAGER

After working in various financial management positions at the same federal agency for a number of years, I hit a dead end; it became clear that I was not going to advance any further at that agency. It was time to find greener pastures.

AN ALTERNATIVE STRATEGY

I applied for a number of jobs through USAJOBS. But none of my applications panned out. So I decided to try an entirely different strategy that involved two prongs. The first prong of this strategy involved consulting a licensed social worker/career coach through the Employee Assistance Program (EAP) at my agency. (Every federal agency has an EAP that provides counseling to federal employees at no charge.) My EAP counselor helped me get into a positive, job seeking mind-set. She also helped me analyze my career, understand why I had run into career obstacles, and figure out how to steer clear of such obstacles in the future.

The second prong of my strategy involved aggressive networking. I joined and became active in numerous organizations in the Washington DC area, including a sailing club and a ski club. At the same time, I completed my MBA, and prepared to take the Certified Public Accountant and the Certified Management Accountant exams.

A CHANCE TO SHINE

My volunteer and professional activities required significant time commitments. But I am a very social and outgoing person, so I enjoyed them. And these activities exposed me to dozens and dozens of professionals whom I would not have otherwise met. In addition, the positive feedback that I received from the people I met in these activities helped boost my confidence for my job search.

Moreover, I ultimately assumed leadership roles in the clubs that I joined. In these positions, I displayed my abilities to my volunteer contacts; put my ideas into action; and proved that I am knowledgeable, energetic and conscientious. In short, my volunteer contacts watched me in action, and I showed them that I handled myself well in responsible positions.

THE PAYOFF

I attended a fund-raiser that was organized by a friend whom I met through one of my volunteer activities. The guitarist of the band playing at the fundraiser asked me for my resume, and passed it on to the management of a new federal agency. A few interviews later, I was hired by that agency as a GS-15 Program Analyst in Financial Management.

If not for my networking, I never would have landed this position, which is a promotion over my previous position. The moral of my story is that if you identify your strengths and pursue a strategy that plays on them, you will probably also be successful in your job search.

FOLLOW THE MONEY: FIND FEDERAL CONTRACT JOBS

Many federal contractors work on federal projects without being full-fledged federal employees. That is, these contractors do federal work, are supervised by federal managers, and are based in the offices of federal agencies. But such agency-based federal contractors are not employed or directly paid by the federal government. Instead, they are employed and paid by another organization that hired them and holds a contract with the federal government.

Because agency-based federal contractors work cheek-to-jowl with federal employees, agency-based contracting assignments provide ideal opportunities for networking, gaining government experience and earning a salary while you job search. Indeed, many agency-based federal contractors are eventually hired into full-time federal positions.

There are two major types of federal contractors:

1. Contractors who work for consulting firms that have contracted with a federal agency to provide specific services. The federal government is currently spinning off more and more projects into federal contracts that are awarded to such consulting firms.

    You can find job openings with federal contractors by checking job websites such as *monster.com* and *http://hotjobs.yahoo.com*, and the Sunday classified sections of newspapers, particularly *The Washington Post*, which occasionally includes a special section devoted to government contracting jobs. In addition, you can search *The Washington Post's* listing of current job openings for Government Contractors, which is posted at *washingtonpost.com/wp-dyn/politics/fedpage*. (Look for the "Quick Search" box in the lower right hand corner of the page.) These listings include jobs that are located inside as well as outside of Washington DC.

2. Professionals who work for employment agencies that have contracted to help a federal agency fulfill its short-term staffing needs for various types of professionals including Accountants, Contract Managers, Writers, IT Professionals and Administrative Assistants, among many other types of professionals. Note that contracts between employment agencies and federal agencies may change quickly, as federal staffing needs evolve.

    Employment agencies (which may go by such names as temporary staffing or human resources agencies) advertise their contract openings on job websites and the Sunday classified sections of newspapers. In addition, you may find employment agencies that have contracts with federal agencies by calling employment agencies that are listed in your local phone book, and asking whether they help federal agencies staff up.

Here are some other tips for finding temp agencies that contract with the federal government: The Department of State posts contact information for its temporary contracting firms at *state.gov/m/dghr/flo/rsrcs/pubs/7248.htm*. In addition, PoliTemps provides staffing services to some of the top political consultants, public relations firms, associations and non-profits in the Washington DC area. (See *politemps.com*.) Other temporary firms that help staff federal agencies include Adecco (*adecco.com/Channels/adecco/home/home1.asp*); Hire Standard Staffing (*hirestandard.com*); Answer Staffing Services (*answerstaffingservices.com*); and Legal Personnel, Inc., (*legalpersonnelinc.com*). GCS specializes in providing staff to government contactors. (See *gcsinfo.com/services.htm*.)

Be sure to treat your application for temporary work as seriously as you would an application for a permanent position. Most employment agencies look for the same qualities in applicants as do other employers.

T E M P · J O B · S U C C E S S · S T O R Y

I GOT THE JOB!

BY BARRY PHELPS, WRITER/EDITOR

Not long after I was laid off from my job as communications director of a nonprofit company that lost its funding, an ad on an Internet job website caught my eye. The ad, which had been placed by Adecco, a temporary placement firm, was looking for a temporary Writer/Editor job at a federal agency.

I followed up on the ad and things moved quickly. I interviewed with Adecco on a Friday, and I was working at the federal agency by the very next Monday. When my three month contract was over, the agency offered me a full-time federal job. The salary negotiations went well. I am now making more than I made at the nonprofit and at several other federal jobs I have previously had.

The type of seamless segue that I experienced from a temporary contract position to a federal position is not unusual because the federal government has special, streamlined procedures for filling positions that address critical needs.

FIND OUT WHO'S IN THE MONEY

It is a good bet that a consulting firm that has *just* won a new federal contract will soon be staffing up. Therefore, such firms — flush with federal funds — provide strategic targets for searches for contracting jobs.

You can identify companies that have just won federal contracts by:

➡ Regularly scanning your local newspapers for articles mentioning the winners of new federal contracts.

➠ Referring to *The Washington Post's* lists of companies located in Virginia, Maryland, and Washington DC that have just won multi-million dollar federal contracts. These lists appear in the back of the Business section of *The Washington Post's* Monday editions under the heading "Federal Contracts," and are posted on the web at *washingtonpost.com/wp-dyn/business/washingtonbusiness/federalcontracts.*

Once you identify a company that has just won a new federal contract that jives with your skills and interests, call the company's personnel office, and ask for the manager of the new contract. Then, call the contract manager and explain why you would be an asset to the company's contracting team. If you act quickly, you may even reach contract managers before they start recruiting. You may thereby elbow out your potential competition.

BE A NEWS JUNKIE

It is a good idea for all government wannabes to stay abreast of the national agenda, which often influences the hiring practices of federal agencies. After all, the priorities of Congress and the President help determine which federal agencies are hiring. And so too do the headlines. For example, scandals in 2001 involving Enron and other corporate giants compelled agencies that address corporate finance to quickly staff up. Moreover, since 9/11, many defense and intelligence agencies as well as defense contractors have been expanding.

WANTED: INTELLIGENCE AND LANGUAGE EXPERTS

H O T • T I P

In the wake of 9/11, many federal agencies are aggressively recruiting intelligence and language experts. Here are some examples of these recruitment efforts:

• **The National Security Agency is hiring 1,500 new staffers per year** — and offering signing bonuses worth up to $7,500. The agency is particularly interested in experts in languages, intelligence analysis, signals analysis, math, computer science, the physical sciences and acquisition. Non-technical professionals are also being recruited. Go to *NSA.gov;* then click on "Careers."

• **The National Geographic Geospatial-Intelligence Agency**, which studies imagery from spy satellites and other systems, will hire about 900 analysts by 2009. The Defense Intelligence Agency and the Department of Homeland Security will also hire large numbers of intelligence specialists and other professionals in the coming years.

• **The Central Intelligence Agency's Corporate Language Hiring Bonus Program** offers some language specialists hiring bonuses worth up to $35,000. Go to *cia.gov;* the click on the following sequence of links: "CIA Careers"..."Language Positions"..."Foreign Language at the CIA."

• **Federal agencies engaged in Iraqi reconstruction efforts** can use special, fast-track hiring procedures to hire individuals whose fluency in Arabic or other related Middle Eastern languages would support those efforts.

POLITICAL APPOINTMENTS

Granted, you probably won't be named Secretary of State if you don't already have serious inside pull and instant name recognition. But take heart: many of the 7,000 political jobs in the federal government are filled by ordinary, hard-working professionals whose names have never graced *People* magazine.

WHAT THEY ARE

Political appointees include ambassadors, Cabinet members, agency heads, members of regulatory commissions, judges, lawyers and policy specialists. Many of the assistants and members of the immediate staffs of high-ranking officials are also political appointees.

All political jobs in the federal government are filled via nominations from the White House. (Some political jobs require Senate confirmation.) Professionals who have strong affiliations with the President, an administration staffer or the President's political party have the best chances of landing political jobs. But many accomplished professionals who have no inside track land political jobs simply by applying for them.

Political appointees usually spend most of their time designing and advocating administrative policies and working closely with key officials. *READ:* power, influence and prestige.

But the flip side to political positions is that they offer little job security, and most appointees lose their jobs when the administration changes. And the stresses experienced by political appointees are reflected in memoir titles such as *Leaving Town Alive* by former National Endowment for the Arts Chairman John Frohnmayer and *Locked in the Cabinet* by former Labor Secretary Robert Reich.

APPLYING

If you apply for a political appointment, treat your quest like a campaign. The more endorsements you get from powerful advocates, the better. Exploit any White House connections — even distant ones — that you have. Perhaps, for example, your Congressman works closely with an administration official. Recommendations from associations, nonprofits, unions, academics and business leaders will also help.

The best time to apply for political positions is right after a Presidential election. Nevertheless, many political positions turn over between elections.

RESOURCES

A list of political positions is available in *The Plum Book*, which is published after each Presidential election. See *gpoaccess.gov/plumbook/2004*. *A Survivor's Guide for Presidential Nominees* is posted at *brookings.edu/gs/pai/20001511survivorguide.htm*. Applications for political appointments are posted at *whitehouse.gov/appointments*.

THE ENFORCERS

If you are looking for a security or law enforcement job, focus your search on these agencies:

- The Federal Bureau of Investigation
- Immigration and Naturalization Service
- Drug Enforcement Administration
- Federal Bureau of Prisons
- Federal Protection Services
- The Customs Service
- United States Secret Service
- Bureau of Alcohol, Tobacco and Firearms
- Internal Revenue Service
- The Mint
- Bureau of Printing and Engraving
- President's Council on Integrity and Efficiency
- Federal Aviation Administration
- General Services Administration
- The Coast Guard
- The Park Police
- Social Security Administration
- The Marshals Service
- The Capitol Police
- Transportation Security Administration
- The State Department (diplomatic security positions)
- The Intelligence Community
- Department of Justice
- Federal Transit Administration
- The Library of Congress
- Government Printing Office
- US Supreme Court

The Washington Post's collection of articles about careers in law enforcement is posted at *washingtonpost.com/wp-dyn/jobs/governmentcareers/security*. The salaries of federal law enforcement officers vary from agency to agency. For more information about federal law enforcement salaries, see Chapter 12.

CHAPTER 3:
OODLES OF INTERNSHIPS, STUDENT JOBS & FELLOWSHIPS

fpmi

CHAPTER 3: OODLES OF INTERNSHIPS, STUDENT JOBS & FELLOWSHIPS

That summer pretty much settled things. I think I knew from that point on that I was going to be a physicist.

— Deborah Jin, winner of the MacArthur "Genius" Award, discussing in *The Washington Post* her summer job during college conducting research at the Goddard Space Flight Center.

"Let me through! I'm an intern!"

www.cartoonstock.com.

The best way to learn about a field is through a total immersion experience — like those provided by federal internships and student jobs. The federal government currently employs more than 50,000 students and interns. Federal internships and student jobs for undergrads, grad students, law students and recent grads are based all over the nation and overseas. The federal government also offers some well-paying fellowships for seasoned medical researchers, journalists, economists, public policy experts and other mid-career professionals.

In this chapter, you will learn how an internship or student job could jump-start your career, and where to find programs that jive with your interests. All of the programs listed here are paying programs, not volunteer programs — proof that even if you are just starting your career, you don't have to slave for free! This chapter also directs you to some of the most dynamic fellowships in the federal government.

WHATEVER FLOATS YOUR BOAT

Whether your passion is space exploration or more earthly concerns like business, information technology, ecology, law or art history, the federal government runs a career-boosting internship for you.

WHY WORK AN INTERNSHIP OR STUDENT JOB?

Through an internship or student job, you can:

→ **Have eye-opening experiences:** Meet people and learn about issues that are entirely new to you. These exposures may steer you onto career paths that you would not otherwise have known anything about.

→ **Get the real deal:** The best way to learn about an occupation is to work it. An internship or student job may show you whether a particular type of career is all that it's cracked up to be, or whether you want to detour onto another one.

→ **Expand your mind:** Many internships and student jobs involve training.

→ **Enhance your marketability:** An internship or student job will give you expertise that is valued in private industry, the non-profit sector and government. In addition, many internships and student jobs may segue into permanent jobs — like "rental with option to buy" contracts.

→ **Change the world:** Interns and student employees weigh in on important issues, such as environmental problems, medical research, international relations and corporate finance.

Nora Vasquez, a recent college graduate, conducts research at the National Institutes of Health (NIH).
(Photo courtesy of NIH.)

→ **Rub elbows:** Interns work shoulder-to-shoulder with scientists, economists, diplomats, business experts, writers and other professionals who serve as mentors and can provide references for you in the future.

→ **Escape the cubicle farm:** Many internships are based in the world's most magnificent parks, forests and marine sanctuaries and most dynamic museums, libraries, laboratories and embassies.

→ **Last but definitely not least.....Earn a competitive salary.** Some internships, as noted in the internship descriptions on the following pages, even provide housing and cover transportation costs to and from internship programs.

GOVERNMENT-WIDE INTERNSHIPS

The biggest federal internship programs place recent graduates of undergraduate and advanced degree programs in federal agencies throughout the federal government. These programs are:

→ **Federal Career Internship Program:** This program offers two-year assignments, which involve some training, to college graduates. Federal Career Internships may lead to permanent positions. For general program information, see *opm.gov/career intern/index.asp.*

HOT • TIP

BE AN EARLY BIRD

Avoid the manic panic of last minute scrambles for summer internships and jobs. Start scouting for a summer position in the fall and winter.

Unfortunately, the federal government does not centralize information about agency Career Internship Programs. Therefore, to obtain information about agency programs, you must contact agencies individually, search the career sections of agency websites for program information, or conduct online searches using keywords, such as Federal Career Internship Program.

→ **Outstanding Scholar Program:** Eligibility for this program is limited to college graduates who had at least a 3.5 grade point average or who graduated in the upper 10 percent of their class or university subdivision. For program information, see *thejobpage.gov/starting.asp* and *opm.gov/employ/luevano.htm.* Unfortunately, the federal government does not centralize information about agency Outstanding Scholar Programs. Therefore, to obtain information about agency programs, you must use the same methods discussed above in the discussion of the Federal Career Internship Program.

Although the Outstanding Scholar Program is open to professionals of all backgrounds, one of the program's purposes is to increase the representation of minorities in the federal workforce.

→ **Presidential Management Fellows Program:** This program offers highly competitive, prestigious two-year assignments designed to groom talented people for upper management. The program includes training, mentoring and rotational assignments. Because of new flexibilities recently added to the program, Fellows can be appointed anywhere between the GS-9 and GS-12 levels, or their equivalents, and may be promoted without regard to time-in-grade re-

ATTENTION!

ATTENTION MINORITIES, WOMEN AND DISABLED APPLICANTS!

Descriptions of internships and fellowships that are exclusively devoted to minority, disabled or women applicants, or that have components emphasizing such groups are highlighted in this chapter.

quirements. Fellows may also benefit from recruitment incentives, such as student loan repayment programs. Only graduate students who are in their final year of study and who are nominated by their school are eligible to participate in this program. After successful completion of internships, Fellows may be converted into full-time federal employees. See *pmi.opm.gov*. Also see description of Senior Presidential Management Fellows Program under Fellowships for Experienced Professionals in this chapter.

↪ **Workforce Recruitment Program For College Students with Disabilities:** This program recruits substantially disabled college students, graduate students and law students for summer and full-time employment in the federal government and private sector. Interested students can only apply to the program by working through their colleges or universities. See *dol.gov/odep/programs/workforc.htm*.

AGENCY INTERNSHIPS AND RECRUITMENT PROGRAMS

Many federal agencies run internships and special recruitment programs for college grads, grad students, law students and recent grads. Each of these programs has a unique design. This means that application requirements, salaries, training opportunities, the duration of programs and opportunities for advancement differ from program to program. Some programs are located in Washington DC; others are based at locations throughout the US or overseas.

In addition, some non-government organizations place college and grad students in federal offices on internships and student jobs. Participants in these programs work in federal offices, but are recruited and paid by the sponsoring organization. Such programs are just as exciting and enriching as programs that are directly run by federal agencies.

Provided below are descriptions of some of the hottest, most dynamic paying internships and recruitment programs in the federal government. Programs that are run by nongovernment organizations are denoted with an asterisk.

1. **African Development Foundation (ADF) Internship:** ADF seeks applications/proposals for special projects or research to be conducted in Washington DC during the summer. This opportunity is ideal for students who are interested in Africa and are majoring in international affairs, economics, law or other development-related fields. College students, recent grads and grad students are eligible. Go to *adf.gov*, then click on "Employment" and "Internship Opportunities."

2. ***American Association for People With Disabilities (AAPD) Internship Programs:** Two programs place disabled college and university students in summer internships in Congressional offices and federal agencies. One program focuses on Information Technology. See *aapd-dc.org*.

3. ***American Indian Science and Engineering Society Internships:** Summer programs place college and graduate students in federal agencies. Overseas positions with the State Department are available. See *aises.org/highered/internships.*

4. ***American Planning Association Congressional Planning Fellowships:** Fellowships lasting six months are available to grad students and recent grads in planning or related fields. Fellows work directly with Congressional staff in a Capitol Hill office. Projects include conducting policy and legislative research, drafting policy briefs, developing briefings and resources for Congressional staff on planning and livability issues, and serving as liaison to Congressional staff and advocacy organizations interested in planning and smart growth. See *planning.org/institutions/scholarship.htm#1.*

Up a creek without a paddle: Environmental Careers Organization (ECO) Interns Lindsay Kneten and April Barajas travel via airboat through Prime Hook National Wildlife Refuge in Delaware. (Photo courtesy of ECO.)

5. ***American University American Indian Program:** Summer, fall and spring programs are available. Interns take credit courses, work in federal agencies, Congressional offices and Native organizations, and participate in cultural and social activities. Open to American Indians and Alaska Natives who are college students or graduate students. See *american.edu/wins.*

6. **Army Materiel Command (AMC) Programs:** Various internship and management training programs for civilians with the Army's premier provider of materiel readiness. The AMC Fellows Program is a five-year, fast-track program that trains college grads to become managers in logistics, contracting, intelligence, safety and other fields. Paid graduate education (earn while you learn) is offered. See *amccareers.com.*

7. ***Asian Pacific American Institute for Congressional Studies Programs:** Various year-round and summer programs place college students in Congressional offices and federal agencies. See *apaics.org.*

8. **Central Intelligence Agency Programs:** The Graduate Studies Program is open to grad students focusing on international affairs, languages, economics, geography, cartography, physical sciences, engineering and more. Participants become acquainted with the work of professional Intelligence Analysts by contributing to projects. Selected pieces of participants' work may be distributed throughout the intelligence community. See *cia.gov/employment/jobs/students_grad.html.* The Corporate Language Hiring Bonus Program offers some language specialists hiring bonuses worth up to $35,000. Go to *cia.gov;* the click on the following sequence of links: "CIA Careers"…"Language Positions"…"Foreign Language at the CIA."

9. **Central Intelligence Agency DO Undergraduate and Graduate Intern Programs:** Assignments lasting six months are available supporting intelligence and the CIA's overseas stations. Positions may lead to careers in the agency. See *cia.gov/employment/student.html#dousp.*

10. **Central Intelligence Agency Undergraduate Internship Program:** This program favors undergraduates who are a member of a minority or who have a disability. Interns work with highly-skilled professionals and observe first-hand the support provided by the CIA to US officials who design foreign policy. Interns are required to work one semester and one summer, or two 90-day summer internships, in Washington DC. The program favors majors in engineering, computer science, mathematics, economics, physical sciences, foreign languages, area studies, business administration, accounting, international relations, finance, logistics, human resources, geography, national security, studies, military and foreign affairs, political science and graphic design. See *cia.gov/employment/student.html.*

Why spend your summer flipping burgers when you could be hobnobbing with power brokers? (Photo courtesy of the HACU Program.)

11. **Congressional Black Caucus Foundation, Inc Internships:** This program assigns undergraduates to positions in the offices of Congressional Black Caucus Members. Full-time summer positions and part-time spring and fall positions available. See *http://cbcfinc.org/Congressional_Internships.html.*

12. **Congressional Budget Office Internships:** Summer positions are available for graduates of advanced degree programs and undergraduates. This program favors specialists in public policy, economics and public administration. See *cbo.gov/Intern.cfm.*

13. ***Congressional Hispanic Caucus Institute Internships:** Two-month summer positions in Congress for undergraduates. See *chci.org.*

14. **Congressional Research Service (CRS) Law Recruit Program:** CRS provides nonpartisan research, analysis and information that supports informed decision-making by Congress. Third year law students may apply for positions as legislative attorneys. Bar membership must be obtained within 14 months of being hired. See *loc.gov/crsinfo/law2004.html.*

15. **Congressional Research Service Student Diversity Internship Program:** Minority students help experts research varied issues that are on the Congressional agenda, and advise Congress on these subjects. See *loc.gov/crsinfo/internships/#Diversity.*

16. **Defense Intelligence Agency:** Various summer and year-round internships available for college students and grad students. One program focuses on financial management. Go to *dia.mil;* then click on "Careers" and "Student Employment Programs." Minorities, women and the disabled are in demand.

17. **Department of Commerce Summer Legal Internships:** Program is open to law students. Interns address varied issues including trade, labor law, litigation, the environment, patent law, telecommunications and economics. Located in Washington DC, this program features lunches with experts and other social activities. See *ogc.doc.gov/internSummer_info.html.*

Texas Representative Solomon P. Ortiz with interns. (Photo courtesy of the HACU Program.)

18. **Department of Health & Human Services (HHS) Internships and Student Jobs:** Dozens of summer and year-round opportunities are available for high school students, undergraduates and graduate students. See *hhs.gov/careers/students.html.* HHS's Emerging Leaders Program provides particularly appealing opportunities. This two-year program includes extensive training, mentoring, rotational assignments and exposure to high level officials. Program participants pursue scientific, public health, IT, social science or administrative career tracks. Applicants should have a BA and work experience, or a JD, Masters, or Ph.D. See *hhs.gov/jobs/elp.*

19. **Department of Interior Internships:** Three programs offer enhanced development opportunities for high-potential future leaders: The Governmentwide Acquisition Management Intern Program, the Office of the Secretary Management Intern Program, and the Financial Management Career Intern Program. Each internship involves rotational assignments, training and mentoring, and lasts for two years. Applicants must be college graduates. Internships are designed to lead to permanent federal positions. See *doi.gov/doijobs/employ5.html.*

20. **Department of Justice Programs for Lawyers:** The Summer Law Intern Program is a highly competitive summer internship program for law students. The Attorney General's Honors Program is the Department's recruitment program for entry-level attorneys. See *usdoj.gov/careers.*

21. **Department of Labor MBA Fellows Program:** This is a comprehensive, entry level, two-year career development program designed to recruit and nurture the next generation of Department of Labor leaders. This program includes an orientation, rotational assignments, mentoring and networking activities. Applicants should have an MBA, a masters or equivalent and/or business experience. Successful completion of the program may lead to a full-time permanent federal job. See *dol.gov/oasam/doljobs/mba_outreach_program/mba_rotate_ prgm.htm.*

22. **Department of Transportation Internship Program for Diverse Groups:** Promotes the entry of women, people with disabilities, and members of diverse groups into transportation careers. Undergraduates, graduate students and law students address engineering, planning, economics, hazardous materials, environment, criminal justice, aviation and other fields. Interns may work in Washington DC, or in selected field offices around the country during summer programs. They participate in field trips to transportation related organizations and facilities, discuss current transportation issues with key officials and attend seminars. See *flhwa.dot.gov/education/stipdg.htm.*

23. ***Diversity Leadership Internship Programs:** Several programs place minority and disabled college students in Congressional and other government offices. Fall, spring and summer positions available. See *twc.edu.*

24. ***Environmental Careers Organization Internships:** Places college students in federal agencies to work on projects addressing environmental issues. Year-round and summer internships available at locations throughout the nation. Diversity Initiative is devoted to minority recruitment. Greater Research Opportunities Undergraduate Student Fellowships provide generous academic support and summer internships to minority students. See *eco.org.*

A National Zoo intern feeds one of Washington DC's non-political animals. (Photo courtesy of the National Zoo.)

25. **Environmental Protection Agency (EPA) Internships:** The Internship Program is a two-year development program for college grads in diverse fields. It features rotational assignments, networking, mentoring, site visits and group projects. Minorities and other underrepresented groups are aggressively recruited for this program. Under EPA's National Network for Environmental Management Studies, undergraduate and graduate students work full-time during the summer and/or part-time during the school year on environmental policy, regulation and law; environmental management and administration; environmental science; public relations and communications; or computer programming and development. Positions are located throughout the nation. Under EPA's Student Environmental Associate Program and Diversity Initiative, students from varied communities and tribes complete paid on-site trainings lasting three to six months. See the career section of *epa.gov.*

26. **Federal Bureau of Investigation (FBI) Honors Internship:** Undergraduates and graduate students participate in an orientation, and then work side-by-side with Special Agents on important cases in Washington DC or the FBI's forensics laboratory in Quantico, Va. Women and minorities are in particular demand. See *fbi.gov/employment/honors.htm.*

27. **Federal Reserve Board Internships:** Positions are available for undergraduates and graduate students specializing in economics, finance and computer science. Interns work in banking supervision and regulation, economic research and Information Technology. See *federalreserve. gov/careers/info.cfm?whichcategory=8.*

28. **Federal Highway Administration Career Intern Program:** This two-year long program is for college grads interested in the engineering, accounting or administrative aspects of transportation management, design and safety. Interns participate in training and development assignments located throughout the nation, and training in Washington DC. Recruitment bonuses are available. See *flhwa.dot.gov/vacancy/career1.htm.*

29. **Government Accountability Office Programs:** A summer student internship program is for college and graduate students and a two-year Professional Development Program (PDP) is for recent grads. Participants in both programs help investigate federal agencies for Congress and issue recommendations to improve efficiency. Both programs feature training, mentoring, rotational assignments, speakers and special events — both social and professional. Both programs are based in Washington DC and other nationwide locations. Participants in PDP are eligible for promotions every six months. See the careers section of *gao.gov*.

FBI interns analyze forensics. (Photo courtesy of the FBI.)

30. **Global Change Education Program Summer Undergraduate Research Experience:** Undergraduates participate in an orientation, and then spend the rest of the summer working at a national laboratory or university conducting global change research. Each student is assigned a mentor. Participants receive travel and housing support in addition to a stipend. All qualified students are encouraged to apply, but minority and female students are in particularly high demand. See *atmos.anl.gov/gcep*.

31. ***Hispanic Association of Colleges & Universities National Internship Program (HACU):** Offers spring, summer and fall student internships with federal agencies and private corporations nationwide. College students are matched with internships based on their interests and the requests of federal and corporate partners. The program helps interns find housing, hosts an extensive orientation in Washington DC for them, provides round-trip air travel, and arranges various professional, social and cultural activities. See *www.hnip.net*.

32. ***INROADS/Greater Washington Internships:** Places high school, college and graduate students in summer internships in federal agencies located throughout the nation. Interns receive year-round personal coaching and formalized training by INROADS staff. During the summer, interns receive career development training in communication, self/time management, business sophistication and management/leadership skills. In addition, their academic progress is monitored through monthly coaching sessions with an INROADS staff advisor and reviews of college transcripts. Each intern also receives mentoring. See *inroads.org*.

33. **International Monetary Fund (IMF) Internships:** Under the supervision of an economist, grad students in economics or a related field research topics that are of special interest to IMF. Internships last 10 to 13 weeks, and begin throughout the year in Washington DC. Nationals from countries in the southern hemisphere studying in universities located in the southern hemisphere are strongly encouraged to apply. For more information, go to *imf.org*, and then click on "Job Opportunities" and "IMF Internship Program."

34. **John A. Volpe Transportation Internships:** Grad students in engineering, the sciences or the social sciences alternate periods of work and academic study, or continuously work part-time at the Volpe National Transportation Systems Center in Cambridge, Mass. Each intern works side-by-side with transportation leaders and receives a salary plus travel reimbursements and up to $10,000 for tuition. Internships may lead to permanent jobs. See *volpe.dot.gov/career/ intrn-pro.html.*

35. **Legal Honors Intern Programs:** Almost every federal agency has a legal department that hires law students and recent graduates for summer and permanent jobs. Information about the Housing and Urban Development's program is posted at *hud.gov/offices/adm/jobs/ internship.cfm.* (Also see this chapter's description of the Department of Justice's Programs.)

36. **Library of Congress Internships and Fellowships:** Undergraduate and graduate students work on important book, paper, photograph and preventive conservation projects. See *loc.gov/ preserv/servpubs.html* and *loc.gov/rr/jrfell.* The Junior Fellows Program particularly encourages applications from women, minorities and people with disabilities. See *loc.gov/rr/jrfell.*

37. **Martin Luther King, Jr. Scholars Program:** Undergraduates and graduate students who are interested in education policy or public policy work on education policy in the Office of the Secretary of Education in Washington DC during the summer. To obtain information about this program, conduct a keyword search using the program name at *ed.gov.*

38. **Mickey Leland Energy Fellowships:** Summer internships for students in science, engineering or the geosciences who are African Americans, Hispanic or Native Americans. Positions available at Department of Energy facilities located throughout the nation. See *fossil.energy.gov/ education/lelandfellowships.*

39. ***Minority Access, Inc.:** Places minority undergraduates and graduate students in federal agencies for fall, spring or winter assignments. Internships available in Washington DC and in other nationwide locations. Applicants must have at least a 3.0 average. Interns receive travel expenses in addition to salary and are guided in their housing search. This program includes pre-employment training, assistance in financial management and professional development. See *minorityaccess.org.*

40. **Morris K. Udall Foundation's Native American Congressional Internships:** Interns work in Congressional offices or agencies on varied projects from administrative support to report preparation. They also network with decision-makers and attend Congressional hearings, lectures and receptions. The program is for college and grad students, aw students, and recent grads of tribal colleges. Roundtrip airfare to Washington DC, housing and stipends are provided. See *udall.gov/p_internships.asp.*

41. **NASA's Student Temporary Employment Program at the Ames Research Center:** High school students, undergraduates and graduate students work full-time/part-time at any time during the year in a laboratory located in the heart of Silicon Valley on projects addressing

business administration, acquisitions and contract administration, financial management, human resources, computer sciences, electrical engineering and aerospace engineering. All qualified candidates may apply, but racial/ethnic minorities, women, physically disabled people and veterans are in particular demand. See *huminfo.arc.nasa.gov/students/step.html*.

42. **National Academy of Sciences Science & Technology Policy Graduate Fellowships:** Law students and grad students in the sciences, engineering or medicine address the intersections between science, policy and government. The program features mentoring, lectures and seminars. Fellowships are based in Washington DC, last at least ten weeks and begin in the summer, fall and winter. Interns receive travel expenses and stipends. See *http://www7.national academies.org/policyfellows/index.html*.

43. **National Academy of Science Internships:** Graduate students in science, engineering, medicine, veterinary science or business, and law students work on science and technology policy. Seminars and mentoring are featured. Travel stipends to and from Washington DC are provided in addition to cost-of-living stipends. Winter and summer positions available. See *http://www7.nationalacademies.org/internship*.

44. **National Aeronautics and Space Administration (NASA) Contracting Intern Program:** Full-time positions with rotational opportunities at multiple NASA centers located throughout the nation are available to college graduates who have degrees in business related fields. See *nasa.hq.nasa.gov/office/procurement/co-op/hqcoop.html*.

45. **National Aeronautics and Space Administration (NASA) Undergraduate Research Program:** Mentored research experiences at NASA Centers located throughout the nation are available. College students studying engineering, mathematics, computer science or physical/life sciences are eligible. Fall and summer sessions are available. See *http://education.nasa.gov/usrp*.

46. ***National Association for Equal Opportunity in Higher Education (NAFEO):** Places students in federal offices. See *http://www.nafeo.org*.

47. **National Cancer Institute Health Communications Internships:** Graduate students work on health communications and science writing in Bethesda, Md. Internships last at least six months and begin in July or January. See *http://internship.cancer.gov*.

48. **National Centers for Coastal Ocean Science Internship Programs:** Various summer and year-round programs enabling undergraduate and graduate students to contribute to research at various locations. Many interns come from minority-serving institutions. See *nccos.noaa.gov/opportunities/internships.html*.

49. **National Endowment for the Humanities:** College students with strong humanities backgrounds spend the summer in Washington DC. Past interns have written articles for *Humanities* magazine, researched emerging issues in the humanities, and developed Internet tools for gathering humanities-related information. See *neh.gov/interns/guidelines.html*.

50. **National Gallery of Art Internships:** Summer and general internships available in Washington DC to college graduates of all backgrounds and graduate students. Positions available as curators, lecturers and museum professionals. See *nga.gov/education/interned.htm*.

51. **National Institutes of Health Internship Programs:** High school students, undergraduates and graduate students conduct biomedical research in the nation's premier research laboratories and attend seminars and other trainings near Washington DC during the summer. Recent college grads can spend one year working side-by-side with leading biomedical researchers. See *training.nih.gov*. Find other internships by typing "internships" into the search window at *nih.gov* and by checking the site's career section.

FBI interns conduct legal research. (Photo courtesy of the FBI.)

52. **National Laboratories:** Dozens of opportunities for high school students, college students and undergraduates in science and engineering research, science writing and teaching at federal laboratories located throughout the nation. See *nei.org/index.asp?catnum=3&catid=757*.

53. **National Park Service (NPS):** The Historic Preservation Internship Program assigns undergraduate and graduate students to research and administrative projects in the National Park Service during the summer or school year. See *www2.cr.nps.gov/tps/hpit_p.htm*. Several types of other NPS internships an jobs are listed at *http://www.cr.nps.gov/getinvol.htm*.

Many other types of internships and seasonal jobs are offered in parks across the nation. But because these opportunities are administered by individual parks and various NPS centers and offices, NPS does not maintain a master list of them. To find them, do a keyword search on internships on NPS's website at *nps.gov/search.htm*.

Alternatively, identify your target parks, and then contact each of them directly. You can access hyperlinked lists of national parks at NPS's website at *nps.gov/parks.html*. You can also conduct online searches for websites about internships with keywords, such as "internship", "student jobs" and "summer positions" together with a park name. In addition, NPS's Seasonal Employment Program website is *sep.nps.gov*.

The National Parks and Conservation Association (NPCA), a nonprofit organization that is independent of the federal government, also offers internships. See *npca.org/jobs*.

54. **National Security Agency Programs:** 1) Cryptanalysts Intern Program: Designed to produce professional cryptanalysts. Interns receive training, and rotate through various assignments. 2) Summer and Semester Intern Programs: Undergrads and recent grads receive training and

work on projects involving languages, math, computer science, information assurance or other topics. Travel expenses are covered. 3) Cooperative Education Program: Undergrad majors in computer science, electrical engineering, computer engineering, business or accounting alternate semesters of full-time work with full-time study. 4) Graduate Student Program: College grads earn a salary while earning a Master's degree in computer science, electrical engineering, computer engineering, systems engineering or information operations at the Air Force Institute of Technology in Dayton, Ohio or at the Naval Postgraduate School in Monterey, Calif. 5) The National Physical Science Consortium: Ph.D. students in math, computer sciences or physics receive funding for their studies as well as at least

Interns from Significant Opportunities in Atmospheric Research and Science (SOARS) near the National Center for Atmospheric Research in Boulder, Colorado. (Photo courtesy of SOARS.)

two summers of employment and two years of post-doctoral employment. Women and other minorities are favored. See *nsa.gov*.

55. **National Security Agency's Language Enhancement Program:** Graduating foreign language students and professional linguists learn new languages and enhance current language proficiencies. New NSA employees enjoy signing bonuses worth up to $7,500. Go to *nsa.gov*, and then click on "Careers" and "Foreign Languages."

56. **National Zoo and Friends of the National Zoo Internships:** Assignments available to undergraduates, graduate students and teachers in research, animal management, conservation, veterinary medicine, animal programs, communications, education and other fields in Washington DC. See *http://natzoo.si.edu/undergradinternships*.

57. **Oak Ridge Institute for Science and Education Programs:** Dozens of student jobs, internships and research opportunities for undergrads, grad students, recent grads and postdocs located throughout the nation. Many opportunities are for minorities. See *orau.gov/orise/educ.htm*.

58. **Office of Management and Budget Summer Internships:** Summer positions are available for graduate students in public policy, business, information systems, computer science, economics, law or related fields. See *whitehouse.gov/omb/recruitment/internships.html*.

59. *****Organization of Chinese American's Congressional and Government Internships:** Summer programs place college and graduate students in Congressional offices and federal agencies. Go to *ocanatl.org;* and then click on "Programs" and "Internships."

60. **Overseas Private Investment Corporation (OPIC) Internships:** Summer, spring and fall internships available for law students interested in finance, international law and development. Summer internships available for college and grad students. See *opic.gov/hrm/internships.htm.*

61. **Sandia National Laboratories Internships:** High school students, undergrads and grad students work with mentors in a variety of technical and business fields. They also attend lectures, seminars and social activities on a lively campus. On-campus housing is available. Interns receive stipends plus travel expenses. Summer and year-round positions are based in Livermore, Calif. (the Bay Area) and Albuquerque, NM. See *http://education.ca.sandia.gov/internships/index.lhtml.*

62. **Science Undergraduate Laboratory Internships:** College and graduate students work with scientists and engineers on research projects at facilities throughout the nation. Summer and year-round positions. See *scied.science.doe.gov/scied/erulf/about.html.*

63. **Securities and Exchange Commission Advanced Commitment Program:** Entry level attorneys with high academic qualifications address corporate finance, enforcement, market regulation and investment management. Positions available in Washington DC, New York and Chicago. See *sec.gov/jobs/advcomm.htm.*

64. **Significant Opportunities in Atmospheric Research and Science (SOARS):** Dedicated to increasing the participation of African American, American Indian and Hispanic students in the study of atmospheric sciences. Undergraduates and graduate students spend summers working at the National Center for Atmospheric Research in Boulder, Colo., or another national laboratory; they participate in research, science writing workshops and other trainings. Participants also benefit from long-term mentoring from respected scientists. Salaries increase during each year of participation. Furnished apartments and round-trip airfares to summer work sites are provided at no charge. Participants may also receive funding for graduate study. See *ucar.edu/soars/index.html.*

65. **Smithsonian Environmental Research Center (SERC) Internship Program in Environmental Studies:** Undergraduate and graduate students research global change, ecology, environmental engineering and environmental education near Annapolis, Md. Interns also attend educational lectures and field trips. See *serc.si.edu/internship.*

66. **Smithsonian Institution Internships:** Dozens of summer and general internships available to students, college graduates and graduate students focusing on African American culture, air and space, American Indian history, art, archeology, architecture, ecology, design, history, horticulture, Native American culture, natural history and tropical resources, among other fields. Most positions are located in Washington DC, but positions in other domestic and international locations are also available. See *www.si.edu/ofg/internopp.htm.*

67. **Smithsonian Institution Minority Internship Program:** Designed to increase participation of minority groups in Smithsonian programs. Undergraduates and beginning graduate students conduct research or work on other museum-related projects under the supervision of research and professional staff members at the Smithsonian's many museums, research institutes and offices. See *si.edu/ofg/applications/mip/mipapp.htm.*

68. **Smithsonian Institution Native American Visiting Student and Internship Programs:** Appointments available for Native American undergraduates and graduate students. See *si.edu/ofg/applications/nap/napapp.htm.*

69. **State Department's Fascell Fellowship Program:** One-year or two-year assignments at various overseas locations in support of a diplomatic or consular mission are available. Most fellowships are intended for, but are not limited to teachers, scholars, academics and graduates of advanced-level programs focused on Eastern European, Slavic or Mandarin languages. Fellows must be fluent in the language of the country in which they want to be posted; enrolled in or be a graduate of a relevant advanced degree program focused on language or areas studies; be able to obtain a top secret clearance; and meet medical requirements. Experience may substitute for a degree. See "Student Programs" in the career section of *state.gov.*

70. **United Nations Population Fund Programs:** A Junior Professional Program is open to professionals up to 30 years old who have masters degrees, and an Internship Program is open to students. Both programs provide practical experience in development programs. The Junior Professional Program is based overseas and the Internship Program is based in New York City. Both programs are open to nationals of developing countries and nationals of donor countries. See *unfpa.org/about/employment/index.htm.*

71. **United Negro College Fund Special Programs (UNCFSP) and US Department of Energy Mentorship for Environmental Scholars (MES) Internship Programs:** Students in environmental science, the natural sciences, computer science, engineering or technology spend 10 weeks at a national lab. Each intern works on research relevant to their interests and is mentored by a scientist. Interns receive stipends plus housing and travel expenses. The program is designed for groups that are underrepresented in environmental and technological fields. See *uncfsp.org/bes/mes.asp.*

72. **United States Air Force:** Two civilian training programs in financial management and contracting for undergraduate business students, MBAs, accountants and recent graduates. See *afpc.Randolph.af.mil/cp/fmcp/paqweb.htm* and *afpc.randolph.af.mil/cp/CCP/copperc.htm.* Other internships in the Department of Defense are posted at *dodvets.com/intern.asp.*

73. **United States Department of Agriculture (USDA) Programs:** 1) Undergrads and grad students serve as assistants to professional, administrative and technical staffers at nationwide locations. See *usda.gov/da/employ/intern.htm.* 2) College grads and grads with advanced degrees are eligible for the Sciences Intern Program and the Administrative Intern Program. Each internship lasts for two years and features training and rotations. Openings are available throughout the nation. Selections are made year round. See *usda.gov/da/employ/CareerInternHowtoApplyProgramOverview.htm.* 3)Post doctoral scientists are eligible for the Food Safety Fellows Program, which offers recruitment bonuses. See *http://www.fsis.usda.gov/careers/Food_Safety_Fellows/index.asp.* 4) Veterinary students are eligible for the USDA's Veterinary Student Employment Program. *See fsis.usda.gov/careers/application_process/index.asp.*

74. **United States Geological Survey (USGS) Programs:** Find nationwide internship programs by typing "internships" into the search window at *usgs.gov*. Student jobs are discussed at *usgs.gov/ ohr/student*. The Jack Kleinman Internship for Volcano Research provides support to undergrads and grad students. Find information about this program by typing the program name into the search window at *www.usgs.gov*.

75. **United States Holocaust Museum:** Semester internships available to work on publications, exhibits, photo archives and other projects in Washington DC. Obtain information about this program by conducting a keyword search on the word "intern" at *ushmm.org*.

76. **United States National Arboretum:** Interns participate in educational programs and field trips, and work on horticulture, botany, research, education and administration in Washington DC during the summer. See *usna.usda.gov/Education/intern.html*.

77. **United States Postal Service Programs:** 1) Summer internships are open to students. 2) The Management Intern Program offers two years of rotating assignments in plant processing, delivery and retailing, and puts interns on a fast track into executive management. Applicants should have an MBA or a masters degree in management, finance, logistics, supply-chain management, operations, engineering management or the equivalent. See *usps.com/employment/ internships.htm*.

78. **U.S. Agency for International Development's (USAID) International Development Intern (IDI) and New Entry Professional (NEP) Programs:** These programs serve as pipelines for new recruits into the Foreign Service, which provides a career-long system of rotational assignments in Washington DC and overseas. NEP participants have more technical backgrounds than IDI participants. Training for both programs is based in Washington DC and lasts up to 18 months. This training includes an introduction to USAID's methods, the development of Individual Training Plans (ITPs), rotational assignments, classroom training and language training. Overseas assignments follow. Specialty areas include democracy and governance, environment/natural resources/energy, financial management, population/health/nutrition, project management, contract management, law, education, business, agriculture and economics. See *usaid.gov/careers/nepbro.html* and.*usaid.gov/careers/nepanno2.html*.

79. **U.S. Public Health Service Commissioned Corps:** The Junior Commissioned Officer Student Training and Extern Program places students in assignments throughout the country during school breaks and the summer. Upon graduation, the student is assigned to an agency that addresses health care, toxic substances, disease control, regulation, environmental problems or other health-related issues. The Senior Commissioned Officer Student Training and Extern Program provides financial assistance to students during their final year of school in return for an agreement to work for the Public Health Service after graduation. See *usphs.gov;* then click on "Students."

80. *The Washington Center's Diversity in Congress Program:** Places minority college students who are interested in public service in Congressional offices. See *http://twc.edu*.

81. ***Women & Public Policy Internship Program:** Places college and graduate students in challenging public policy internships with research, government and advocacy organizations. Students receive individualized attention in the placement process and throughout the internship from women leaders who are outstanding mentors and role models. Interns frequently engage in research and writing projects. Weekly seminars and opportunities to earn academic credit provided. Summer, spring and fall positions available. See *plen.org/interns/program.shtml.*

H O T • T I P

HOUSING HELP FOR OUT-OF-TOWNERS

If you are moving to a new location for an internship or job, ask your employer for leads on how to find housing. Also check the housing listings at local colleges. In addition, the University Career Action Network has an online listing of subletting opportunities throughout the nation. See *cdc.richmond.edu:591/ucan.*

If your internship is in Washington DC, the Washington Intern Student Housing may help you find housing. See *internsdc.com.*

82. ***Women's Research and Education Institute for Women and Public Policy:** Positions available for graduate students or recent graduates of advanced degree programs who have a proven commitment to equity for women and interest in public policy. Fellows work as Congressional legislative aids from January to August. They are expected to be articulate and adaptable. See *wrei.org.*

83. **World Bank Programs:** Summer and year-round internships are open to college students, and two-year entry level recruitment programs are open to graduates of masters and Ph.D. programs. Expertise in a development-related field and language skills are required. These programs offer exposure to the challenges of development and poverty alleviation and may serve as a stepping stone to a career in the World Bank or other government agencies, consulting, the private sector or academia. Go to the Jobs/Careers section of the World Bank's website at *worldbank.org.*

STUDENT JOBS

The Student Temporary Employment Program and the Student Career Experience Program (SCEP) place high school and college students and recent graduates throughout the federal government.

→ **Student Temporary Employment Program (STEP):** STEP provides students who are at least 18 years old with part-time work during the school year and full-time work during the summer. One of STEP's purposes is to increase the representation of minorities in the federal workforce. See *opm.gov/employ/students/index.asp.*

→ **Student Career Experience Program (SCEP):** SCEP is similar to STEP, but offers work experience that is directly related to the employee's academic studies. Unfortunately, however, the federal government does not centralize information about agency SCEP programs. Therefore, to obtain information about agency SCEP programs, you must contact agencies individu-

> ### BOOKMARK THIS SITE
>
> *The Washington Post's* collection of articles about student jobs, internships and fellowships is posted at *washingtonpost.com/wl/jobs/Content?Content=/communities/CareerStages/firstjobs/cover.htm.*

ally, search agency websites for program information or conduct online searches. (Use "SCEP" and "federal" as keywords in online searches.)

You can get more information about student jobs from these sites:

→ A hyperlinked list of federal student jobs programs at *thejobpage.gov/students.asp#.*

→ An overview of the Student Educational Employment Program at *opm.gov/employ/students.*

→ A database of student jobs openings and a gateway to the websites of federal agencies that offer student jobs at *studentjobs.gov.*

FINDING MORE INTERNSHIPS AND STUDENT JOBS

You can find other opportunities by referring to these resources:

→ The federal government's hyperlinked lists of agency internships at *thejobpage.gov/starting.asp* and *studentjobs.gov/e-scholar.asp.*

→ The House of Representatives' lists of agency internships. Find these lists by typing "internships" into the search window at *house.gov.*

→ Lists of internships and recruitment programs provided by the Partnership for Public Service, a non-profit devoted to promoting federal careers. To access these lists, go to *ourpublicservice.org;* then click on "Call to Serve" and "Internships." Excellent resources for young professionals are also provided under the other "Call To Serve" tabs.

→ The websites of members of Congress. (But most Congressional internships are unpaid.)

→ Your career counselor at your college or university.

→ *USAJOBS.gov* and *studentjobs.gov*: Conduct keyword searches on these sites using the word 'summer." Also conduct other Internet searches on keywords such as "internships", "student jobs", "federal", along with the name of the agency or facility that interests you.

→ The employment sections of the websites of federal agencies, museums, libraries, parks, forests and marine sanctuaries.

→ Advocacy organizations for minorities and people with disabilities, professional associations, publications and nonprofits.

FELLOWSHIPS FOR EXPERIENCED PROFESSIONALS

Like federal internships, fellowships for positions in the federal government provide ideal networking opportunities, hands-on experience in legislative, judicial and regulatory processes and inside tracks to permanent federal jobs. But while internships are usually filled by entry level professionals, fellowships are filled by experienced professionals. Therefore, fellowships pay better than internships.

Some federal fellowships are listed at *studentjobs.gov/d_fellowship.asp*. Provided below are descriptions of some sample fellowships. Fellowship titles that are highlighted indicate programs that are devoted to minorities or that have components emphasizing such groups.

1. **AAAS Science & Technology Policy Fellowships:** This program places scientists and engineers for one year on Congressional staffs, working as special legislative assistants in legislative and policy areas requiring scientific and technical input. The program includes an orientation on Congressional and executive branch operations, and a year-long seminar series on issues involving science and public policy. Applications are invited from individuals in any physical, biological or social science, any field of engineering or any relevant interdisciplinary field. Applicants must have a Ph.D. or equivalent, or a master's degree in engineering and at least three years of post-degree professional experience. Access information about this program by conducting a keyword search on the program name at *aaas.org*.

> ### GOT THE SEVEN YEAR ITCH?
> If you are primed for a career switch, a fellowship can help you make the change. A fellowship on a Congressional staff could, for example, help you segue from a career as a teacher, researcher, academic, clinician or industry scientist into a career in public policy and government.

2. **Albert Einstein Distinguished Educator Fellowship Program:** Outstanding mathematics, science, and technology teachers work as professional staff members in Congressional offices, the Department of Energy, NASA, the National Institute for Standards and Technology or the National Science Foundation. This program provides an opportunity for classroom teachers to impact national educational policy and to learn about the political process and agency programs. See *triangle-coalition.org/programs.htm.*

President Bush with an intern from the HACU Program. (Photo courtesy of the HACU Program.)

3. **American Chemical Society Fellowships:** Two programs place chemists in one-year positions on Congressional staffs and the executive branch. Access information about this program by conducting a keyword search on "fellowships" at *http://www.chemistry.org.*

4. **American Geophysical Union Fellowships:** Places scientists, engineers and other professionals in Congressional offices for one-year assignments. Fellows address high-profile issues such as water policy, climate research and energy conservation. Applicants should have a broad background in science. They should also be articulate, literate, flexible and able to work on a variety of public policy problems with people from diverse professional backgrounds. See *agu.org/sci_soc/policy/congress_fellows03.html.*

5. **American Institute of Physics State Department Science Fellowship Program:** This program offers one-year appointments in the State Department to physicists. Applicants must have a Ph.D. in physics or a closely related field, or equivalent research experience. Applicants should also be familiar with the scientific or technical aspects of foreign policy. Physicists with excellent scientific credentials, outstanding interpersonal and communications skills, sound judgment, and maturity in decision-making are in particularly high demand. See *aip.org.*

Fellows from the Albert Einstein Distinguished Educator Fellowship Program with a statue of Albert Einstein. (Photo courtesy of Albert Einstein Distinguished Educator Program.)

6. **American Psychological Association Congressional Fellowship Program:** Professionals who have a doctorate in psychology or at least two years of post-doctoral experience work for one year as legislative assistants on Congressional staffs. Activities may involve conducting legislative or oversight work, assisting in Congressional hearings and debates, preparing briefs and writing speeches. Fellows also participate in an orientation on Congressional and executive branch operations and a year-long seminar series on science and public policy issues. See *apa.org/ppo/funding/congfell.html.*

7. **American Physical Society (APS) Congressional Science Fellowships:** This program involves a one-year fellowship, usually running September through August. Following a two-week orientation and interviews on Capitol Hill, fellows choose a Congressional office where they wish to serve. Fellows handle varied assignments, both technical and non-technical. (Many former fellows are currently in influential positions in Washington DC). Applicants must have a Ph.D. in physics or a closely related field, a strong interest in science and technology policy and some experience in applying scientific knowledge toward the solution of societal problems. In exceptional cases, the Ph.D. requirement may be waived for compensating experience. See *aps.org/public_affairs/fellow*.

AAAS Fellow Michael Eichberg (holding the sign) helps announce the RAPID Cures Act — a bill designed to counter biological weapons. Eichberg, who holds a Ph.D. in chemistry, wrote the bill. With Eichberg are Representatives Sheila Lee and Jim Turner. (Photo courtesy of Michael Eichberg.)

8. **American Society for Microbiology Congressional Science Fellowships:** Postdoctoral to mid-career microbiologists spend one year on a Congressional staff. This program includes an orientation, a placement process and weekly seminars throughout the year. A Ph.D. in microbiology is required. See *asm.org*.

9. **American Political Science Association (APSA) Congressional Fellowship Program:** This is a highly selective nine-month program that enables seasoned political scientists, journalists, doctors, federal executives, health policy experts and international scholars to serve on Congressional staffs. See *apsanet.org/about/cfp/index.cfm*.

10. **Excellence in Government Fellowships:** Participants in the Excellence In Government Fellows and E-Government Fellows Programs gain the core qualifications required for membership in the Senior Executive Service. These year-long programs are open to current federal and state mid-level professionals (GS-13 through GS-15 or equivalent). While remaining in their current jobs, fellows participate in workshops, site visits to various organizations, seminars, networking opportunities and team meetings. Fellows must either be based in Washington DC or able to travel there for monthly meetings. These programs do involve tuition, but tuition and travel costs are usually covered by each fellow's home agency. Go to *excelgov.org*, then click on "Programs."

11. **Institute of Electrical and Electronics Engineers (IEEE) Government Fellows Programs:** Places engineers on Congressional staffs and staffs of executive branch decisions-makers for one year. See *ieeeusa.org*.

12. **LEGIS Fellows Programs:** Places current federal employees in Congressional offices. See *http://web.em.doe.gov/emtrain/legis.html*.

13. **National Laboratories:** Dozens of opportunities are available for science writers, teachers, scientists and engineers at federal laboratories throughout the nation. See *nei.org/index.asp?catnum=3&catid=757.*

14. **Senior Presidential Management Fellows Program:** Highly competitive, prestigious two-year assignments that are similar to assignments in the Presidential Management Fellows Program described on page 42, but are designed for experienced managers. The program includes training, mentoring and development assignments. Senior fellows can be appointed to the GS-13, 14 or 15 levels or their equivalents. Participants in this program may be recruited from inside or outside of the federal government. See *pmi.opm.gov.*

AAAS Fellow Julie March discusses food distribution methods with relief workers at a refugee camp in Rwanda. March, who has a Ph.D. in ecology, works for Food for Peace, which is part of the United States Agency for International Development. (Photo courtesy of Julie March.)

15. **Smithsonian Institution Fellowships:** Dozens of opportunities are available for scholars in American history, American Indian studies, anthropology, art, astrophysics, communication, aviation and space history, cultural heritage, design, ecology, education, evolution, library science, marine science, materials research, natural history, molecular biology and tropical resources. Opportunities in the US and abroad. Latino Studies Fellowship Program also available. See *http://www.si.edu/ofg/fell.htm.*

16. **Smithsonian Institution Native American Community Scholar Awards:** Appointments in residence at the Smithsonian are awarded to Native Americans who are formally or informally related to a Native American community to undertake projects on Native American subjects and use the Native American resources of the Institution. See *si.edu/ofg/applications/nap/napapp.htm.*

17. **Supreme Court Judicial Fellows Program:** This program offers one-year appointments in the Office of the Administrative Assistant to the Chief Justice. Fellows research background information for the Chief Justice's speeches and reports; prepare analytical reports on legal and managerial issues; assist Judicial Conference committees; work with the Administrative Office, the Federal Judicial Center and the United States Sentencing Commission on special projects, and develop programs that enhance public understanding of the Supreme Court. Fellows also attend special seminars, lectures and social activities. Candidates must have at least one post-graduate degree, two or more years of professional experience with a record of high performance and multi-disciplinary training and experience, including familiarity with judicial processes. See *fellows.supremecourtus.gov.*

18. **USDA Graduate School Congressional Fellowship Program:** Places current federal employees in Congressional offices for six months or one year. See *grad.usda.gov/cgi-bin/sb/nav.cgi?nav=100389.*

19. **White House Fellows Program:** This is America's most prestigious program for leadership and public service. The program offers exceptional young men and women first-hand experience working at the highest levels of the federal government. These jobs pay very well! Fellows typically spend a year working as full-time, paid special assistants to senior White House staff, the Vice President, cabinet secretaries and other top-ranking officials. Fellows also participate in an education program consisting of roundtable discussions with renowned leaders from the private and public sectors and trips to study US policy in action both domestically and internationally. This program seeks candidates who have exceptional writing ability, a positive attitude, strong management skills and the ability to work well with others. See *whitehouse.gov/fellows/about/faq.html.*

AAAS Fellow Rosemarie Szostak (with raised arm) rolls along with Department of Defense staffers during Marine training. Szostak, a former chemistry professor, helps the Defense Sciences Office develop high-tech equipment that withstands sand, grit and heat. (Photo courtesy of Rosemarie Szostak.)

CHAPTER 4:
THOSE !@#! VACANCY ANNOUNCEMENTS
fpmi

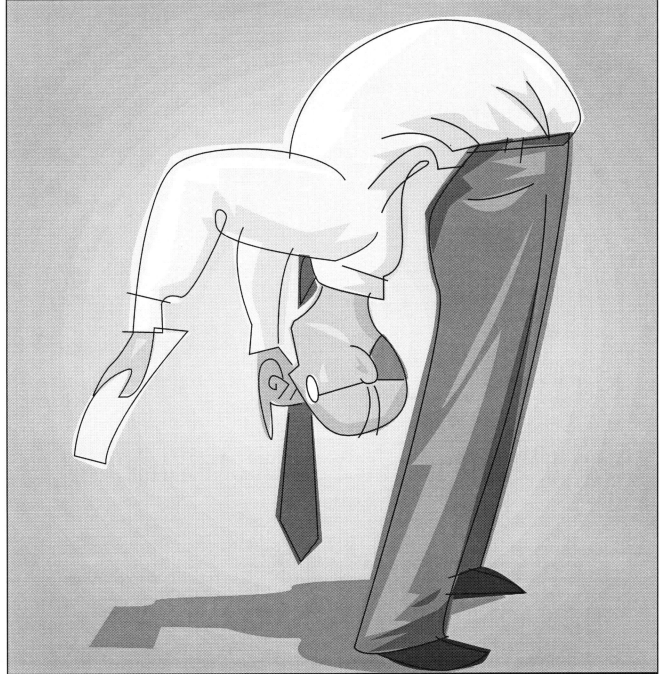

CHAPTER 4: THOSE !@#! VACANCY ANNOUNCEMENTS

There is no short cut to a place worth going.

— *Beverly Sills,* Opera Singer

So you've found a juicy job opening(s), and you're rarin' to apply...right? Well, not so quick. First, you've got to figure out if you have enough time to apply and if the job would be a good fit for you. And to do that, you have to decipher those dense announcements of federal jobs, which are known as vacancy announcements; this task is commonly associated with a syndrome called docu-trauma.

You can prevent docu-trauma by reading this chapter. This chapter explains everything you need to know in order to understand and use vacancy announcements, including:

- ☛ What types of information about job openings are provided in vacancy announcements.
- ☛ How to decide which openings to pursue.
- ☛ The various mechanisms used by the federal government to hire employees.
- ☛ The basic components of applications for federal jobs.

HOW TO READ VACANCY ANNOUNCEMENTS

Vacancy announcements are flat-out confusing, boring and long-winded. And those are the user-friendly ones!

But even many of the most plum federal positions are announced in seemingly impenetrable announcements. So you shouldn't judge a job by its vacancy announcement. In other words, don't lose interest in a juicy position that meets your salary and geographic requirements just because it is wrapped in rambling verbiage.

And don't be intimidated by the length of vacancy announcements. Much of their hulk and bulk is generated by legal filler satisfying regulations that probably don't concern you.

STEPS FOR READING A VACANCY ANNOUNCEMENT

Once you find a vacancy announcement that piques your interest and meets your salary and location criteria, decide whether you should apply by:

1. Checking whether you fulfill the "Who May Apply" criteria. Some openings are open to all US citizens. But some openings are restricted to current or former federal employees or to the hiring agency's current employees. (In government lingo, most current employees at federal agencies have what is known as "Status," or "Competitive Status," or "Civil Service Status;" most former employees have what is known as "reinstatement eligibility.") In rare cases, openings may be open to non-US citizens.

2. Ensuring that you can meet the application deadline, known as the "closing date." A few caveats about closing dates:

   ☞ Sometimes the closing date specifies the date by which the application must be received, and sometimes specifies the date by which an application must be postmarked if paper applications are accepted. If you are unsure of which type of deadline applies to your target job, get in touch with the contact person listed on the target job's vacancy announcement.

   ☞ Agencies occasionally extend the closing date of a job. So if you need more time to work on your application, check whether your target job's closing date has been extended.

   WHO WRITES THESE THINGS ANYWAY?

   Most vacancy announcements are written by human resources (HR) staffers who are generally overworked and not necessarily familiar with the professional demands of the opening. More often than not, program managers are only minimally involved, at best, in preparing vacancy announcements. The federal government is currently working to make vacancy announcements easier to understand, but this effort will never be criticized for progressing too rapidly.

   ☞ Applications that are submitted via automated hiring systems are usually due by midnight Eastern Standard Time (EST) of the closing date. To meet such deadlines, you must hit the "send" or "submit" key for your electronic application by midnight of the closing date. Unfortunately, many applicants mistakenly believe that they will be able to slip their application under the wire if they have logged into the hiring agency's automated hiring system by midnight. Not so. An electronic application that is sent after midnight EST of the closing date will likely be automatically rejected by the automated hiring system.

3. Checking whether you meet the basic or minimum qualifications for the job. If you don't meet these qualifications, your time is better spent applying to other openings.

4. Reading the vacancy announcement and crossing out any information that is irrelevant to your needs. This chapter's glossary of terms can help you decipher hard-to-understand passages and eliminate those that are irrelevant to you.

5. Evaluating the job description and whatever knowledge, skills and abilities (KSAs) or Executive Core Qualifications (ECQs) questions are included in the announcement to determine whether you really want this job. (More information about KSAs and ECQs is provided later in this chapter, and in Chapter 7.)

THE REAL DEAL ON PRESELECTED JOBS

Many job-seekers wrongly believe that any federal job that is only open for a short time, such as two weeks or less, is pre-selected or rigged. According to this myth, the short window of opportunity for applying reflects the hiring agency's desire to minimize the number of doomed applications that will ultimately have to be processed.

Granted: Some federal jobs — albeit a minority — are initially targeted to selected candidates. But stories abound of candidates who failed to apply for openings that were targeted to them. Moreover, enough checks and balances are built into federal hiring procedures to usually ensure that even openings that may be initially targeted are eventually filled by the most qualified applicants. Therefore, some targeted openings really are up for grabs. The weight given to veterans preference in selections also complicates efforts to preselect federal openings.

And the supposed two-week red flag is really a red herring. In fact, many agencies keep *all* of their vacancy announcements open for only two weeks or less so that they can fill openings quickly. (Too bad that the federal government's reputation for sluggishness is so entrenched that its quick response policies are apparently almost enough to spawn conspiracy theories!)

The truth is that there is simply no sure way to distinguish preselected jobs from vacancy announcements. (A vacancy announcement will not surrender her secrets easily!) Nevertheless, a vacancy announcement that describes job responsibilities that are so specific that they could only be fulfilled by one or two people in the United States is more likely to be preselected than one that describes job responsibilities that are reasonably broad. In addition, an opening that has been filled without the hiring agency conducting any interviews is suspect.

Conversely, a vacancy announcement that advertises multiple openings is less likely to be pre-selected than one that announces a single opening. But the chances of being thwarted by preselections are too remote and vacancy announcements for multiple openings are too few for either of these phenomena to provide the sole basis for any sensible job search. Bottom line: You should apply for every opening that would be a good fit for you.

6. Ensuring that you meet any background, licensing, physical or medical requirements or other conditions of employment specified for the job.

7. Listing everything you have to do and submit in order to apply for the job. Gather this information from the "How To Apply" section of the vacancy announcement, as well as from other sections of the vacancy announcement that specify additional requirements.

8. Calling the contact person named on the vacancy announcement if you have procedural questions about applying or substantive questions about the job. Such contacts are potentially invaluable sources of information that are overlooked by many applicants.

WAYS THAT FEDERAL JOBS ARE FILLED

There are two major ways that the federal government fills jobs: Through competitive appointments and noncompetitive appointments. It may be helpful for you to quickly familiarize yourself with the basics of how competitive and noncompetitive appointments work so that you will understand the associated terminology included in most vacancy announcements.

COMPETITIVE APPOINTMENTS

Most federal jobs are filled through open competitions. In an open competition, applicants are rated and ranked based upon their qualifications and veterans preference, and then the best qualified candidate is selected to fill the job. (Note that in some cases the spouse or mother of a veteran may claim veterans preference. For more information about veterans preference, see Appendix 1.) Federal jobs that are filled through open competitions are called competitive appointments.

NONCOMPETITIVE APPOINTMENTS

Some federal jobs are filled through noncompetitive appointments. When an agency fills a job through a noncompetitive appointment, it bypasses requirements to hold an open competition and to award the job to the most qualified candidate. Instead, the agency awards the job to an applicant who meets or exceeds the basic qualifications for the job *and* meets certain, other specified criteria.

Noncompetitive appointments are most commonly awarded to:

☛ **Veterans:** Veterans are eligible for noncompetitive appointments to federal jobs under the Veterans' Employment Opportunities Act of 1998 (VEOA), the 30 Percent or More Disabled Program or the Veterans Recruitment Appointment. For more information about these and other special hiring opportunities for veterans, see Appendix 1.

☛ **People With Disabilities:** People who have severe physical, cognitive or emotional disabilities may receive noncompetitive appointments to certain positions under Schedule A Appointments. To be eligible for such appointments, an applicant must have a certification letter from a state vocational rehabilitation office or the Department of Veterans Affairs. See Appendix 2.

☛ **Displaced Federal Employees:** Federal employees who have been laid-off or whose jobs have moved are eligible for noncompetitive appointments to some federal jobs through the Career Transition Assistance Program (CTAP) and Interagency Career Transition Program (ITAP). (A federal lay-off is called a RIF — short for reduction-in-force.)

☛ **Returned Peace Corps Volunteers (RPCVs):** May receive noncompetitive appointments during the first year after completion of their tour of duty. See "Resources for Returned Volunteers" at *peacecorps.gov.*

☛ **Bilingual/Bicultural Program:** The Bilingual/Bicultural Program gives preference to applicants who are fluent in English and Spanish or another language or who are knowledgeable about the Hispanic culture or another underrepresented culture. This program is used to recruit for some entry-level jobs that require bilingual skills or special cultural knowledge. You can find some of these jobs by conducting keyword searches on the program name on *usajobs.opm.gov.*

Also note that because Hispanics are particularly underrepresented in the federal government, many federal agencies are particularly eager to recruit Hispanics. In addition, many security and law enforcement agencies are particularly eager to hire professionals who are fluent in Arabic or other languages, or who are familiar with Muslim, Mid-East and other cultures. So if your target job requires language or cultural skills but its announcement does not specifically specify the Bilingual/Bicultural program, call the contact listed on the announcement and ask if the agency will consider hiring you under this program.

☛ **Applicants to Internships and Student Jobs Programs:** Participants in most internships and student jobs programs discussed in Chapter 3 are hired through noncompetitive appointments.

☛ **Former Federal Employees:** May receive noncompetitive appointments if they have reinstatement eligibility and if they seek reinstatement at a grade that is equal or lower than their previous grade.

Note that even applicants who fall into one of the categories listed above are never guaranteed noncompetitive appointments; no agency is ever required to hire any particular applicant.

Why do federal agencies sometimes opt to fill jobs through noncompetitive appointments rather than through competitive appointments? For one thing, noncompetitive appointments help the federal government meet its obligations to hire the types of employees that are listed above. In addition, noncompetitive appointments are much faster and easier to process than competitive appointments.

More information about the various categories of applicants discussed in this section can be accessed by going to *opm.gov*, and then clicking on the following sequence of links: "Career Opportunities" ... "Job FAQs."

FINDING NONCOMPETITIVE OPENINGS

Each vacancy announcement posted on USAJOBS lists the types of noncompetitive appointments that can be used to fill the opening. Therefore, you can use the name of a noncompetitive appointment in a keyword search of vacancy announcements on USAJOBS to find those that meet your requirements.

Some federal jobs that can be filled through noncompetitive appointments are not advertised. To find them, contact the Selective Placement Coordinator in the Human Resources Office of the agency that interests you.

You can access a list of these Coordinators by clicking on the following sequence of links on USAJOBS: "Federal Employment of People with Disabilities" ... "Applicants and Employees" ... "Selective Placement Coordinators." If you are a student, your placement office may also be able to help connect you with federal agencies that have noncompetitive appointments available.

IF YOU APPLY FOR A NONCOMPETITIVE APPOINTMENT...

ATTENTION!

1. Specifically, state your request for a noncompetitive appointment in the cover letter of a paper application, and in the body of an electronic application that does not accommodate a cover letter.

2. Answer all application questions, just as you would if were not requesting a noncompetitive appointment. Even though you don't necessarily have to be the most qualified candidate to land a noncompetitive appointment, the better your application is, the better your chances will be for receiving an offer.

THE MEAT OF MOST APPLICATIONS

Some vacancy announcements include the entire job application for the opening. Other vacancy announcements contain only some components of the job application in the document itself and instruct applicants how to access other components of the job application. These components may include automated application systems that must be accessed, or tests that must be taken to apply for the job.

Whether or not the entire application for a job opening is included in the vacancy announcement itself, the applications of most entry-level and mid-level federal jobs include some combination of the following components:

☛ **Knowledge, Skills and Abilities (KSAs):** KSAs are the single most important part of any application that has them. Why are KSAs so important? Because they define the criteria used to rate applications; the rating that your application receives in the selection process will be based upon how well it demonstrates your competency, experience and education in the areas identified by KSAs. You should respond to each KSA with an essay describing how your experience and education satisfies the KSA.

A few caveats about KSAs:

- KSAs have many aliases in vacancy announcements. They may be labeled in vacancy announcements as Competency Factors, Supplemental Statements, Evaluation Criteria, Ranking Factors, Selective Factors or a variety of other names. And some vacancy announcements do not label KSAs by any name at all.

- Most vacancy announcements that include KSAs also specifically say that an essay addressing each KSA is required. But some vacancy announcements include KSAs without specifically saying that KSA essays responding to them are required. If you are applying for a vacancy announcement that has KSAs but doesn't specifically ask for responses to them, you should include essay responses anyway — or else your application will not be seriously considered. Instructions on writing effective essays are included in Chapter 7.

How can you identify KSAs when they are unlabeled and when an essay addressing them is not specifically requested in the vacancy announcement? By their format: They are usually presented as a numbered list. KSAs may also be identified by their wording: Each item in a list of KSAs usually beings with words, such as "Knowledge of…," "Skill in…," "Ability to…" or "Experience in…"

☞ **A series of short answer questions about your qualifications:** Short answer questions are a primary feature of many Internet-based automated applications. They are akin to "mini KSAs."

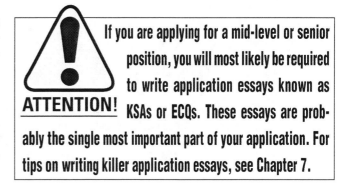

ATTENTION! If you are applying for a mid-level or senior position, you will most likely be required to write application essays known as KSAs or ECQs. These essays are probably the single most important part of your application. For tips on writing killer application essays, see Chapter 7.

Short answer questions are usually formatted as yes/no questions or multiple-choice questions that ask applicants to evaluate their proficiency in various skills. For example, a multiple choice question about oral communication might ask you whether you have experience presenting information to others. You would be able to choose from five multiple-choice ratings ranging from "I have not had education, training or experience performing this task" to "I am regularly consulted by others as an expert in this task."

Be aware that your answers to short answer, mini KSAs will help determine your rating in the selection. The higher you score yourself on these questions, the higher your rating in the selection will be. So be sure to rate your skills as highly as you truthfully can.

☞ **A choice of a federal resume or Optional Form 612 (OF-612).** The OF-612 is a form that asks for all of the information required in a federal resume. The federal government does not officially favor a federal resume over the OF-612; these documents officially receive the same weight.

However, the overwhelming majority of hiring managers prefer reading well-formatted resumes which — as explained in Chapter 8 — can be tailored to prominently brandish your most important qualifications, rather than cumbersome OF-612 forms, which are laid out in a stodgy, difficult-to-read format. But if you do not have the time or will to prepare a well formatted resume, the OF-612 may be your best bet. You can download the OF-612 from USAJOBS.

Note that federal resumes require more information than resumes accepted by other types of employers. See Chapter 8 for more information about federal resumes.

The federal government also accepts the Standard Form-171 (SF-171) in lieu of federal resumes or the OF-612. But the SF-171 — another resume form — is so stodgy and antiquated that the federal government does not even produce them any longer. So if you have an old SF-171, you should probably transfer that information over to a federal resume or OF-612.

☞ **Tests:** Applications for most government jobs don't require tests anymore. Tests are only currently required to apply for a few types of entry-level positions.

THE MEAT OF APPLICATIONS FOR SENIOR POSITIONS

The federal government's corps of about 6,000 executive managers is called the Senior Executive Service (SES). SESers are the big enchiladas…the top brass…the muckety mucks of the federal government.

Vacancy announcements for SES jobs are available from the same sources as those for entry-level and mid-level jobs. Applications for SES jobs are similar to those for entry-level and mid-level jobs — except that applications for SES jobs also require essays addressing:

- ☛ Three to six "Technical Factors" or "Technical Qualifications." These factors vary from job to job.
- ☛ Five Executive Core Qualifications (ECQs). Every SES application has the same five ECQs.

  - ✓ Leading Change
  - ✓ Leading People
  - ✓ Results Driven
  - ✓ Business Acumen
  - ✓ Building Coalitions/Communication

So between the Technical Factors and the ECQs, an SES application can require a total of more than 10 essays. Well, even if nowhere else, federal muckety mucks earn their big bucks just by toiling through such lengthy applications!

More essay-writing advice for applicants for SES jobs is provided in Chapter 7.

OPP'Y OF A LIFETIME

Fast-growing midtown corp needs bright, articulate M/F to reorganize 760,000 files from top to bottom, fire four people nobody else will, and take care of children aged three and one. Must be certified in UNEX, GOM, SYSCO, CREM, LEM, ZOT, FENIX, JOD, and FRON. Own car a necessity, also up-to-date trucking license. Knowledge of quantum physics, short-order cookery helpful. Can you type? Even better. If you have $250,000 cash and are not afraid of large dogs, we're looking for YOU. At least twelve years' experience required. Personable, attractive college grads only call 555-2121 for appt. Starting salary 9K. Great benefits.

H O T • T I P

IF YOU DON'T OWN A COMPUTER...

You can access Internet-equipped computers at many public libraries and unemployment offices for free. In addition, you can rent in-store computers by the hour for reasonable rates at some office supply stores, such as Kinko's Inc., and set up free e-mail accounts from many Internet providers, such as Yahoo and Hotmail.

Each federal agency is required to provide job-seekers who are without computer or Internet access a way to apply for its openings. Here are some of the ways that federal agencies are reaching out to unplugged applicants:

- Many agencies still accept paper applications. (Some agencies don't accept electronic applications at all.)

- Some agencies help applicants submit applications online. For example, the Transportation Security Administration's (TSA) Call Center Representatives accept the application information of unplugged applicants over the phone and submit it for them online. The telephone numbers for TSA's Call Center are 1-800-887-1895 and TYY at 1-800-887-5506.

- Some agencies, such as the Environmental Protection Agency, give job-seekers access to computers in their Human Resources offices.

Federal agencies do not necessarily specify application alternatives for unplugged applicants on their vacancy announcements. So if you need help applying for a federal job because you lack a computer or Internet access, call the contact person named on the vacancy announcement of your target opening, and ask what type of support the hiring agency provides for applicants like you.

CAUTION: FOLLOW DIRECTIONS

About half of all job applications received by the federal government are rejected merely because they violate instructions by missing the deadline or omitting required information. (Hey, it would be a lot easier for applicants to follow directions if those !@!#! vacancy announcements were clearer!)

Unfortunately, if your application is missing required information, the hiring agency will not inform you of the problem. In addition, late applications almost always get kicked out of the competition, and applications that are missing required information frequently get kicked out of the competition. So keep your application out of the circular file by ensuring that it includes all required information and documents, and by submitting it by the closing date. Also be sure to follow all directions in the vacancy announcement's "How To Apply" section. **If you must submit some documents separately from your application via FAX, make sure that your FAX includes enough identifying information for it to be matched to your application.**

One more thing: Every time that you apply for a new job via an automated application, check the accuracy of any information that you previously entered on the system. In particular, make sure that your contact information and the description of your most recent job on your resume is still current.

CHAPTER 5:
HOW APPLICATIONS ARE SCREENED
fpmi

CHAPTER 5:
HOW APPLICATIONS ARE SCREENED

I want to hire someone who <u>really</u> wants the job. If an applicant doesn't want the job enough to spend a couple of hours tailoring their application to the opening, then they don't want it enough to deserve to be hired.

— A Federal Hiring Manager

Many job-seekers use the mass mailing approach to apply for jobs: They send out the same, generic application to every federal job and private sector job that they can get their hands (or mouse) on. Although the mass mailing approach is the easiest method, it's also the least productive method. DON'T BE A MASS MAILER!

Why not? Because many federal job openings draw dozens if not hundreds of applications. If you fail to tailor your application to your target job, there is bound to be a gap between what the job asks for and what your generic application says you offer — a gap big enough for an army of competing applications to fill. Moreover, the selection process used by the federal government is unique. If your application fails to cater to this process, it will almost certainly be overshadowed by more accommodating applications.

Yes, it does take more time and effort to tailor applications to job openings than to send out mass mailings. But it is way more efficient to spend eight hours preparing a single stellar application that fits the opening than to spend the same amount of time submitting multiple generic applications that will all miss their mark.

Moreover, think about all of the blood, sweat and tears that you've already devoted to your career. Isn't your career worth a few more hours of work? Don't scrimp on the last few hours of labor required to tailor your application to the position and to the federal selection process — hours that could keep your application out of the circular file and guarantee its place in the "let's interview these people" file.

In order to understand how to tailor your job to particular jobs and the federal selection process, you must understand how the federal selection process works and the special demands that it places on applicants. This chapter provides this strategically essential information.

SELECTION THE OLD FASHIONED WAY: PEER REVIEW PANELS

In agencies that have not automated their screening processes, most applications are rated through a three-step procedure:

1. **SCREEN FOR BASIC QUALIFICATIONS:** Think of the screen for basic qualifications as a laugh test: If you can't imagine a hiring manager saying that you are qualified for the opening with a straight face, your application probably won't survive this hurdle.

   During the screen for basic qualifications, a human resources staffer compares each application to the "basic qualifications" defined in the job's vacancy announcement. Applications that meet basic qualifications survive; those that don't are kicked out of the competition.

   Because the standards for the screen for basic qualifications are relatively low, most applications are forwarded onto the panel screen for further evaluation.

2. **THE PANEL SCREEN:** All applications that meet basic qualifications are reviewed by a panel of subject matter experts. These subject matter experts are agency employees whose jobs are similar to the opening. Nevertheless, because every federal job is somewhat unique, panelists are not always thoroughly versed in the ins-and-outs of jobs that they screen.

   Few panelists volunteer to serve on panels. Rather, they are usually drafted onto panels by superiors. (I have been frequently told by human resources staffers that I may be the only person in western civilization to ever have volunteered to serve on a selection panel; I frequently do so in order to gain insights into how to impress hiring managers.)

   Panelists are good people. They take their panel assignments seriously. But they are busy — always. And like most jurors, they regard their side stints on peer review panels as unwelcome interruptions that distract them from their "real work," which is piling up in their absence.

   How do panelists rate applications? Each panelist usually receives a stack of applications containing dozens or even hundreds of applications. They rush through this stack because:

   → The longer the panel assignment lasts, the more real work will greet them upon their return to their regular jobs.

→ Panelists are rarely tempted to linger over applications that, by and large, are remarkably similar to one another and are well. . .boring. After all, the typical federal job opening draws umpteen vague, mushy resumes and cover letters from professionals who are looking for "a challenging and rewarding position that provides opportunity for growth" and are "convinced that you will consider me a perfect fit for the position." They also draw about a gazillion *War and Peace*-sized essays that are formatted with minuscule margins, tiny, eye-squinting fonts and mile-long paragraphs that are overflowing with credentials that have nothing to do with the opening. Panelists are supposed to read all of them. Some fun.

→ The time crunch: A single federal application, including a long-winded resume and pages and pages of essays, may exceed 10 pages. So 10 times the number of applicants for the job equals the number of pages that each panelist must review — usually by tomorrow. So how much time does each page get? Well, you can do the math. (I don't want to be the bearer of bad news.)

During the panel screen, each panelist rates each application essay (known as a KSA or ECQ) submitted by each applicant. (See sample rating sheet on page 79.) Then, all panelists' rating sheets are integrated into a total score for each applicant. Next, applications claiming veterans preference receive additional points as warranted. Finally, a "cut off" threshold is identified; applications that score below this threshold are kicked out of the competition, and those that score above the threshold are added onto a certification list of "most qualified candidates" or "best qualified candidates." In government lingo, these surviving applications have "made the cert."

3. **THE FINAL CUT:** The certification list of most qualified candidates is submitted to the selecting official — who is usually the manager who will supervise the new employee. But because selecting officials may rise through the ranks through almost any profession, they are not necessarily in the same profession as applicants for the opening. For example, the director of a marketing office whose background is in advertising could serve as the selecting official for an opening for a graphic artist who would work within the marketing office.

Depending upon agency policy, the selecting official may interview all, some or none of the applicants on the certification list. (Phone interviews are allowed.) Based upon the selecting official's impression of the quality of applications, interviews and references, s/he picks the winner of the competition who is offered the job. If the winner rejects the offer, another qualified candidate is usually offered the job.

SAMPLE PANEL RATING SHEET

NAME OF APPLICANT	KSA #1	KSA #2	KSA #3	KSA #4	Veterans Preference	TOTAL POINTS

NAME OF PANEL MEMBER _____

Each panelist grades each applicant on each of his/her responses to application essays known as KSAs or ECQs identified in the vacancy announcement, and records scores on a sheet like this one. Notice that scores are based on essays and veterans preference; resumes are not specifically scored. Hence, the importance of application essays.

HOW SENIOR POSITIONS ARE FILLED

Each agency decides how to fill its own openings in the Senior Executive Service (SES). One common method is to advertise the SES opening, and then rate and rank applicants through peer review panels similar to the way that entry level and mid-level federal jobs are rated and ranked — but with one additional step: The selected applicant must be approved by the Qualifications Review Board (QRB), which is a panel of executives run by the Office of Personnel Management, the federal government's human resources agency. You can find openings for SES positions on USAJOBS.

An agency may also fill an SES position by appointing without competition a QRB-certified graduate of an agency-run Senior Executive Candidate Program. Agency-run Senior Executive Candidate Programs, which last 18 to 24 months, are specifically designed to groom mid-level government professionals for the SES; they are usually open only to current federal employees. Each agency has its own Candidate Development Program. For general information about the SES program, see *opm.gov/ses*.

HOT • TIP

BECOME SENIOR EXECUTIVE SERVICE MATERIAL

One way to gain credentials required for getting into the Senior Executive Service is to participate in the Council for Excellence in Government's Fellows and E-Government Fellows Programs. These programs are described in the Fellowship section of Chapter 3 and on the Council for Excellence in Government's website. Go to *excelgov.org;* then click on "Programs."

Federal agencies will also hire graduates of the Office of Personnel Management's Candidate Development Program (CDC). Graduates of the CDC program will be certified by the SES Qualifications Review Board and will be eligible to be selected for SES positions in any federal agency without competition.

The CDC program, which features rotational assignments, formal training and mentoring lasting 14 months, is open to professionals at the GS-14 and GS-15 levels or equivalents. And unlike agency SES programs, the CDC program recruits nonfederal employees.

One of the goals of the CDC program is to train women, minorities, people with disabilities and veterans for the SES.

For more information about the CDC program, see *leadership.opm.gov/content.cfm?CAT=SESFCD.*

TAKING THE HUMAN OUT OF HUMAN RESOURCES: MACHINE SCREENS

ELECTRONIC VS. PAPER APPLICATIONS

Some federal agencies still only accept paper applications, but more and more federal agencies — automating some or all of the selection process — only accept e-mailed applications or electronic applications that are submitted via the agency's Internet-based automated hiring system. Still other federal agencies allow applicants to choose for themselves whether to submit a paper or electronic application.

Automated hiring systems offer several important advantages: They can slash the time needed to process applications. In addition, they enable more people for apply to more jobs with less hassle. **But if you are applying for a job that gives you a choice between submitting a paper application or an electronic application, choose the paper option.** Why? Because:

➔ Most automated applications do not accommodate text formatting features, such as bold, underlining, bullets and various font types and sizes. Therefore, KSAs submitted via/on these systems invariably print out as dense slabs of tiny, featureless text. For hiring managers, the task of reading such texts is comparable to reading page after page of the telephone book. By contrast, well formatted paper applications are considerably more alluring to hiring managers. Thus, paper applications tend to receive more attention from hiring managers than electronic applications.

➔ Electronic applications sometimes include short essay questions that are not required in hard-copy applications for the same job! These extra questions unnecessarily lengthen applications, which further alienates hiring managers.

➔ Some automated applications do not offer a spell checker function. Therefore, applications created on these systems are prone to spelling errors and typos that can — by themselves — doom an application. By contrast, paper applications that can be spell checked and easily printed out for proofreading are more likely to be error free.

The raw reality is that, in the overwhelming majority of cases, when time-pressured hiring managers confront piles of applications that include concise, well-formatted paper applications as well as dense, long-winded, hard-to-read electronic applications, the electronic applications sink to the bottom of the pile; at most they receive quick skims. Such half-hearted attention does not bode well for the hiring prospects of their authors.

As one hiring manager said (with rolling eyes), "PEEEUUUU! I hate those automated applications. Page after page of long, unbroken paragraphs in tiny print remind me of the warning inserts that come with prescriptions. Nobody reads them thoroughly because they are unreadable!"

TYPES OF AUTOMATED SYSTEMS

Among the types of automated application systems currently used by federal agencies are various customized versions of Resumix, QuickHire and USA Staffing. In addition, the Department of Commerce has its own system, which is called the Department of Commerce Opportunities On-Line (COOL).

HOW AUTOMATED SYSTEMS WORK

Each federal agency's automated application system is separate and unique; your registration on one system will not carry over to another. Therefore, you must register on as many agency systems as you use, and log in to each system before each session.

Each agency determines the criteria used by its automated system for rating and ranking applicants. For example, some automated systems rate applicants based on their answers to multiple choice questions that ask applicants to rate their proficiency in various skills. Other automated systems rate applicants based on the presence of keywords in resumes.

Because the automated application systems that conduct such keyword searches incorporate huge thesauruses, they understand synonyms. For example, such systems understand that, "I am a teacher" may mean the same thing as "I am an educator." These systems also analyze meaning based upon context. For example, they would be able to distinguish between the sentence, "I live on Harvard Street" and the sentence, "I attended Harvard University."

STOP THE INSANITY!

The federal government is currently working to **STOP THE INSANITY** of the multiplicity of automated application systems and the resulting redundancy of effort required by them. USAJOBS will eventually serve as a centralized, one-stop-shop application center that will accept standardized electronic applications, and provide on-line status checking of automated applications.

The federal government posts updates of its efforts to standardize automated application systems on USAJOBS at: *opm.gov/egov/recruitment_status.asp.*

Each automated system rates applicants' skills on a point system and then adds points for veterans preference as warranted. The system then ranks applicants and generates a list of high-scorers of "most qualified" or "best qualified candidates," just as peer review panels do under the traditional system.

The applications of high-scorers are submitted to a selecting official, just as they are under the traditional panel review system. Also like under the traditional system, the selecting official reviews these applications and may interview applicants if he/she wants to. Based upon their impression of interviews and applications, the selecting officials make the final selection, just as they do under the traditional system.

Bear in mind that just because an agency accepts electronic applications does not mean that its applications are necessarily screened by automated systems; many agencies use peer review panels to screen applications that are submitted via automated application systems.

CANCELLED VACANCY ANNOUNCEMENTS

The overwhelming majority of federal jobs that are announced to the public are filled by applicants who have answered the announcements for these jobs. Nevertheless, a federal agency may cancel a vacancy announcement during any stage of the selection process without hiring anyone. In other words, the fact that an agency invites applications for a job does not necessarily guarantee that it will eventually hire anyone from the resulting applicant pool. Such bait-and-switch maneuvering may be compelled by budget constraints, changes in programmatic priorities, dissatisfaction with the quality of applications or other factors.

The potential cancellation of vacancy announcements provides an extra reason why you shouldn't take it personally if you are rejected from a government job: It is possible that the vacancy announcement was cancelled, and so the job never really existed at all. Take heart: You shouldn't feel slighted about not being picked for a nonexistent job. But unfortunately, if the agency advertises the position again later, the original applicants must reapply in order to be considered during the second go-round.

WHAT MAKES A SUCCESSFUL APPLICATION

Whether your application will be screened by a peer panel or an automated system, the federal selection process incorporates several important principles that should guide your preparation of KSAs. The first principle of application preparation is that KSAs, mini-KSAs and short answer self-rating questions are the most important parts of applications that include them. So submitting an application without required KSAs or mini-KSAs is like hitting the third rail of the federal application process; don't even *THINK* about doing it. In addition, if your application asks you to rate yourself on your proficiency on certain skills, give yourself the highest self-rating that you can truthfully claim. (Warning: The keyword here is "truthfully." Remember: Lying on a federal application can get you in biiiig trouble. See "Resume Padders Need Not Apply" on page 181.)

Another important principle of the federal selection process is that hiring managers are plucked from the masses to serve on hiring panels. Selecting officials are ordinary Joes, too. Because of this principle, you can be sure that hiring managers are in no way constitutionally or organically different from anyone else. In other words, today's cube neighbor is tomorrow's hiring manager; yesterday's hiring manager is today's cube neighbor. Therefore, you can preview what hiring managers will think of your application by soliciting feedback on it from friends, colleagues and relatives. By incorporating this feedback into your application, you will significantly boost your chances of impressing hiring managers.

Other important principles of the federal selection process are the following:

BECOME AN INSIDER

Do you want to get behind closed doors where hiring decisions are made? You can do so by volunteering to:

- Serve on peer review panels if you currently work for the federal government. Discuss your interest in such an assignment with your supervisor and Human Resources Office. They will probably enthusiastically welcome your offer.

- Review applicants' resumes if you currently work for a nonprofit or private organization.

Such an assignment will probably claim several days of your time. But for your investment, you will be repaid in spades by what you learn about how job applications are evaluated and how job-seekers present themselves to employers. You will gain a whole new perspective on the hiring process by participating in it from the other side.

→ Most hiring managers rush through thick stacks of applications, spending at most five or 10 minutes on each application.

→ Panelists never write the questions on applications; selecting officials only rarely contribute to them. Without pride of ownership in application questions, panelists and selecting officials almost never have a specific "right" answer in mind — no magic credential that will automatically seal the deal for an applicant; there is rarely a "Eureka!" moment for hiring managers.

However, hiring managers <u>and</u> automated application systems are almost always most impressed with applicants whose previous achievements closely match those demanded by the job opening and who have worked at or above the level of the opening. In other words, applicants who have already done the same job as the opening, done it well, and done it for muckety mucks tend to rate highest in the selection process.

→ Because most federal job applications are long, boring and similar to one another, hiring managers usually have trouble
distinguishing them from
one another and even
more trouble re-
membering them.

→ Hiring managers are
not necessarily ex-
perts in the jobs that they
screen. Nor are they necessarily familiar with the particular types of projects that applicants' experience is built upon.

→ Panelists and selecting officials do
not read applications to enjoy them.
They read them solely to get through
the pile, solely with a desire to *dismiss* applications and whittle down the pile to a
few choice candidates. And believe me, they
look for any reason they can to eliminate applicants, down to grammatical errors and typos.

Only by heeding these principles will you be able
to craft an application that is attention-grabbing,
impressive and memorable to harried, time-pres-
sured hiring managers. How can you heed these principles? By designing an application that will
STAND OUT and WAKE UP hiring managers because it is:

→ Interesting
→ Concise
→ Packed full of relevant, high level achievements
→ Formatted to be eye-catching, and to support fast reading and skimming
→ Easy-to-understand, and written for non-specialists
→ Error free

Fortunately for you, only a relatively small minority of applications for federal jobs meet these
criteria. Part II of this book will teach you how to craft KSAs, resumes and cover letters that will be
among the few that *will* meet these criteria and therefore stand out from the pack for all of the right
reasons.

SECTION II: CRANKING OUT YOUR APPLICATION

fpmi

Excuse me for being anatomically correct, but your job application is your brain on paper. Yes, your job application is the *only* version of you that hiring managers will see when they decide who to interview.

In other words, whatever qualities your application conveys are the qualities that *you* will convey to hiring managers. If for example, your application is disorganized and sloppy, then hiring managers will assume that *you* are disorganized and sloppy. But if, on the other hand, your application is logical, organized and describes impressive achievements, then hiring managers will assume that *you* are logical, organized and will produce impressive achievements.

Section II of the book will teach you how to convey all of your winning qualities in your application documents, including application essays, resumes and cover letters.

CHAPTER 6: YOUR BRAGGING WRITES

> *You can't sit around and wait for inspiration. You have to go after it with a club.*
> — **Jack London, Writer**

In order to be a highly successful federal job-seeker, you must pack your resumes, Knowledge, Skills and Abilities (KSA) essays and interviews with descriptions of impressive achievements that are relevant to the demands of your target job.

This type of "packing" is difficult for many job-seekers. I know this because the most common and most serious strategic problem that I have observed in the hundreds of job-seekers whom I have counseled is their inclination to undersell themselves: They emphasize relatively minor achievements that have nothing to do with their target job while omitting major and relevant achievements, and they describe their achievements in forgettable, bland terms instead of in wowing, attention-grabbing terms.

These problems are caused by common tendencies. For example, most of us:

➥ Remember too little about ourselves: After all, it's hard enough to keep track of everything that is going on now let alone remember assignments that were finished months or years ago.

➥ Know too much about ourselves; we are all so involved in everything we do that we can hardly distinguish what is important to us from what would be important to potential employers.

➥ Believe that inventorying our successes will make us sound like egocentric blow-hards.

➥ Don't know how to express achievements in terms that capture their magnitude.

This chapter will help you overcome these tendencies. It walks you through a step-by-step process for mining your qualifications for golden selling points and describing them in impressive, unforgettable terms—without sounding egocentric. This process is supported by exercises and tip sheets that will jog your memory and help you separate the wheat from the chaff, and by pep talks that will rev your confidence. Consider these tools as the "club" that the writer Jack London described as essential to inspiration.

You will be able to incorporate the skills and achievements that you identify and describe with the help of this chapter into your cover letter, resume, application essays and interviews. Put another way, this chapter will help you to create a reservoir of selling points that you can draw from throughout the application process.

SELLING YOURSELF

Guess what: If you are looking for a job, you are in sales — even if, during your whole life, you have never galloped your fingers over the keys of a cash register, asked a shopper, "would you like that in paper or plastic?" or processed a credit card payment. Huh? Yes, if you are looking for a job, you are in sales: The big ticket product that you are selling is yourself, and your potential buyers are your target employers.

Because you are in sales, you would be wise to take a few pages out of the playbooks of persuasive sellers. As any good seller will tell you:

1. A winning sales pitch addresses the *buyer's* needs — not the *seller's* needs. After all, you wouldn't buy a car from a seller whose sales pitch focused on how much profit the dealership would make from selling you a car instead of how a particular car fits *your* needs. Likewise, an employer is unlikely to hire you if you harp on why *you* want the job, instead of how you are going to solve *the employer's* problems. Put another way: On your job application and in your interview, you should ask not what an employer can do for you…you should tell what you can do for the employer.

And in order to effectively address an employer's needs, you must tailor your descriptions of your achievements to the employer's needs, as defined in the vacancy announcement of each job.

2.   A subtle sales pitch is a losing sales pitch. Just as a sensible shopper wouldn't buy a consumer product without understanding its virtues, an employer is not going to hire you without understanding your qualifications. And the only way to make an employer understand your qualifications is by describing them loud and clear on your job application and in your interviews. (Remember, if *you* don't describe your qualifications and sing your own praises, nobody will.)

If you are at all shy about singing your own praises, also keep in mind that:

1.   The questions on job applications and most interview questions solicit information about applicants' qualifications; they are basically invitations to toot your own horn. If your answers provide less than thorough assessments of your qualifications, they simply won't be answering the questions correctly.

2.   You simply cannot expect time-pressured, harried hiring managers to sleuth out hidden or subtle messages on written applications or interpret the hints of reticent interviewees. In most cases, it takes nothing less than the verbal or written equivalents of knock-out punches just to get and keep the attention of harried, time-pressured hiring managers.

3.   If you don't persuasively sell the product — you — you can't expect employers to buy it.

But don't mistake an aggressive sales pitch for an egocentric sales pitch; you *can* toot your own horn without sounding brassy, self-serving or cocky. To do so, you must describe what you have accomplished and why it was important and successful — without asserting how wonderful or valuable you are, predicting how impressed hiring managers will be with your applications, or describing yourself in unqualified, grandiose statements. Instead, provide specific examples of your achievements, and support descriptions of your results with hard data and objective validation of your results. In short, present yourself in factual, specific terms; let your achievements and credentials speak for themselves.

By doing so, you will provide evidence of your high-value that will naturally lead employers to the conclusion that you are a prize. This is a more convincing and less braggy strategy than directly proclaiming yourself as such.

What follows is a step-by-step approach for developing factual, specific and action-oriented descriptions of achievements.

STEP #1: THE PAPER CHASE

Collect the documents that can help you identify your golden selling points. These include:

- The vacancy announcement for your target job.

- A recent resume, if you have one. If you don't have a recent resume, list your jobs from the last 10 to 15 years, and describe your main successes at each one. Include special assignments, details, task forces and committees on which you served.

- List of professional training courses that you have taken.

- Copies of your performance evaluations from the last 10 to 15 years.

- Any academic/professional awards, professional honors or letters of commendation you have received. For government employees, this includes the write-ups accompanying performance awards and Quality Step Increases (QSIs).

- Letters of commendation and complimentary e-mails from superiors, stakeholders, clients, customers, trainees, contractors or conference participants. (Don't restrict yourself to positive feedback that you received from your supervisor.) And don't restrict yourself to positive feedback that you received in writing. Any positive feedback — whether it was delivered in an oral or written format, is fair game for you to cite in your resume, application essays or interviews.

- Positive evaluations that you received from attendees of training classes or other events.

- Products from your projects, such as documents or web pages that you helped produce.

- List of teams, task forces or other work groups that you were specially selected to serve on because of your skills or knowledge.

- List of your presentations, speeches and other public speaking engagements, including conference presentations and poster presentations.

- List of your publications.

- List of websites that you contributed to.

- List of awards or honors that you helped your organization earn.

- Clips in the popular press or trade publications covering projects that you contributed to.

•❖ List of professional organizations that you participate in.

•❖ Professional licenses and certifications.

•❖ List of your volunteer and community work.

•❖ Record of your military service.

•❖ List of computer hardware and software systems that you are can use.

•❖ Languages in which you are proficient or fluent.

STUDENTS AND RECENT GRADUATES

Collect the documents that can help you identify your golden selling points. These include:

•❖ Your academic transcripts: Compute your overall GPA and your GPA in your major.

•❖ List of your major papers, class projects, presentations, independent study projects, student grants, fellowships, your grades on these projects and any positive verbal praise that you received on these projects.

H O T • T I P

KEEP TRACK OF YOUR SUCCESSES...

It will be easy for you to inventory your golden selling points in the future if you create a file for storing the types of documents listed in "The Paper Chase." Update this file every time you finish another project or receive written or oral positive feedback on your work.

•❖ List of your honors and awards. Of course, if you were valedictorian and/or gave a commencement speech, note this stellar achievement.

•❖ List of your conference presentations, major speeches and public speaking engagements and any associated positive feedback that you received.

•❖ List of your articles in the popular press or trade publications.

•❖ List of your student jobs, teaching assistantships, tutoring jobs, summer jobs, internships and positive feedback that you received in these positions, such as praising evaluations, promotions and invitations to return to summer jobs.

•❖ Extracurricular activities, including positions in student government and newspapers, athletic activities, artistic and theater activities and volunteer work. Be sure to cite your leadership positions, such as any elected positions you held or any clubs or teams that you led.

•❖ List of websites that you helped produce.

➥ Record of military service.

➥ List of computer hardware and software systems that you can use.

➥ Languages in which you are proficient or fluent.

STEP #2: BRAINSTORM YOUR ACHIEVEMENTS

You may be one of the few job-seekers who is blessed with an ability to spontaneously reel off lists of impressive achievements and skills. But if you are like most job-seekers, you need additional coaching. So review the documents that you collected in Step #1, the Idea Generator provided on page 98, and the accompanying "before and after" examples of achievements provided on page 99, and then experiment with the five brainstorming methods suggested here for identifying your achievements.

One warning before you begin: Avoid vague statements from job descriptions that begin with phrases like "My responsibilities include…" or "My duties include…" Why? Because such statements don't necessarily reflect your activities. After all, just because you were assigned a responsibility on a job description doesn't mean that, in real life, that is what you actually did. But even more importantly, job descriptions convey vague areas of responsibility; they do not capture your most important selling points — your specific successes and results.

METHOD #1: ASK YOURSELF WHAT MAKES YOU…*YOU*

We each have received different training, and we each have our own biases and personalities. Our unique training, perspectives and personalities are reflected in almost everything we do.

Think about it: If two equally ranked professionals were to complete the same project, they would probably produce two totally different work products. Both results might be good, but they would certainly be different. For example, suppose two web designers were instructed to produce a website showcasing a government project. One designer might produce a site with fancy, moving graphics and lots of color. Another designer might produce a classic website in striking black and white that had no moving graphics. Both sites might be eye-catching, informative and impressive, but they would certainly convey different looks.

Even the simplest, everyday tasks reflect our uniqueness. Even two administrative assistants manage the phone differently. One might answer calls with a more cheerful and friendly greeting; the other might be more likely to check the answering machine.

Apply the uniqueness principle to yourself by figuring out what makes you...*you*. What makes you different from your colleagues and less experienced professionals? What makes you special? And then describe your uniqueness in brain-catching terms.

METHOD #2: GET INTERVIEWED

Ask colleagues, friends or relatives to interview you about your professional achievements. Include among your interviewers those who are familiar with your job history as well as those who are unfamiliar with your job history. Encourage your interviewers to include probing questions in their interviews. If you feel comfortable doing so, show the documents that you collected in Step #1 to your interviewers.

This brainstorming method may sound like a "Mickey Mouse" kind of exercise. But believe me, it works. Why? For one thing, the dynamic give-and-take of conversation may fire your brain and revive memories of important achievements better than will the solitary experience of sitting in front of an intimidating blank piece of paper. In addition, colleagues, friends and relatives who are familiar with your work will remind you of achievements and associated positive feedback that you may have forgotten. And friends and relatives who are unfamiliar with your work will help you recognize extraordinary aspects of your achievements that you take for granted.

METHOD #3: DO YOU DESERVE A PROMOTION?

When I lead "how-to-land-a-government-job" seminars, I frequently ask job-seeking attendees whether they deserve a promotion. In response, usually about 90 percent of these job-seekers answer "yes." Then, I ask them why they deserve a promotion. In response, long lists of stellar achievements invariably roll off their tongues; they usually cite achievements such as their:

- Creation of expansive, popular programs on their own initiative without supervision.

- Ability to simultaneously manage multiple projects — each with a difficult-to-meet, non-negotiable deadline.

- High productivity levels.

- Substantive knowledge, high quality-control standards and dogged work ethic that has significantly improved the quality of audits, investigations, publications, regulations or other work products.

•◆ Reputation as the "go-to" person for important projects that have strict deadlines and strict accuracy requirements.

A few minutes after asking these job-seekers why they deserve promotions, I usually ask them to name their most important skills or achievements. They invariably respond to this request with tongue-tied silence and heads that are bowed in "please-don't-call-on-me" postures — not even realizing that they had just answered the question a few minutes earlier when it had been phrased differently.

My classroom observations suggest that the easiest way for you to identify your best credentials may be to simply ask yourself why you deserve a promotion. Then, write down all of your skills and achievements that pour forth. By doing so, you will go a long way towards mining your qualifications for some gem-like achievements.

METHOD #4: PRETEND YOU'RE SOMEONE ELSE

Are you one of those professionals who is great at selling anything or anyone except yourself? If so, conquer your inhibitions by slipping your own skin for a few minutes: Pretend that you are the President of the Official "your name goes here" Fan Club. Then, through this alternative identity, review the documents that you collected during Step #1, and explain to a potential employer why they should hire you.

This kind of detached, out-of-body-experience may free you to abandon your modesty, and give yourself the glowing sales pitch that you deserve.

METHOD #5: TAKE SOMEONE ELSE'S LEAD

Ask a colleague, friend or relative to describe their achievements to you. Use their descriptions to get your creative juices flowing enough to describe your own achievements.

METHOD #6: SEEK A SECOND OPINION

No matter what initial brainstorming method you use…after you have created a list of your accomplishments, show it to colleagues, relatives or friends. Use their suggestions to improve your descriptions.

THE IDEA GENERATOR: IDENTIFY YOUR ACHIEVEMENTS

- Which of my projects or achievements mirror those demanded by my target job, and/or address the issues and stakeholders that my target job will address?

- What would I like to be asked about in a job interview? (Instead of passively waiting to be asked about an achievement in an interview, enthusiastically sing it out in your application.)

- Which achievements am I most proud of?

- Which of my achievements have drawn recognition, such as awards, promotions, bonuses or written or oral praise?

- How do I do my job differently or better than colleagues with the same job title or colleagues who have much less experience?

- When have I wisely used my judgment, discretion or creativity?

- Is there something that I have worked on mightily to accomplish?

- What special knowledge/skills do I have? What is unique about my education, training or experience?

- What am I an expert or fanatic about?

- What makes my job interesting or important?

- How have I shown initiative and gone the extra mile?

- How would my employer's services and the office atmosphere be different if I had never worked for this organization?

- Which of my achievements involved high-pressure, high-profile, high-dollar or high-priority projects?

- Which of my achievements helped or impacted the most people?

- Which of my achievements benefited or involved high-ranking officials?

- Have I managed politically sensitive situations, confidential information or top secret information?

- How have I helped save time or money or improved the efficiency of procedures?

- Do any of my accomplishments rank as "the first," "the only," "the best," "the fastest" or in the top tier? You don't have to be the first person to climb Mt. Everest in order to have an important "first," "only" or "best" under your belt. You should, for example, brandish your innovation if you have created a new filing system, designed a new priority system for answering correspondence of phones, initiated a new training course, identified the need for a new document or program, or implemented a new software system.

- Have I helped pioneer a new approach?

- Am I the only employee, or one of the only employees, qualified/entrusted to conduct an important activity because of my special skills or knowledge?

- Do I have special language skills?

- Do I have special computer skills?

USING THE IDEA GENERATOR: ACHIEVEMENTS GO FROM FIZZLE TO SIZZLE

BEFORE	AFTER
1. File documents.	1. Developed company's first electronic filing system giving company's 200 employees quick access to commonly used forms.
2. Write manuals.	2. Expert in translating technical information into easy-to-understand manuals.
3. Take orders over the phone.	3. Process product orders over high-volume call lines. Consistently exceed average processing volume of company sales representatives by 30 percent.
4. Develop contracts.	4. Developed company's first incentives-based supply contracts that give contractors incentives for beating deadlines.
5. Manage the books.	5. Closed company's books within three days of end of month for first time in company's history.
6. Deal with customer complaints.	6. I have earned a reputation for using tact, diplomacy and my programmatic knowledge to transform dissatisfied customers — whose hard-to-resolve complaints are not adequately addressed by more junior staffers — into satisfied, repeat customers.
7. Perform data entry functions.	7. Serve as sole customer care agent qualified to resolve orders that have been flagged for potential problems by credit card companies. (Entrusted with this task because of my reputation as an exceedingly accurate data processor and because of my thorough system knowledge.)
8. Help users solve computer problems.	8. Specialize in trouble-shooting "impossible-to-solve" problems.
9. Run Alternative Dispute Resolution Program.	9. Expanded company's Alternative Dispute Resolution program that now saves $2 million annually in legal costs.
10. Manage internship program.	10. Manage internship program employing 50 high school students per year. Program has reduced drop-out rate of participants by 30 percent and improved company's stature in the community.

STEP #3: QUANTIFY YOUR ACHIEVEMENTS

Hiring managers love descriptions of achievements that are supported by statistics, measurements, counts and other numbers because they usually sound scientific, indisputable and objective. They also usually sound massive, weighty and hefty.

Even if you don't work in a technical or scientific field, you can almost certainly quantify your activities and results. The Number Generator can help.

THE NUMBER GENERATOR ($,#,%)

TIME
- Number of years of experience you have.
- Number of hours of training you received.
- Time-savings that you produced by streamlining or implementing new procedures.
- Tight deadlines that you met.
- Number of days, weeks, months or years by which you shortened the production time of work products.

NUMBER OF PEOPLE IMPACTED BY YOUR ACTIVITIES
- Number of employees you supervise or train.
- Number of people attending your trainings or conferences you organize.
- Number of people receiving a product that you produced or packaging you designed.
- Number of managers whose calls you screen or whose travel you arrange.
- Number of people whom you recruited.
- Circulation of publication that you work on, or number of hits per day received by your website.
- Number of people or organizations that must comply with a regulation you produced or enforce.
- Reductions in the number or rate of deaths, injuries, accidents or illnesses within a specified time.
- Number of correspondences you send out per week/month.
- Number of customers/clients that you serve within a specified time period.
- Number of technical support calls that you answer within a specified time period, and average length of time it takes you to resolve each request.
- Number of users on computer or other high-tech system that you manage.

GEOGRAPHY
- Number of regional offices, states or countries within your sales or management jurisdiction.
- Number of square feet of building space that you manage.
- Size of acreage that you manage.

MONEY
- Dollar value of contracts or grants that you are authorized to award or manage.
- Dollar value or percentage of cost savings you produced or contributed to.
- Dollar value of property or equipment that you manage or protect.
- Dollar value of merchandise you sell per day, week or month.
- Dollar value or percentage increase in production or sales you produced.
- Dollar value of budget you manage.
- Dollar value of revenue generated by catalogue that you produced or contributed to.
- Dollar value of legal cases that you manage or won.
- Revenues of company that you help manage. (For example, "Direct accounting operations of $400 million investment firm that serves domestic and international clients.)

OTHER
- ➡ Percentage or other measure demonstrating how you improved the accuracy of a work product.
- ➡ Number of your suggestions or regulations that you implemented.
- ➡ Numbers or percentages documenting your reduction of a backlog of work.
- ➡ Number of high-level conference calls that you organize per week/month.
- ➡ Size of database you manage.
- ➡ Improvements in survey results that you helped bring about.
- ➡ Number of international or domestic trips that you arrange within a specified time.
- ➡ Number of articles, reports or other documents you published.
- ➡ Number of users on system that you manage.

USING THE NUMBER GENERATOR: ACHIEVEMENTS GO FROM FIZZLE TO SIZZLE

BEFORE	AFTER
1. Serve as time-keeper.	1. Manage all payroll and time-keeping records of 200 employees. Accurately perform bi-weekly updates. Answer dozens of questions about time and attendance regulations from managers daily.
2. Solve IT problems.	2. Answer about 30 calls to technical support hotline per week. Usually solve each caller's problem within 10 minutes.
3. Sell catalogue products.	3. Sell about $500 worth of collectible coins, jewelry and medals per day over the Mint's customer care hotline.
4. Manage property.	4. Manage 100,000 square feet of commercial office space.
5. Answer the telephone and word process.	5. Screen calls for five associate directors, and format and finalize 40 controlled letters per week.
6. Directed the transportation of equipment during Gulf War.	6. Directed transportation of 500,000 pounds of explosive weapons, 1,000,000 troops and 50,000 pounds of perishable food from Kentucky to Kuwait during Gulf War.
7. Manage important accounts.	7. Manage five bulk corporate accounts that are each worth more than $5 million per year.
8. Provide computer support.	8. Update software and virus-proof 30 laptops per week.
9. Help produce website.	9. Research and write content for the Small Business Administration's (SBA) Intranet, which is accessible to all of SBA's 3,000 employees. Write articles under tight deadlines.
10. Guard property.	10. Guard $73 million worth of gold and silver at Fort Knox.

STEP #4: NAME-DROP

Applicants who are perched on the highest rungs on the corporate or government ladder usually impress hiring managers the most. How can you prove that you occupy a lofty position in the hierarchy? By mentioning in your resume, application essays and interviews the highest-level managers who have blessed your work as well as the most important projects that you worked on. The common name for this practice is name-dropping.

Although name-dropping is generally a faux pas in social situations, professional name-dropping is an invaluable tool for job-seekers. Why is it so important? Because by name-dropping your high-level associations, you will prove that you can operate successfully in a demanding environment. You will also show that you are adept at the care and feeding of muckety mucks — an important skill in government.

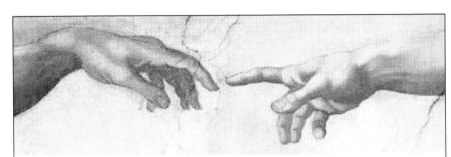

Michelangelo's Creation of Adam fresco shows Adam and God reaching toward one another, arms outstretched, fingers almost touching. The spark of life is evidently leaping from God to Adam across that gap between their fingertips. Just as Adam receives the spark of life from God, your application will receive an electrifying jolt from the almighty, exalted managers that are named-dropped in it.

In addition, by name-dropping your high-level associations, you will demonstrate that you have already fulfilled the trust of senior officials. You will thereby reassure potential employers that it is safe for them to trust you as well.

Don't restrict yourself to name-dropping your immediate supervisor(s). Go as high up the food chain as you can by mentioning the titles of senior staffers who reviewed or approved your work plans or work products, praised you orally or in writing, attended events that you organized, interacted with you, belonged to the target audience of your documents or other work products, or in any way benefited from your toil. Whether your highest-level contact is an Assistant Department Director or the President of the United States, it doesn't matter: Mention them. Also mention the names of high-profile documents or other work products that you contributed to. The name-dropping makeovers on page 103 provide vivid examples of the effective use of this technique.

Also format your resume and KSAs to brandish your own job titles as well as the names of your employers — particularly if they are Fortune 500 corporations, large companies, influential think tanks, Congressional committees and important nonprofits. And mention your titles and employers in interviews.

If you are reluctant to name-drop because it feels forced, remember how hard you worked to earn the approval of your superiors; all of your hard work won't get you very far if your potential employers don't know about it. In the job-searching realm, the squeaky wheel principle applies; the more that you tell your potential employers about your high-level successes, the more likely they will be to hire you.

Moreover, you've worked hard to help make your muckety mucks look good; you've hauled and carried; you've endured the boring meetings; you've knocked yourself out to meet the impossible deadlines; you've trouble-shot the last-minute emergencies; now it's payback time, it's time for your muckety mucks to help make you look good. Go ahead: Bask in their reflected glow.

NAME-DROPPING MAKEOVERS: ACHIEVEMENTS GO FROM FIZZLE TO SIZZLE

BEFORE	AFTER
1. Organize meetings and events.	1. Schedule and coordinate high-level conference calls, weekly management meetings, monthly board meetings and special events attended by dozens of top executives.
2. Arrange travel.	2. Arrange international and domestic travel for five senior attorneys and director of sales and marketing. In a typical month, arrange 10 trips.
3. Develop web content.	3. Write articles for website that is accessed by department's 20 senior managers and 200 staffers.
4. Work as paralegal.	4. Serve as sole paralegal for eight senior attorneys in high-pressure, deadline-driven environment.
5. Answer correspondence.	5. Answer about 50 Congressional inquiries per month about Clean Air Act program covering 50 coal-fired power plants.
6. Help design personnel regulations.	6. Drafted early retirement regulations affecting 2000 General Electric employees.
7. Helped plan unveilings of new coin designs.	7. Played pivotal role in the planning and management of 10 unveilings of new quarters from high-profile, national 50 State Quarters Program. Each event drew more than 500 attendees, including members of Congress, the national media and trade publications.
8. Write reports.	8. Write quarterly reports summarizing national worker safety statistics that are — without fail — approved without substantial revisions by Director of Bureau of Labor Statistics and then scrutinized by Congress.
9. Arrange stakeholder meetings.	9. Arranged annual meetings of the Laboratory Directors Conference attended by 75 directors of national research facilities, including the director of Lawrence Livermore National Laboratory.
10. Pitched stories to the press.	10. Provided story ideas and background information for dozens of articles that appeared in publications including *Government Executive*, *FedWorld*, *Federal Times* and *FedNews*.

STEP #5: VALIDATE YOUR SUCCESS

How many times have you done this? You receive positive feedback at work, such as verbal complaints, exemplary performance evaluations, praising e-mails, or merit-based awards…You feel good about being validated for only about half a day, but it doesn't even occur to you to write down whatever verbal praise you received or save praising documents.

After cashing whatever financial award you may have received, you:

•• Throw away the praising flattering justification, or
•• File the praising flattering justification in an obscure folder that will never again see the light of day.

Then you swiftly forget about the positive feedback you received altogether.

Well, what good is validation that is literally cast aside into eternal oblivion? The positive feedback that you receive at work is among your most important tools for advancement. It's OK to file praising feedback away…in fact, you should store it for safekeeping…But when you start your next job-search, be sure to pull it out again — faster than a sheriff in a western town would draw his gun in a shoot-out.

Use this objective feedback to crown descriptions of your achievements in resumes, KSAs and interviews. By doing so, you will go a long way towards proving that you are a producer by an objective standard, instead of just by your subjective standards. Review the Feedback Generator for ideas on what types of positive feedback and other objective measures to cite.

THE VALIDATION GENERATOR: PROVING THAT YOU ARE A PRODUCER

FORMAL RECOGNITION OF PERFORMANCE/TRUSTWORTHINESS:
•• Superior performance evaluations. For example:
  ✓ *Received glowing performance evaluation for 2004.*
  ✓ *Received superior performance evaluation for four of out of the last five years.*

•• Performance awards (including team awards) and merit-based bonuses.
•• Letters of commendation.
•• Patents.
•• Security clearances.
•• Management of confidential information.
•• Grants.

ADVANCEMENT:
•• Hired from contract or temporary position into permanent position.
•• Rapid advancement. For example:
  ✓ *Accepted into Senior Executive Service after only two years as a federal employee.*
  ✓ *Advanced from a Clerk to Program Manager position in six years.*
  ✓ *Received two merit-based promotions in four years.*

ORAL OR WRITTEN PRAISE:

•• Oral comments or praising e-mails from a supervisor, senior official, stakeholder, client, contractor, customer or your staffers. For example:

  ✓ *Regularly receive letters of appreciation from customers for my swift and effective resolution of problems that had delayed their orders.*

•• Favorable comments on performance evaluations. For example:

  ✓ *Please note these comments from my supervisor on my most recent performance evaluation: "Whenever there is a problem here, John comes up with a fool-proof solution. I often wonder, what we would do without John?"*

FEEDBACK FROM TRAINING, CONFERENCE OR OTHER EVENT:

•• Drawing a large crowd to event.
•• Favorable evaluations, or oral or written praise from attendees or favorable coverage by the press.
•• Standing ovations.

SPECIAL REQUESTS FOR YOUR SERVICES:

•• Requests by customers, clients, stakeholders groups from your participation in projects.
•• Specially selected to serve on details, workgroups, committees or task forces. For example:

  ✓ *Specially selected to serve on the Department of Interior's Communication Task Force due to my superior analytic, problem-solving and writing skills.*

  ✓ *Specially selected by General Electric's CEO to write company's annual report because of my ability to write easy-to-understand, eye-catching documents.*

RECORD OF IMPROVING REPUTATION OF YOUR ORGANIZATION:

•• Praise from an article in press or trade publication for project that reflects your contributions.
•• Your contribution to awards earned by your organization. For example:

  ✓ *Managed Department of Labor's Energy Conservation Program, which won the Department of Energy's "Energy Saver Award" in 2003.*

  ✓ *Played pivotal role in management of accounting records of ABC Company from 2000 to 2004, which received an unqualified audit opinion from an independent public accountant every year during that period.*

MEMBERSHIP IN ELITE, SELECTIVE GROUP:

•• Member of executive management team.
•• Member of Senior Executive Service.
•• Management of elite clients, such as Fortune 500 Companies, high-dollar corporate clients or high-profile clients.
•• Member of the board of a non-profit or other organization.
•• Elected position in a professional or community organization.
•• Experience serving as a team leader.

YOUR STANDING IN THE TOP-TIER OF YOUR JOB CATEGORY OR OFFICE:

•• Receipt of highest possible bonus in your office or among your peers, or regular receipt of high bonuses.
•• Record of beating a quota or goal. (Mention quota or goal to provide reference point.)
•• Number or percentage of cases you have won, if you are a lawyer.
•• Record of exceeding average productivity levels. These measures don't have to be official tallies; you can estimate them yourself. But make sure that your claims are defensible. For example:

  ✓ *Consistently exceed average productivity levels of company Sales Representatives by about 30 percent.*

YOUR ENVIABLE REPUTATION:

•❖ How your work products, advice or strategies are incorporated into office-wide or organization-wide policies, programs or procedures.

•❖ How the methods you used in a project have served as a model or template, or set the standard for subsequent projects.

•❖ Your ability to gain approval of your work by supervisors or senior management without requiring significant revisions and/or without requiring redundant efforts.

•❖ Your record of completing projects under budget, on-time — or even beating budgets or deadlines.

•❖ Your record for accuracy, which eliminates the need for redundant efforts.

•❖ Your ability to smoothly manage operations. Cite for example, your record of running glitch-free teleconferences, large events or computer systems.

•❖ Your successful completing of increasingly responsible, complicated or specialized projects.

•❖ Your record of being consulted by other professionals as an expert.

•❖ Your experience in providing training.

•❖ Your excellent reputation. For example:
   ✓ *Because of my expertise with all Microsoft office software programs, I have earned a reputation as a computer-savvy administrator.*

EVIDENCE OF YOUR TRUSTWORTHINESS:

•❖ Authority to award contracts or allocate grants.
•❖ Authority to manage, disburse cash or checks.
•❖ Management of confidential information.

STUDENTS AND RECENT GRADUATES:

•❖ Overall GPA, GPA in your major, or grades in relevant classes or on relevant assignments — whichever makes you look best.
•❖ Honors and awards.
•❖ Fellowships, scholarships and grants.
•❖ Ability to juggle school and student jobs at the same time.
•❖ Elected position in student government or other student organizations.
•❖ Selection for particularly competitive summer jobs or internships.
•❖ Written and oral praise from professors in response to a thesis defense, exams, papers, independent projects, oral presentations and other projects.
•❖ Positive feedback from participation in extracurricular activities, such as student newspaper, student government, team sports or other pursuits.

FPMI ©2005

STEP #6: ADD POWER WORDS AND PHRASES

Sometimes, you can't hang a specific number, name-drop specific officials or cite objective validation for a project, activity or success. Power words and phrases may help you describe such credentials. Such power words and phrases include:

- I am an award-winning…
- Multi-million dollar
- High-profile
- High-pressure
- High-priority
- High-energy
- High-volume
- High-dollar
- High-visibility

- Fast-paced
- Fast-track
- High-traffic
- Front-line
- Deadline-driven
- I am an expert in…
- I played a pivotal role in….
- I single handedly….
- A significant improvement in….

STEP #7: MATCH YOUR SKILLS AND ACHIEVEMENTS TO THE OPENING

To be effective, job applications and interviews must target the skills
demanded by the opening. This means that you shouldn't serve-up brain dumps of *all* of your
activities and achievements. Instead, you should winnow down your list of activities and achievements to the most relevant ones. To accomplish this task, you should — as explained below —
analyze the skills demanded by the opening, and then match your experience to analyzed skills.

ANALYZE THE OPENING

The skills demanded by each opening are defined in its job description. Granted: More often than
not, these job descriptions are dense, rambling and repetitive. But you can extract their essence by:

1. Highlighting important phrases.

2. Grouping similar skills under categories, if possible. (These categories may help you identify
   redundancies in the vacancy announcement. They may also suggest a framework for organizing your experience in your resume or KSAS.)

3. Consolidating similar skills and eliminate redundancies.

4. Listing remaining categories and skills.

These steps were used to analyze the writer/editor position opening below.

A SKILLS ANALYSIS OF SAMPLE JOB DESCRIPTION

Here is a job description from a vacancy announcement for a writer/editor opening at the Transportation Security Agency. Appearing below the job description is a skills analysis for this job.

The incumbent of this position will report to the manager, communications division within the Office of Security Technology. The incumbent will be the senior writer-editor for the division. This involves a broad spectrum of specialized and complex writing and editing duties related to the mission of the Office of Security Technology. Develops strategies and plans for a communications program to respond to public and congressional inquiries. Researches, identifies and establishes viable communications methods and tools to inform the public and internal agency and department organizations of the Office's policies, programs, services, and activities. Independently writes, edits, creates, and updates materials intended to be definitive descriptions and explanations of the Office's programs, accomplishments, policies, and procedures. Ensures product materials comply with Agency policies, standards, and formats and content is accurate and current. Integrates complex technical material into highly readable documents for a variety of audiences. Analyzes, synthesizes, and integrates a variety of inputs to produce an optimum written communication approach for a designated audience. Interfaces with headquarters offices to analyze, recommend, develop and create Agency written materials, products and web page designs. Coordinates and resolves potential conflicts with internal Office subject matter experts for the creation and development of standard reply information and product materials. Develops standards for paper and electronic responses to public and congressional inquiries and conducts subject and program matter searches to obtain information necessary to support proposed responses. Supports outreach initiatives to meeting internal and external customer requirements, which includes participation in meetings, conferences, and workshops. There will be periods of time when priority deadlines must be met and the incumbent may be asked to work more than 40 hours. Distributing information and reporting results of legislative tracking to senior officials in a timely basis.

SKILLS REQUIRED BY THIS JOB

STRATEGIC PLANNING
- Developing communication strategies for responding to information requests from Congress, the public and other internal and external audiences.
- Developing communication plans.
- Supporting outreach initiatives.

RESEARCHING

- Researching, analyzing, synthesizing technical information from varied sources.
- Legislative tracking.

WRITING

- Independently writing, editing and updating documents including accurate program descriptions that comply with agency requirements.
- Describing programs, accomplishments, policies and procedures.
- Integrating information from various sources.
- Translating complex information into easy-to-understand language.
- Communicating in hardcopy and electronic formats, including web pages.
- Developing standards for content and format.

ORAL COMMUNICATION/PROJECT MANAGEMENT

- Interfacing with various offices to resolve potential conflicts.
- Distributing information and reporting on legislative tracking to senior officials.
- Participating in meetings, conferences and workshops (acting as liason).
- Working extra hours.
- Meeting deadlines.

Of course, the more evidence that you can provide of your ability to apply these skills to transportation issues, the better.

MATCH YOUR SKILLS

To match your skills to those demanded by the opening, review the activities and achievements that you identified in Step #1 through Step #5. Then, select those that fit the skills demanded by your target job, and eliminate those that do not.

Repeat keywords: Your resume and KSAs should repeat keywords from the opening's job description. Suppose, for example, that you were applying for the writer/editor opening provided above, which requires the following skill: Develops communication strategies for responding to information requests from Congress, the public and other internal and external audiences.

If you have previously demonstrated this skill, you would be well advised to include something like the following sentence in your resume and KSAs: *Developed communication strategies for responding to information requests from Congress, the public and other internal and external audiences.*

Some applicants wrongly believe that hiring managers perceive such parroting as contrived or "fishy." Au contraire! (Purge your memory of those images of your grade school teacher wagging her index finger while warning you about the evils of plagiarism.) By parroting keywords in your resume and KSAs, you will boost your rating because:

- Some automated systems rate applications based upon keyword searches.

- Human resources staffers who screen applications for basic qualifications and hiring managers usually favor applicants who have previously done the same job as the opening. By repeating keywords, you will prove that you have this potentially pivotal experience.

Put another way: Each job description and KSA in a vacancy announcement is really a question that asks, "Do you have this experience?" The more ways you can answer this question with, "Yes, I have this experience," the higher your application will rate in the selection process. Echoing keywords on an application is one important way to affirm that your experience is relevant to the opening.

You may wonder why your application should echo keywords from a vacancy announcement when, as discussed in Chapter 5, keyword searches performed by automated application systems can identify synonyms. Because, by echoing keywords, you will maximize the chances that automated systems and hiring managers will understand the parallels between your credentials and the requirements of the opening, and minimize their opportunities for misinterpreting your application.

If your credentials don't exactly match the job description of the opening, just include as many keywords as you can in your resume and KSAs. Also, include your relevant academic experiences. For example, here is an excerpt from a KSA about communication skills that could be submitted by a newly minted graduate student applying for the writer/editor opening discussed on page 108. Keywords from the job description are underlined:

I wrote and edited a paper on mass transit for a graduate level urban planning class. For this assignment, I:

- *Researched mass transit policies,*
- *Tracked transportation legislation throughout 2003,*
- *Synthesized, summarized and translated transit legislation into easy-to-understand language, and communicated results orally and in writing to class.*

I received a B+ on the paper and an A- in the class.

Strengthen Your Descriptions: Don't succumb to the temptation to mechanically regurgitate keywords without adapting them to *your* background, and without quantifying, name-dropping and providing objective evidence of you success. For example, here is an excerpt from a KSA about communication skills for the writer/editor position on page 108 that embeds keywords within strengthened descriptions:

I developed communication strategies for responding to Congressional requests for information about multi-million dollar federal transportation grants to the states. Such efforts involved:

- *Meeting with representatives of Ways and Means Committee, Transportation and Environment Congressional committees at least every other month.*
- *Preparing summaries of legislation that were scrutinized by the Director of the Department of Transportation.*
- *Meeting tight deadlines for producing comprehensive documents by working many weekends and holidays.*

In addition, I received three On-The-Spot Awards for my timely production of rush documents for Congress.

CHAPTER 7:
WRITING KILLER APPLICATION ESSAYS
(KSAs and ECQs)
fpmi

CHAPTER 7: WRITING KILLER APPLICATION ESSAYS (KSAs and ECQs)

Good writing is clear thinking made visible.
— Bill Wheeler, Writer

Most job-seekers would rather eat ground glass than write application essays. (Application essays are frequently called KSAs, short for Knowledge, Skills and Abilities, or ECQs, short for Executive Core Qualifications.) So job seekers often procrastinate their essay writing chore for days, even weeks. Indeed, it is not uncommon for job applicants to live with their application essays hanging over their heads until they either come perilously close to nervous breakdowns or to missing application deadlines — whichever comes first.

When typical job applicants finally do force themselves to work on their application essays, they are invariably overwhelmed by crippling self-doubt...page fright. Most of them have no clear idea what to say in their essays, or how to say it.

The knowledge that essays are probably the single most important part of most federal job applications and the vagueness of most essay questions usually only compounds the pressure for job applicants. With every sentence that job applicants slowly and painstakingly squeeze out of their brains, they wonder, "Is this wrong?....Is this right?...Is there a better way that I should be doing this?"

Worse still, typical job applicants taunt themselves by imagining the competition effortlessly churning out perfect essays (whatever "perfect" is), landing jobs that should rightfully be theirs, and stealing their futures. These unfortu-

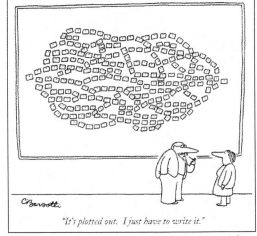

"It's plotted out. I just have to write it."

nates — mired in uncertainty — typically discard draft after draft, only to start over again, each time more defeated and more insecure than the previous time. One step forward...two steps backward.

Although essay preparation does demand some time and thought, its does not *have* to be sooooo painful. In fact, most of the agony and *endlessly* protracted nature of the process is usually rooted in the uncertainty of the assignment. After all, despite the importance of KSAs, federal agencies — with only a few rare exceptions — do not disclose what constitutes "good" essays. Nor do they provide advice on how to write KSAs, distribute model KSAs or warn of common essay blunders.

No wonder the overwhelming majority of KSA and ECQ writers — unguided and without access to example essays — feel like they do not know what they are doing…no one has given them a clue about what they should do.

But this illuminating chapter will finally free you from the feeling that you are flailing around helplessly in the dark when you write application essays. Here you will find specific tips and model essays that will show you how to write essays that are:

➤ Interesting
➤ Concise
➤ Packed full of relevant, high level achievements
➤ Formatted to be eye-catching, and to support fast reading and skimming
➤ Easy-to-understand, and written for nonspecialists
➤ Error free

This guidance will enable you to bypass the bewilderment that typically bogs down KSA and ECQ writers. Liberated from indecision, you will crank out killer KSAs and ECQs that will stand out from the pack for all of the right reasons.

WHY KSAs AND ECQs ARE REQUIRED

Most job-seekers struggle to understand why federal agencies put them through KSA or ECQ hell. Why, they wonder, doesn't the hiring agency just base its selecting decisions on applicants' resumes?

Hiring agencies require KSAs or ECQs in addition to resumes because:

➤ A resume usually lists an applicant's academic and professional credentials in chronological order. In order to evaluate such documents, hiring managers must comb through them, tease out applicants' relevant credentials and gauge their applicability to the opening.

By contrast, essay questions provide applicants with an opportunity to consolidate their most relevant credentials to the target opening, and thereby prove that their credentials and previous triumphs qualify them to solve the hiring agency's current problems. Voila! No teasing, combing or gauging required. Therefore, by requiring KSAs and ECQs, hiring agencies shift the burden of work from hiring managers to applicants.

➤ KSAs and ECQs contain more detail than resumes.

➤ KSAs and ECQs provide a convenient screening device. That is, unmotivated candidates who are unwilling to endure the hassle of preparing these essays weed themselves out of the competition.

THE IMPORTANCE OF STORY TELLING

Most applicants for federal jobs fill their KSAs with job descriptions. (See the sample me-o-centric essay on page 117.) I call these documents "job description KSAs" or "me-o-centric KSAs." Their telltale signature is their repetition of the pronoun "I", the word "me" and clauses, such as "my responsibilities include…" or "my duties include…"

What's wrong with job description KSAs? Dominated by lists of activities that are devoid of a theme or plot, job description KSAs are boring. Put another way: Reading a job description KSA is about as interesting as reading someone else's mile-long "to do" list. And a boring KSA is unlikely to be read, much less remembered. What's more, because job description KSAs focus on what the applicant was supposed to do rather than what s/he actually accomplished or achieved, they are generally unimpressive. (Your job description may say that you will land a rocket on Mars…but did you actually do it?)

SUCCESS STORIES

How can you craft KSAs and ECQs that are impressive and memorable? Specificity and concrete, relevant examples will make your essays distinctive and interesting. Generalities and platitudes that could apply to every other government wannabe, or every other professional with your title, will bore. If you use them, you will just blur into the crowded pack of applicants.

Usually, the best way to convey specificity and examples is by telling a relevant success story — a narrative that describes how you accomplished a specific goal or solved a problem that relates to the opening. No matter what level you have reached in your career — whether you are applying for an entry level or executive position, your KSAs and ECQs should contain success stories because:

1. **Success stories are memorable.** Because success stories are conceptually united by a dramatic narrative, they are like verbal Velcro that wraps around and sticks to the reader's brain. Indeed, even a short essay that describes a single success story will likely be more memorable and impressive than a long job description essay that rattles off paragraph after paragraph of responsibilities that are only linked by the fact that they are performed by the same person.

As the political consultants James Carville and Paul Begala explain in their non-partisan book about succeeding in everyday life, *Buck Up, Suck up…And Come Back When You Foul Up**:

> *Facts tell, but stories sell…If you're not communicating in stories, you're not communicating. You may be presenting a series of facts, many of them perhaps important, but the chances of your audience remembering or being moved by your facts enough to do what you want are nil.*

The memorable, persuasive punch provided by storytelling has compelled almost every successful politician — from Abraham Lincoln, to Ronald Reagan, to Bill Clinton — to use this device to woo votes. You can use this same technique to wow hiring managers.

* Reprinted with permission of Simon & Schuster Adult Publishing Group from BUCK UP, SUCK UP...And Come Back When You Foul Up by James Carville and Paul Begala. Copyright © 2003 by James Carville and Paul Begala.

2. **Success stories are impressive.** By telling success stories that transcend descriptions of ho-hum, day-to-day chores and that highlight your save-the-day moments and your Superman, home run, gold medal achievements, you will prove that you are a producer. You will thereby get hiring managers salivating at the prospect of hiring you to produce at their agencies.

3. **Your success stories will help you stand out from the pack:** By telling success stories that capture the *uniqueness* of your problem-solving and goal-reaching experiences, and de-emphasizing responsibilities that are indistinguishable from those of hundreds of other government employees who have the same job title as you, you will distinguish yourself from the pack.

Don't pressure yourself to find a single blockbuster story that captures all of the credentials that you want to convey in a particular essay. You may answer an essay with more than one story and/or include additional credentials in your essays besides those that are embedded in stories.

POWER LAWYER, GERRY SPENCE, EXPLAINS WHY STORIES PERSUADE
(From the audio version of *How To Argue And Win Every Time* by Gerry Spence)

Gerry Spence is one of the nation's best known and most respected trial lawyers. In practice for more than 40 years, he has never lost a criminal case. His hundreds of victories include many high-profile cases, such as the Karen Silkwood, Imelda Marcos and Randy Weaver cases. Here Spence explains why story-based arguments are so compelling. (Remember that each of your essays is essentially an argument for why you should be offered your target job.)

Photo by DJ Bassett

Every argument in court or out, whether delivered over the supper table or at coffee break, can be reduced to a story. An argument like a house, like the houses of the three little pigs, has structure. Whether it will fall, whether it can be blown down when the wolf huffs and puffs, depends on how it will be built. And the strongest structure for any argument is always story…

Story telling has been the principle means by which we have taught one another from the beginning of time. The campfire. The tribal members gathered around, the little children peeping from behind the adults… The old man — can you hear his crackly voice, telling his stories of days gone by?

We are entertained by the drama of movies. Television and theater are highly developed forms of story telling. The most effective advertisements on television are always mini stories that take little more than half a minute. Jokes are small stories… Christ's parables are stories…

Storytelling is in the genes. Listening to stories is also in the genes. It follows, therefore, that the most effective structure for any argument will always be story…

The story argument is so powerful because it speaks in the language form of the species. Its structure is natural. It permits the storyteller to speak easily, openly from the heart zone. It provokes interest. It is an antidote to the worst poison that can be injected into any argument — the doldrums.

DON'T BE A ME-O-CENTRIC

Have you talked lately with a me-o-centric person — someone who is single-mindedly focused on himself or herself?

If so, chances are that you hardly remember the me-o-centric's words. How come? Because the me-o-centric's preoccupation with "me," without regard for the interests or activities of others, is monotonous and boring. Moreover, the me-o-centric's tendency to begin every sentence with the pronoun "I" offers all of the dynamism of a sleep-inducing white noise machine.

Shortly after starting a conversation with a me-o-centric, most people either physically move away or mentally drift away. Soon after the contact is over, any memory of the me-o-centric's words fades away. Just as forgettable as me-o-centric monologues are me-o-centric essays. Try to slog through, for example, the me-o-centric essay on the next page.

Now, without looking back at the essay, describe the writer's work. Chances are you don't remember much about it. How come? Because, like me-o-centric monologues, this me-o-centric essay is boringly self-absorbed — as reflected in its overuse of the "I" pronoun.

Moreover, any KSA or ECQ that is single-mindedly focused on "I" isn't explaining the benefits to people and programs yielded by the work done by "I." By ignoring their own results and how they benefited their employers, me-o-centrics sacrifice their best selling points. (You might even say that me-o-centrics are victims of their own self-centeredness.)

Also missing from the me-o-centric essay is an overarching theme or framework that unites its content. Disjointed and uncohesive, the essay's facts fail to lodge in the reader's mind. Instead, they slip through the reader's mind like sand through a sieve.

By contrast, success stories are held together by the glue of a plot. Therefore they are more memorable than me-o-centric essays. In addition, success stories are — by definition — focused on results that solved problems or achieved goals impacting organizations and people besides the writer. Therefore, they are more impressive than the dull, this-is-what-I-do-everyday descriptions of me-o-centric essays.

SAMPLE ME-O-CENTRIC KSA

Describe your experience applying procedural knowledge and analyzing policies in performing your job.

__I__ am responsible for developing OGE policy, staffing and recruitment, position classification and position management, pay and allowances, time and attendance, health and life insurance programs, employee relations and discipline. __My__ duty is to function as the agency's Training Officer and conduct career development. __I__ counsel employees on retirement, benefits and TSP. __I__ administer the agency's performance management system. __I__ administer the agency's injury compensation program. The Personnel Office at OGE functions as a Delegated Examining Unit. As the Personnel Officer, __I__ manage all aspects of merit staffing procedures. This involves the ability to analyze jobs to identify the knowledge, skills and abilities required for effective work performance. __I__ analyze, interpret and apply qualification standards to prospective applicants. __I__ develop rating schedules and crediting plans. __I__ write job descriptions, and ensure that vacancy announcements are posted on USAJOBS. __I__ have served on many selection panels. __I__ am responsible for candidates under the terms of OGE's merit promotion plan. __I__ have in-depth knowledge of Title 5 staffing and employment regulations. __I__ have knowledge of personnel rules and regulations relating to staffing, recruitment and benefits. __My__ policies and programs have been used as templates by other offices. __I__ accomplished staffing and recruitment in all targeted areas for the IRS: Examination, Collection, agents, Criminal Investigators, and Taxpayer Service Representatives while serving as a staffing specialist for the IRS. __I__ have knowledge of federal employment rules, regulations, practices and merit principles. __I__ am able to apply these policies to recruitment and selection, and other components of personnel. __I__ consulted with management concerning both the immediate and long-range goals of the organization and developed approaches to improve operations in these areas. __I__ am able to analyze and synthesize a variety of information from IRS functions and devise solutions to staffing and recruitment needs. __I__ have the ability to analyze problems and exercise sound judgment in staffing and classification decisions. __I__ have knowledge of special hiring programs such as Public Law 105-339: Veterans Employment Opportunities of 1998. __I__ have knowledge of the legal authorities used for these types of appointments. __I__ have prepared recruitment packages with materials for varied audiences and cover letters to various universities, law schools and legal journals to recruit attorneys for the Office of Government Ethics. __I__ have also recruited for the positions of Ethics Specialist and Administrative staff using the Internet, professional publications and career fairs. While at IRS, __I__ prepared recruitment packages aimed at recruiting accountants, attorneys and taxpayer service representatives to the organization. __I__ provide expert advice and on matters relating to overall HR programs and processes to employees, applicants and the general public.

DIAGNOSING A ME-O-CENTRIC KSA

Notice how almost every sentence and important clause in this me-o-centric KSA begins with the pronoun "I" or the word "my" — the stylistic signature of the me-o-centric. Notice too how this unformatted essay, which features no paragraphs or headings, looks dense and overwhelming. And since nothing stands out off this KSA, nothing from this KSA will lodge in the memory of a busy, time-pressured hiring manager.

PICKING POWERFUL STORIES

GRIST FOR STORIES

Chapter 6 can help you mine your experience for powerful success stories. Remember to favor stories that closely parallel the demands of your target job, and capture your biggest successes, i.e., those that involved the largest numbers of people, largest amounts of money, approvals or participation of high level officials or most favorable press coverage.

If you are not a new graduate, your stories should primarily come from your work experiences. However, you may also cite non-work stories that are based in your academic experiences, activities in professional organizations, community work, volunteer jobs, hobbies or reading.

Just be sure that your non-work stories, like your work stories, reflect traits demanded by your desired job. For example, you could answer KSAs and ECQs addressing leadership or negotiating skills by discussing how you swayed a jury while serving on jury duty; started a neighborhood crime watch in your neighborhood; or negotiated an economical maintenance contract for your condo complex while serving on the condo board.

WHAT HAVE YOU DONE FOR ME LATELY?

The more recent your power stories, the better. If possible, favor stories that describe events that occurred during the last five or 10 years. Why? Because potential employers are way more interested in learning about who you are now and what you offer now than about who you were and what you did eons ago. And after all, our careers are supposed to reflect an upward momentum. So if your essays hark back to Neanderthal times, employers may — rightly or not — infer that you don't have better recent stories because your career is going downhill instead of uphill.

DANGER ZONES

Steer clear of stories that might offend hiring managers or suggest to them — however wrongly — that you might be a negative, high-maintenance employee. Such stories include those that so much as hint at your:

➤ Religious beliefs
➤ Personal problems or shortcomings
➤ Criticisms of former or current employers, employees or colleagues
➤ Propensity to break rules on the job or elsewhere

Also keep your political views to yourself unless you cite your position as a political appointee as a credential for your target job. In addition, if you cite your position as a staffer for a member of Congress as a credential, tone down the potentially partisan implications of your position by referring to your superiors by title rather than by name. For example, say, "I served as a legislative assistant for a senator from Colorado," rather than, "I served as a legislative assistant for Senator John Doe (R-CO)."

FEATURES OF A POWERFUL STORY

Many story tellers omit critical information that seems self-evident to them but that is not at all obvious to strangers to the situation. These story tellers thereby confuse and alienate their audiences. This is not a good thing to do when you are asking your audience for a job. You can avoid this pitfall by running your stories (as well as the rest of your application) by an objective editor(s) who can tell you whether your train of thought will be clear to hiring mangers who are unfamiliar with your projects.

The critical components of an effective story include:

1. **A CONCRETE PROBLEM OR GOAL:** How much detail about the problem or goal should you provide? First, make sure that you orient the reader by identifying the year, your title and the name of the organization that employed you when you began addressing the problem or goal. Why? Because titles and dates give your story credibility. In addition, titles give you a more authoritative and commanding presence than vague references to "my previous job" or "my current job," which probably means nothing to the strangers who will read your essay.

   If possible, document the existence of the problem or the size of the goal with supporting statistics or other numbers; such figures will help to objectively underscore the importance of your work.

   Also be sure to include enough context in the beginning of your story to set the stage for discussions that will follow about the wisdom of your strategy and the importance of your achievements. Make sure that any additional introductory information that you provide about the problem or goal is truly necessary to help explain your success — and not just extra frill.

Examples of problems suitable for essays include:

➤ An unattended switchboard.
➤ A disorganized filing system.
➤ An unacceptable trend.
➤ The need for a better system for tracking and ordering office supplies.
➤ A high accident or death rate.
➤ Poor sales.
➤ Poor customer service.
➤ High employee turnover, or poor employee morale.
➤ An ineffective or inefficient system or process.
➤ Inadequate profits.
➤ A back-log of letters, product orders or contracts that should be processed.
➤ A disorganized office.
➤ A gap in office capabilities.
➤ An uninformative or outdated website.
➤ The need to purchase software or hardware.
➤ Inappropriate use of an employer's credit cards by employees.
➤ The need to cut costs.

Examples of goals suitable for essays include the need to:

➤ Improve awareness of a problem, situation or event.
➤ Quickly procure goods or services.
➤ Win a legal decision.
➤ Develop a new policy or regulation.
➤ Organize a meeting, conference or other event.
➤ Produce a document.
➤ Conduct an investigation, audit or survey.
➤ Launch a product.
➤ Avoid an anticipated potential catastrophe, such as the Y2K computer threat or a shortage of human capital.
➤ Avoid controversy or confusion when a new regulation is released.

2. **YOUR PROBLEM-SOLVING OR GOAL-REACHING ACTIONS:** Such activities may involve:

➤ Passing or enforcing a regulation.
➤ Creating a team, task force or organization.
➤ Researching alternative solutions to a problem.
➤ Designing and running a marketing or public awareness campaign.
➤ Conducting an investigation, audit or survey.
➤ Improving personnel policies.

- Identifying inefficiencies in a system or processes and fixing them.
- Automating a process.
- Consulting with experts.
- Planning and arranging a meeting, conference or other event.
- Reducing costs or boosting sales.
- Creating/updating documents or websites.
- Arranging or providing training.
- Soliciting the cooperation of stakeholders.
- Putting a contract or other project on a "fast track."
- Proving the cost-effectiveness of a purchase.
- Keeping a project a high-priority by communicating persistently and persuasively with senior management.
- Providing training.
- Securing funding for projects.
- Systematically prioritizing tasks and then completing them.
- Getting "buy-in" for an approach from senior management or regional offices.

3. **CHALLENGES YOU CONQUERED:** Don't feel obliged to pretend that your job is easy. You should, by all means, describe any factors that complicated your project. By doing so, you will help illuminate your tenacity and problem-solving skills.

   But be sure to describe your challenges objectively and in impersonal terms, without reflecting bitterness or resentment towards your employer, boss or colleagues. No grumbling!

   Emphasize what you did — not what was done to you or how you were victimized. That is, focus on how you used your knowledge and creativity to deftly conquer your challenges rather than on how you were personally wronged when the project was assigned to you or as it progressed — no matter how wronged you were.

   Examples of challenges suitable for essays include:

   - Staffing, equipment or geographic constraints.
   - Constraints created by a tough economy or a tight budget.
   - Tight deadlines.
   - Entrenched, change-resistant bureaucracy.
   - Hostile stakeholders or hostile press.
   - Varying perspectives of members of a workgroup that must reach consensus.
   - Lack of consistent commitment from senior management.
   - Last minute schedule or policy-changes that required accommodation.
   - Racial or gender glass ceilings.
   - The inaccessibility of important data.
   - A sensitive political situation.

- A database or computer system that is crippled by bugs.
- Office reorganizations or moves.
- Changing leadership within an office.
- Office closures due to bad weather or other causes.

4. **POSITIVE RESULTS:** Provide evidence that you solved the problem or achieved your goal that you identified in the beginning of your story. (See Chapter 6 for tips on how to quantify your activities and results and how to name-drop your high-level contacts.)

Examples of positive results include:

- Improvements in an alarming trend.
- Improved survey results.
- Improved customer satisfaction.
- Finalization of a regulation.
- Launch of a website that receives many hits per day.
- A successful product launch or improved product sales.
- Resolution of an important question.
- Improvements in customer service.
- Improvements in a system or process.
- A successful meeting, conference or other event.
- The development of consensus on an important issue among experts.
- Increased profits.
- Improved awareness of a problem, situation or impending event.
- The creation or release of an updated website or document.
- The creation of a network of professionals promoting information exchange.
- Acquisition of needed products or services.
- Elimination of a back-log of letters, product orders or contracts.
- Improved office organization.
- The seamless transition to a new geographical location or to a new organizational structure.

Be sure to mention, if possible, any evidence that you exceeded expectations or went beyond the call of duty by, for example:

- Beating a deadline.
- Beating a quota or average production levels.
- Completing a project under budget.
- Attracting a particularly large crowd to a conference, training or other event.
- Working exceedingly long hours.

➤ Maintaining a hectic travel schedule.
➤ Having your documents (or other work products) approved by supervisors or senior officials without drawing any substantive suggested changes or requiring redundant efforts.

5. **FEEDBACK THAT YOU RECEIVED**
    If possible, provide objective evidence of your success. See the Validation Generator on page 104.

FIVE STORY MAKEOVERS

Provided here are five story makeovers, including a "before" and "after" version of each story. These stories are based on stories from real life, winning KSAs and ECQs. (Names of employers, offices and other details have been changed to disguise the identities of their writers.) Even if these example stories are not related to your field, they will give you ideas on how to tell effective success stories, and they will help get your creative, story telling juices flowing.

Notice how the "after" versions are enhanced by their short paragraphs as well as by the following formatting features:

Bolded, Enlarged Headings: Headings help underscore the logic of a document, and encourage the reader's eye to whiz down the page. In addition, the "results" headings in the "after" versions of these KSAs help guarantee that their authors will be pegged as producers by hiring managers who only glance at these documents.

Bulleted or Numbered Lists: KSAs that list an applicant's activities, skills or results in bulleted lists eliminate the need to repeat the me-o-centric word "I" over and over again. Lists also encourage fast reading.

SIDE-BY-SIDE #1: THE ME-O-CENTRIC

Describe your experience in working with methods, procedures and regulations related to civil rights laws.

As a result of my extensive training and daily responsibilities, I have obtained a thorough knowledge of EEO principles, laws, policies and regulations. As EEO counselor, this knowledge allows me to advise employees and applicants seeking guidance on EEO policies and practices and complaint procedures. I have the knowledge required to apply EEO rules and regulations appropriately, allowing the entire process to progress smoothly. I can research various laws and policies relating to the Civil Rights Act of 1963 with complete understanding of its relationship to the issues involved. I understand various authorities relating to persons with disabilities and minorities and women. I have also conducted training explaining employee rights and responsibilities. I act as a coach to my personnel assistant and clerk.

Typical of me-o-centrics, this me-o-centric presumes that her list of responsibilities and areas of knowledge will attract employers. But she has inadvertently overlooked what <u>most</u> attracts employers: Evidence that she <u>fulfills</u> her responsibilities and <u>applies</u> her knowledge to solve specific problems and achieve concrete goals. A few sentences, for example, about how the author skillfully recruited a sought-after lawyer who won important cases for his agency, or about how the author's coaching helped propel her personnel assistant through the ranks would have been more memorable and more impressive than this collection of vague "I"-isms.

SIDE-BY-SIDE #1: THE REFORMED ME-O-CENTRIC

Describe your experience in working with methods, procedures and regulations related to civil rights laws.

As an Equal Employment Opportunity (EEO) counselor at the Equal Opportunities Administration, I am helping to shatter glass ceilings all over Iowa. Most recently, in 2003, I helped the Iowa City Fire Department, which was entirely male, adhere to EEO regulations. I did this by designing and delivering five day-long workshops on EEO regulations for senior managers, who were almost unanimously opposed to hiring women firefighters. These workshops covered:

- All applicable EEO regulations on discrimination.
- Examples of how state agencies were heavily penalized for breaking EEO regulations.
- Testimonials from male firefighters whose lives had been saved by female firefighters.

Results: Within two months of participating in my workshops, the Iowa City Fire Department hired ten female firefighters.

Notice how, in less than 10 sentences, this applicant tells a story that clearly defines a problem, her solution and impressive results. Moreover, by including a bolded "Results" section, the author shrewdly gives her results extra umph and broadcasts them to skimmers.

After reading this essay, turn away from it and try to describe the author's achievements...Chances are you will recall more of this applicant's achievements than of the me-o-centric's achievements. Potential employers will also remember the applicant's achievements.

SIDE-BY-SIDE #2: THE FIXER IN SEARCH OF A PROBLEM

Describe your experience analyzing procedures.

When I assumed responsibility as the deputy director for Intelligence Resources in January 2000, I inherited a problem from my predecessor. I discovered that our command had accrued monthly fees of $800 and had accrued a total of $11,000 in outstanding fees to date for storage of used equipment and furniture. Through extensive research, I found that our organization had made a verbal agreement with the contractor to pay monthly for storage of the items, but had later decided to back out of the agreement. So, for several months, we were receiving bills, but leaving them unpaid. To resolve this issue, I sent a two-person team to inventory the items in storage and find an interim temporary storage facility on the base to house the items. I paid the contractor the amount we had incurred to date and arranged for immediate shipment of the items, which closed out our obligation to the contractor. As a result, I implemented two polices — (1) the command would utilize all items in storage first, prior to ordering new; and (2) made it clear to all members of our command that they would work through the Intelligence Resource Division and our resident military contracting officer before going to any outside commercial contractor for this saves time, money and any potential legal action that could have an adverse effect on performing our mission.

This applicant knows that he confronted some important problems and he is confident that he developed some mighty impressive solutions for them. But he's apparently unsure of which solution addressed which problem. His confusion is exposed by his failure to clearly articulate a problem.

At first blush, the essay's first few sentences seem to be building towards a discussion of the office's inability to pay the $11,000 storage fees or of the bogusness of the fees. But no, as it turns out, those aren't problems at all. The problem — only discernable by reading the essay several times and by reading between the lines — is that the IRD has been wasting money on unnecessary contracts for storage services, and, as the essay's last line implies, for other services as well.

In addition to failing to define this central problem, the author ignores an important problem that he inadvertently introduced: The failure of the IRD to pay its bills on time — not exactly an image-building maneuver. By failing to disclose how he addressed this problem — if at all, the applicant spotlights his own inadequacies. (Someone should tell this guy about his fifth amendment right against self-incrimination.)

SIDE-BY-SIDE #2: THE EFFICIENT FIXER

Describe your experience analyzing procedures.

Since becoming deputy director of the Intelligence Resources Division (IRD) in January 2000, I have saved my office almost $20,000 by eliminating unnecessary contracts.

PROBLEM

I was initially alerted to IRD's over-eagerness for outsourcing by a bill for $11,000 that IRD received from a commercial storage company for storing some of IRD's furniture and equipment. The bill had been accruing for over a year without IRD making a single payment on it. Moreover, because our furniture and equipment was still languishing in the storage facility at $800 per month, the meter was still ticking. So I gave this contract my full and immediate attention.

ACTION

After swiftly verifying that the charges were legitimate, I found space in IRD's own storage facilities for holding the furniture and equipment. Then I worked swiftly to:

- Restore IRD's good standing in the community by sending the storage facility a letter of apology for IRD's delinquency and paying our bill in full.

- Stop further unnecessary storage fees from accruing by arranging for the transfer of the stored furniture and equipment to IRD's storage facility.

- Ensure that the stored furniture and equipment be distributed to IRD staffers before we purchased any additional pieces.

- Establish regulations that channel all of the base's contracting requests through my office for stringent screening. Since these regulations took effect, my office has identified and cancelled many other unnecessary contracts for storing equipment, renting vehicles and obtaining plumbing services.

RECOGNITION

Please note these comments from the Assistant Secretary for Intelligence on my 2001 performance appraisal: "With his ability to sniff out unnecessary contracts, Bill has helped transform this office from a chaotic free-for-all into a well-oiled-machine."

This applicant wisely hits readers with his best shot up front: His $20,000 savings. (Notice how he quantified and tallied his savings to yield an impressive total figure.) Then the applicant methodically defines the problem and his solution to it. And by quoting praise from his performance evaluation, he provides vivid proof of his supervisor's satisfaction with his results. (Note that this applicant name-dropped his supervisor's impressive title.)

SIDE-BY-SIDE #3: THE ABUSED EMPLOYEE

Describe your experience managing financial data.

In 1999, the US Postal Service awarded the Breast Cancer Stamp to a new advertising agency. This is a high profile contract with a very large dollar value, $15 million per year.

I inherited a major problem because the advertising agency had never before handled a government contract. It had no idea how to do invoices. The accounting department refused to review them and higher-grade Brand Managers were too busy, so this process was pushed on me. By the beginning of 2003, the situation was so bad that the contract was at the center of a major lawsuit. For each month, there were 508 binders, which I had to review at least 3 times and create a discrepancy list to wipe out basic errors. The work is so enormous that we are still processing last year's invoices.

The vendor does not have knowledge of cost accounting standards. The vendor submits disorderly invoices that have no regular format (no spreadsheet, no accounting codes). Annually submit 60 to 70 task orders and this is not computer entered and I must keep this in my mind and delve into a pile of binders and read each page and detect hidden errors with my eagle eye. Materials are often entered without unit price or quantity. And only through individual research I prevented the US Postal Service from overspending. Provided discrepancy lists that assisted in the contract being rescued at that time, meanwhile saved money to a large extent, which influenced savings of 17K after second review.

This type of review I single-handedly created and implemented in order to deal with the crisis. During my vacation in 2001, management could not find a single person to process the last quarters' (October – December 2000) invoices, as a result they had to get 4 people from across the divisions to receive the invoices in PeopleSoft for me and when I returned, unfortunately for me everything was entered wrong.

Woe! This applicant sounds like he is primed for workplace violence!

No matter how justified his anger may be, the appropriate venue for venting is not an application essay. His resentment will only backfire by arousing suspicions that he is the problem — not everyone around him, as he claims. It's been said that the sweetest revenge is success. This applicant would better serve his cause by channeling his energy into writing a positive, dispassionate account of what he achieved under difficult circumstances, rather than into writing a treatise of the injustices foisted upon him.

SIDE-BY-SIDE #3: THE RECOVERED ABUSED EMPLOYEE

Describe your experience managing financial data.

PROBLEM

As an accountant, I manage financial records for the US Postal Service's high-profile $15 million-a-year Breast Cancer Stamp Program. About 50 million breast cancer stamps are currently sold annually. Records management for this high-dollar project — already labor intensive — has been particularly challenging since 1999, when advertising for the program was contracted out to an agency that had never before handled a government contract.

SOLUTION

Because the contracting advertising agency's invoices and task orders almost always deviate from standard accounting protocol and are prone to costly errors, I single-handedly process them according to a unique and painstaking accounting protocol. My protocol involves:

- Reviewing hundreds of invoices that are submitted each month at least twice, scrutinizing them for errors and cross-checking them against previous invoices to ensure that we are not being charged more than once for the same service.

- Conducting daily reviews of 60 to 70 hard-copy task orders and cross-checking them against previous orders.

- Researching accounting codes, unit prices and quantities of purchased products, which are almost always omitted from task orders and invoices.

- Accurately entering all invoices and task orders into accounting records stored in PeopleSoft.

RESULTS

By regularly identifying and doggedly pursing financial discrepancies and over-charges, I helped save the US Postal Service $17,000 in unwarranted changes since 1999. Through my contributions to this project, I have earned a reputation as an exceedingly conscientious and eagle-eyed financial manager.

Notice how "the recovered abused employee" — unlike "the abused employee" — explicitly mentions his involvement in the important Breast Cancer Stamp Program in the very first paragraph of the essay.

Moreover, the applicant factually states what he did . . . not what was done to him. Untarnished by his resentful comments, his accomplishments shine brightly.

SIDE-BY-SIDE #4: THE WALLFLOWER

Describe your experience leading change.

I served as the representative of the Internal Revenue Service's Congressional Task Force for Improving Government, an interagency taskforce. I facilitated partnerships among high-level federal officials from a number of executive agencies and representatives of a network of community-based organizations that are dedicated to encouraging life-long learning for adults. This involved organizing meetings and developing and revitalizing several websites, including *workers.gov*, *plainlanguage.gov*, and *FirstGov.gov*.

This wallflower is too afraid of the spotlight to even provide his title or to define the problem that he addressed. In addition, he only glosses over his activities without explaining their importance. These flaws minimize his stature and achievements.

SIDE-BY-SIDE #4: THE REFORMED WALLFLOWER

Describe your experience leading change.

PROBLEM

In the year 2020, 60% of all jobs in the US will require technical skills that are possessed by only 22% of today's workers, according to the US Department of Commerce.

ACTION

As Director of the Congressional Task Force for Improving Government's 21st Century Workforce Team from May 1999 to January 2000, I worked to narrow the nation's skills gap by:

- Forging and fostering partnerships between 20 community-based organizations (Workforce Network Partners) that encourage lifelong learning and Assistant Secretaries from appropriate federal agencies, including the Departments of Labor, Education and Commerce.

- Advising Workforce Network Partners how to secure federal grants to sustain and expand their adult education and lifelong learning programs.

- Developing and revitalizing interactive websites that provide information on best practices for improving adult education and lifelong learning programs. (These sites include *workers.gov*, *plainlanguage.gov*, and *FirstGov.gov*.)

- Managing a high-traffic list-serve that helped Workforce Network Partners exchange best practices information — despite the geographical distance between many of them and our program's tight budget.

WORKFORCE RESULTS

Under my leadership, the 21st Century Workforce Team and our partners built an electronic and organizational infrastructure that will help community-based organizations encourage lifelong learning and adult education for years to come. (The Workforce Team's websites, for example, currently receive tens of thousands of hits every day.) By propelling American workers into high-skill, high-wage jobs, this infrastructure will contribute to US competitiveness.

Oh! What a shot of courage can do! By starting the story with a hard-hitting statistic, this applicant establishes the national importance of his project. By stating his title, the full name of his organization and the dates he worked there, this applicant gives himself authority and credibility. In addition, by explaining that he collaborated with Assistant Secretaries, this applicant proves that he has worked at a very senior level. All of the bullets in this essay reflect an energetic, multi-talented individual. And this essay's "Results" section describes how he left a lasting and important legacy that will continue to address the problem introduced in his story's first sentence.

SIDE-BY-SIDE #5: THE RAMBLER

Describe your experience leading change.

For more than 30 years, most small construction sites in the United States employing fewer than 20 workers have been essentially exempt from requirements to provide safety training to their employees. These requirements are implemented by the Occupational Safety and Health Administration (OSHA). This exemption was implemented as a result of a deal brokered by several construction operators and lobbyists. It has remained in effect due to various examples of fancy political legwork.

During the 1990s, fatalities at small construction sites climbed. Congress held several sets of hearings on the topic. Many editorials on the topic were published in newspapers. CNN did a special on construction safety. Safety at small constructions sites had clearly become an important problem. Something needed to be done about it. Finally, the OSHA leadership attempted to get rid of the exemption. As part of this effort, Congress authorized the expenditure of funds to provide safety training to construction workers at small construction sites.

We held 11 hearings before we inaugurated the Small Construction Site Training Program. These hearings were designed to collect comments from interested parties. They were held in many cities including New York, Boston, Washington DC, Denver, Mexico City and Los Angeles. Transcripts were made of public meetings and published on OSHA's website to allow those who had been unable to attend hearings to participate in the process.

The safety training program was delivered by the congressionally mandated deadline and was well received. It took effect a year later. Since 2000, fatalities at small construction sites had fallen significantly from their all-time high level. Achieving "buy-in" has proven to be critical to increased performance and has been the basis for rewarding employees for their work and innovation. This project was regarded as a great success, and OSHA received suggestions that the Part 56 experience be used as a model in other regulatory projects.

Get out the gong bell! This applicant was apparently too involved with his project to distinguish important from unimportant information. The politics described in the first few paragraphs are boring. They are also irrelevant because we don't need this information to understand the applicant's actions or achievements.

Also notice that the final two paragraphs are mired in repetitious and technical information (what is Part 56?) that obscure — rather than enhance — the applicant's achievements. Moreover, the essay's final paragraph fails to identify who regarded the project as a great success. (For all we know, this applicant's fan is none other than his own mother!)

SIDE-BY-SIDE #5: THE REFORMED RAMBLER

Describe your experience leading change.

PROBLEM

Every year, hundreds of construction workers are killed by electrocutions, collapsing structures and collisions between gigantic trucks. Nevertheless, construction operations that employ fewer than 20 construction workers have traditionally not been required to provide safety training to their employees.

But because of the long hours and lack of safety training at small construction sites, accidents soared at these facilities during the construction boom of the 1990s. In 1999, fatalities at such sites reached a record high of 200 deaths — many of which could have been prevented by basic safety training. In response, in 2000, Congress ordered the Occupational Safety and Health Administration (OSHA) to develop a safety training program for small construction sites by 2001.

SOLUTION

As Chief of OSHA's new Small Construction Site Training Program since its creation in 2001, I directed the kick-off of the Small Construction Site Safety Program and currently manage this program. So far, this program has:

- Produced an attention-grabbing video reviewing construction safety methods. This video, which was distributed to 50,000 construction sites, won the Occupational Safety Video of the Year Award in 2003.

- Created a new website on construction safety for small construction operators. This site, which is updated daily, receives more than 500 hits per day. Its offerings include free, downloadable scripts for construction safety trainings on varied topics from vehicle safety to electrical safety.

- Finalized requirements that every worker at a small construction site receive safety training by a certified construction safety trainer at least once every six months.

To battle the popular misconception among many labor organizations that the training program would reflect undue industry influence, I invited all interested parties to comment on my office's efforts at 10 public, nationwide meetings held in 2001. At these meetings, a total of 98 construction workers, union representatives, safety trainers, members of academia and construction operators provided suggestions — many of which were incorporated by the safety program.

RESULTS

Under my leadership, OSHA initiated the Small Construction Site Training Program in record time and met Congress's tight one-year deadline. As a result, more than 100,000 construction workers now receive effective workplace safety training. Since the Small Construction Site Training Program began in 2001, workplace deaths among construction workers at small operations declined by almost 50 percent, from 200 fatalities in 1999 to about 105 fatalities in 2001.

For my leadership role in the training program, I received the Secretary of Labor's Spectacular Achievement Award. In addition, the program was praised by organized labor, federal officials and union representatives at a ceremony hosted by Secretary of Labor Elaine Chao. Also, the union publication, *Construction Safety Today*, hailed the training program as "a giant step forward." Furthermore, construction operators have regularly suggested that the cooperative process used in developing the program serve as a model for the development of other training programs.

This story's opening is attention-grabbing and briskly establishes the problem's life-or-death importance. Moreover, the "Results" section quantifies the applicant's achievement and portrays the applicant's accomplishments in a precedent-setting light. Nice name-dropping too. Bullets and headings dramatically encourage fast-reading.

WORKSHEET FOR TELLING A COMPELLING STORY

PROBLEM OR GOAL: _____
_____
_____
_____
_____
_____

MY ACTIONS: _____
_____
_____
_____
_____
_____

OBSTACLES I OVERCAME: _____
_____
_____
_____
_____

RESULTS AND POSITIVE FEEDBACK: _____
_____
_____
_____
_____

TIPS FOR WRITING KILLER KSAs and ECQs

There are practically an infinite number of ways to structure an application essay. In some cases, for example, you may be able to answer an essay question simply by telling one or two success stories. But in other cases, you may need to include additional credentials besides just success story(s) in an application essay. In still other cases, a bulleted list of achievements may make the best answer to an essay question.

But whatever strategy you choose, it is important to remember that the typically harried, time-pressured hiring manager may spend only five or 10 minutes on your application before s/he succumbs to the siren song of the next application in his/her huge stack of applications. You can craft perfect essays that will quickly impress hiring managers by following the tips provided below for planning, writing and editing application essays.

"I wrote another five hundred words. Can I have another cookie?"

PLANNING ESSAYS

1. **Don't leave your application to the last minute!** It is virtually impossible to dash off a quality essay, resume or cover letter in a single sitting. Most writers need at least several sittings to develop the perfect structure, content and wording for application documents, and to debug them of typos as well as punctuation, spelling and grammatical errors. So build enough time into your application preparation schedule to enable you to work through several revisions of your KSAs and ECQs.

2. **Identify your relevant credentials:** Kick-off your essay writing session by reviewing Chapter 6 to generate ideas on what credentials to cover in your essay, and how to describe them in impressive terms.

3. **Map out your ideas for each essay:** Write down each question and list your relevant credentials and stories that closely match the demands of your target job.

4. **Answer the question you are actually asked — not the question that you wish you were asked.** Although politicians commonly get away with question-dodging, job applicants rarely do. Nevertheless, hiring managers observe no shortage of KSA and ECQ essays that discuss topics unrelated to the associated question and cite experience that is unrelated to the opening. Beware! Such off-target applications are usually the first to be eliminated from consideration.

Tell hiring managers what they want to hear by explaining how your credentials match the requirements of your target job. If you are suffering from page fright, pretend that your essay questions are interview questions; talk out your answers, then write down and edit your verbal answers. Other tips for getting your creative juices flowing are provided in Chapter 6.

5. **Hit your readers with your best shot up top:** Readers remember best what they read first. So, if possible, include your most impressive credentials in your first essay.

6. **Include stories in at least some of your essays:** You need not necessarily include a story in each essay, but most of your essays should have at least one story.

7. **Make sure that, taken together, your KSAs and ECQs fully represent you without your resume:** This means that all credentials that you want considered should be featured in your essays, including your education, training classes and relevant work experience. Don't omit credentials from your essays just because they are featured in your resume. You simply can't assume that hiring managers who are racing through applications will cross-check your essays against your resume. For the sake of consistency, also make sure that every job that you discuss in your essays is also covered in your resume.

8. **Provide recent examples:** Emphasize in your essays your work experiences from the last 10 or, at most, 15 years. Only review older experiences if they are ultra-relevant to your target job.

9. **Include your education:** Mention your undergraduate and graduate degrees and training courses in one of your essays, if they are relevant to your target opening. (Bear in mind that college and graduate degrees are almost always relevant to essay questions addressing communication skills. After all, it's pretty hard to earn a degree without being able to speak or write.)

10. **Do not leave a KSA or ECQ blank:** As explained in Chapter 5, essays are rated according to a point system. This point system assigns zero points to a blank essay, but assigns at least some points to a weak answer. Therefore, you will earn more points by providing a weak answer than by providing no answer to a KSA or ECQ. If you do not have any work or nonwork experience that fulfills a KSA or ECQ, do some reading or interview relevant professionals about the topic. Then describe these activities and what you learned from them in your essay.

    If most of your essays are strong, they may earn enough points to compensate for one weak answer. However, if all of essays are weak, your time would probably be better invested in applying for another position for which you are better qualified.

11. **Strategically parcel out your credentials among essays:** If the issues addressed by some essay questions for a job overlap with one another, parcel out your credentials among your essays in whatever way makes you look best. That is, include your best credentials in your first essay, and then distribute the rest of your credentials among your essays without leaving any essay blank. It is preferable not to repeat the exact same credential in multiple essays. But if you must cover the same project or type of experience in more than one essay, give it a different angle or emphasis each time you cover it.

12. **Outline each essay:** There are no definitive rules on how to sequence information in essays. But be sure to sequence each essay logically. If you don't have a good reason for sequencing your sentences as you did, rethink their order. Make your logic apparent to readers by distinguishing each section of each essay with a heading. Be sure to set off descriptions of your "results" and "recognition" with headings. By doing so, you will emphasize your reputation as a producer and make your successes apparent even to hiring managers who only skim your essays.

See the example stories on pages 124 to 134 and the example essays on pages 151 to 160 for ideas on organizing your essays.

ESSENTIAL TIP FOR WRITING ESSAYS IN AUTOMATED APPLICATION SYSTEMS

The planning, editing and revising of KSAs and ECQs in some automated application systems is complicated by the following constraints:

➤ The essay questions contained in automated applications for some openings vary slightly from those contained on the opening's vacancy announcement. Therefore, in some cases, you must access the automated application in order to access all essay questions for the opening.

➤ Some automated application systems do not allow users to save an application that is only partially completed. This constraint prevents users from completing part of an application during one session, and then completing other parts of the application during subsequent sessions.

➤ Some automated application systems require users to provide certain, required answers before allowing them to advance to other application questions.

Without a work-around mechanism, these constraints would prevent users from previewing all essay questions before answering them, and from repeatedly editing and revising draft essays, as necessary for producing high-quality essays.

But you can work around these constraints. Here is what you need to know to do so: On automated application systems, you can override a previously submitted application by submitting another application for the same job anytime before midnight of the job's closing date. You may usually repeat this process as many times as you like.

Therefore, you can enter an automated application on a trial run, merely to scope the essay questions. During such a trial run, you may provide nonsense answers to required questions, so that you will be allowed to access questions that follow them. After you retrieve your essay questions, you can write, edit and revise your answers outside of the automated application system. Then, once you are satisfied with your answers, you can reenter the automated system and submit another application that includes your carefully crafted answers. By doing so, you will override a previous submission.

WRITING ESSAYS

1. **Orient your readers:** Remember that hiring managers know *nothing* about you…until you tell them. In particular, they are keenly interested in what your profession is as well as where you currently and previously worked. So just as you would introduce yourself to an interviewer whom you have never met before, you should introduce yourself on paper to hiring managers by identifying your titles, employers and dates for every position or story that you describe in your essays.

CONFUSING	ORIENTING
In my current position, I…	As a contract manager at the Immigration and Naturalization Service since 1997, I……
In my previous position, I…	In 1998, when I worked as a contract manager at the Bureau of Land Management, I…. OR As a contract manager at the Bureau of Land Management from 1998-2002, I….

2. **Write interesting openers:** Distinguish your essays — or at least your first essay — from a typical essay that begins with a boring introductory sentence, such as "Throughout my career, I have written many important documents." Granted, such an opener is not technically wrong, and probably wouldn't, by itself, dash your chances of landing a job. But nor would such a bland, yawn-provoking lead sentence likely engage or stick in the craw of a hiring manager who reads dozens of KSAs that all begin with similar sentences.

Rather than waste your first sentences of essays on ho-hum sentences, try to open your essays (and stories) with lively leads that will reel in readers with a hard-hitting statistic that defines a problem that you have addressed, a vivid image, a quote, a reference to a high-profile news event that overlaps with your work, or another dramatic device. Here are several other examples of stand-out essay openers:

➢ *As a customer care operator at the US Postal Service, my switchboards typically stay lit up like a Christmas tree throughout the Christmas season. I keep up with my heavy workload during the busy holiday season by…*

➢ *As a contract manager at the Federal Reserve since 1993, I design contracts that get the agency the biggest bang for the buck and draw upon the newest buying strategies for saving money. For example…*

➢ *"Golda Meir said, "You cannot shake hands with a clenched fist." I cite this quote at the beginning of each Alternative Dispute Resolution (ADR) negotiating session that I lead between employees and management as an ADR Counselor at the Department of Labor. During negotiating sessions, I also…"*

➤ *Coin collectors often describe coins as "time capsules" that preserve history. More than ever, this concept came alive for me when, as a program analyst at the US Mint, I helped organize a presidential ceremony held on July 26, 2001 honoring the Navajo Code Talkers of World War II who used their native language as an unbreakable military code. My contributions to this event included…*

➤ *Nothing boosts organizational morale like an active incentives award program. As human resources director of Data Consulting Inc., I innovated low cost ways to reward our most productive staffers. For example….*

➤ *If your staff suffers from meeting overload, I have the cure! As a conference planner and facilitator at Meeting Managers Inc. since 1988, I have been running effective, productive and even fun meetings and conferences that make disorganized, pointless and endless events a thing of the past. Here's how I do it….*

➤ *On January 1, 2003, as I arrived at my job as a senior attorney at the United Nations, my boss ran up to me and said, "I need you to deliver an opening statement at the war tribunals trial in the Hague by January 30. Can I count on you?" The challenges of this assignment included…"*

3. **Reel in your readers:** Keep your first paragraph particularly short — two or three sentences at most.

4. **Enliven your essays:** Express what you like about your job, what drives you, and/or why you believe it is important. For example:

➤ *As a software engineer, I consider nothing more gratifying than digging into a vexing technical problem that has stymied everyone else — and no matter what it takes — solving it. Here are some examples of impossible-to-solve problems that I have cracked:*

H O T • T I P

SHOW YOUR PASSION

Passion is a primary element of effective communication. In fact, in a recent article in *O, The Oprah Magazine*, about how to communicate effectively, trial attorney Johnnie Cochran said, "passion and preparation are unbeatable if you're to be an effective advocate."

By conveying passion and humanity in your essays, you will make your essays interesting *and* convince hiring managers that you are the kind of self-motivated, low maintenance employee who any supervisor would treasure.

➤ *Journalism suits me to a "T" because I am inveterately curious. I can't stop asking questions.*

➤ *My work is more than just a job for me. It is a passion. Every time I help the Consumer Product Safety Commission pull a defective toy from the market, I know that I may be saving a child's life.*

> ➤ *I earned a B.A. in International Relations because diplomatic strategies have prevented many wars. I hope that by pursuing a career at the State Department, I can help defuse heated international conflicts.*

5. **Specify frequency:** For example, if you represent your office at meetings, state whether these meetings are held on a weekly, monthly or bimonthly basis. Alternatively, if you write reports, state how frequently you produce them.

6. **Don't put yourself or anyone else down:** Many applicants mistakenly believe that they will somehow impress hiring managers by putting themselves down in an essay. NOT! Unless an essay question specifically asks applicants to fess to their weaknesses — and I have yet to see such an essay question — there is no way that an applicant can earn additional points for volunteering information about their shortcomings, botched projects, missed deadlines or other failures on an essay. Nevertheless, many job applicants include confessional information in their essays. I even read one KSA by a NASA employee who personally accepted some responsibility for the Challenger accident. As if any hiring manager would hire a walking disaster!

    Never reveal unflattering information about yourself in an essay. Remember: In the US, you have a fifth amendment right against self-incrimination; you don't even have to testify against yourself when you commit murder, let alone when you innocently apply for a job. Moreover, take some advice from my mother, Dr. Dorit Whiteman, who is a clinical psychologist:

    "Don't ever put yourself down in public. There are enough people out there who are more than willing to belittle you. Don't ever make it easy for them."

    So instead of giving potential employers ammunition against you when they aren't even asking for it, spin your stories whichever way makes you look best, as long as the information that you provide is truthful. Here is an example of effective spin in a KSA that removes self-incriminating information about a missed deadline:

BEFORE: SELF-INCRIMMINATING	AFTER: INNOCENT AND IMPRESSIVE
I managed a $5 million renovation of 15,000 square feet of office space in the National Federal Center in Washington DC. Unfortunately, we missed the three-month deadline for the project.	I managed a $5 million renovation of 15,000 square feet of office space in the National Federal Center in Washington DC. This project was complicated by the unexpected discovery of asbestos in the building's ceiling paint. To safely remove the ceiling paint, I quickly met the many administrative requirements for hiring asbestos-removal contractors. Because of my effective project management, my three-person team and I completed the entire project in only ninety-seven days and within budget, despite the unanticipated expenses.

Also be careful not to criticize your employer, boss, or colleagues in essays. See pages 128 and 129 for more guidance on staying positive in essays.

7. **Maximize your stature:** Include credentials in your KSAs and ECQs that maximize your stature by reflecting the highest level of responsibility at which you have operated; exclude credentials that diminish your stature be reflecting relatively low level responsibilities. For example, try to identify which activity — by its relatively low level of responsibility — reduces the applicant's standing in the following KSA excerpt:

> *As Director of Communications for the Vice President of the United States, I prepared position papers on issues such as partial-birth abortions, Middle East peace talks and national environmental regulations, and I wrote Boy Scout congratulatory notes.*

8. **Favor specific terms over vague, mealy words:** For example, the wimpy verbs *to help, to participate in, to join* and the equally unimpressive "*to be involved with*" can usually be replaced by terms that more precisely define what exactly was accomplished. By providing this specific information, you will portray yourself as a mover and shaker rather than as a hauler and carrier whose greatest contribution amounted to little more than just being there.

BEFORE: VAGUE	AFTER: SPECIFIC
I help my supervisor keep track of ongoing cases.	On my own initiative, I created a case tracking system that identifies each open case, the attorney managing it, and the dates of impending case milestones.

To improve is another vague verb. Replace it with terms that define exactly what was improved.

BEFORE: VAGUE	AFTER: PRECISE
Under my leadership, the Office of Sales and Marketing improved customer service.	Under my leadership, the Office of Sales and Marketing slashed average order delivery times from eight to four days.

Here are two more examples of credentials that sound more impressive when they are described in precise terms.

BEFORE: VAGUE	AFTER: PRECISE
I have briefed Congressional staffers.	During the last two years, I briefed the Director of Communications of the House Ways & Means Committee six times about the Security and Exchange Commission's budget requests.
I handled some major contracts.	I successfully directed cradle-to-grave contracts for four multi-year, multi-million dollar contracts for staffing Environ's computer help desk.

In addition, by replacing vague terms with precise terms, you will create verbal pictures that will lodge more securely in the minds of hiring managers than vague descriptions that rarely gain traction. Aren't the following "after" versions more memorable than their "before" versions?

BEFORE: VAGUE	AFTER: PRECISE
I produced a catalogue.	I designed the layout and all graphics for a 75-page, full-color catalogue that was packed with photographs of electronics products. The catalogue generated $5 million in revenues in two months.
My communication skills have been important to my career.	My ability to convey technical information to general audiences has helped me advance from a GS-5 position to a GS-14 position in 6 years.

Here are several examples of vague sentences from real-life KSAs that created more questions than they answered:

➤ *The agency is working to achieve its vision of its mission in the community.* (Huh? This sentence is composed of a meaningless string of buzzwords.)

➤ *My credentials speak for themselves.* (They do?)

➤ *As Deputy of the Foreign Press Bureau in Croatia in the early 1990s, I was responsible for recruiting, training and supervising a corps of novice press officers under the most demanding circumstances imaginable.* (Oh! What juicy, impressive war stories this applicant would have told if only he had understood that most hiring managers weren't in Croatia during wartime, and so couldn't possibly imagine what conditions there were like.)

9. **Use keywords:** As discussed in Chapter 5 and Chapter 6, you should sprinkle your essays and resume with keywords from the job description of your target job.

10. **Write in plain language:** If a layman would be able to understand your essay on the first read, your essay is probably in plain language. If, on the other hand, a layman would need multiple passes to understand your essay, it is probably in bureaucratese, legalese or scientificese. Why is it important for essays to be in plain language? Because:

➤ Your application may be judged by nonspecialists who are strangers to your field, as discussed in Chapter 5. Moreover, even hiring managers who are experts in your field may be unfamiliar with the regulations, programs, procedures, databases and computer systems that are incorporated into your projects. Hiring managers who do not understand an essay on the first pass are probably not going to take the time to study it until they "get it." And an essay that confuses hiring managers is unlikely to earn a high rating. Therefore, by writing your essay in plain language, you will increase its chances of impressing hiring managers.

➤ Studies prove that people — whether experts or nonexperts — read plain language explanations faster and remember them better than explanations that are written in bureaucratese, legalese or scientificese. Therefore, by writing your essays in plain language, you will enable harried, time-pressured hiring managers to quickly read, skim and remember them.

➤ You will express your big ideas more persuasively and compellingly through small, everyday words than through pompous, specialized terms. After all, the great speeches of history, such as those by Abraham Lincoln, Franklin Roosevelt and John Kennedy, were all built upon small, everyday words that are easy to understand and that convey a human voice. By contrast, documents and speeches that are built upon pompous inflated language almost never make it into the history books because they are boring and forgettable. (I have yet to see a list of great books that includes an edition of the *Code of Federal Regulations*.) Although no one expects your KSAs or ECQs to have the resonance of a presidential speech, they will be more accessible and memorable if they are — like other memorable texts — built upon everyday words.

Many applicants wrongly believe that their essays will sound unprofessional if they exclude professional jargon. But studies show that even subject matter experts, such as lawyers and scientists, are more impressed by the writers of explanations of easy-to-understand, plain language texts than texts that are written in traditional bureaucratese, legalese and scientificese. Likewise, hiring managers will be more impressed by your essays if they are conveyed in easy-to-understand terms rather than in specialized terms.

ALBERT EINSTEIN ON PLAIN LANGUAGE

Most of the fundamental ideas of science are essentially simple, and may, as a rule, be expressed in a language comprehensible to everyone.

— Albert Einstein

Many applicants also wrongly believe that their work is too specialized or too technical to be explained in plain language. But there is hardly any topic that is too technical or specialized to be summarized in plain language. Consider, for example, publications like *The Wall Street Journal, Newsweek* and *Time.* They regularly cover specialized fields like business, medical research and regulatory issues in plain language without sacrificing accuracy. Likewise, no matter how technical your work is, you can convey it in easy-to-understand terms so that it will appeal to hiring managers who have diverse backgrounds.

Translate your KSAs or ECQs into plain language by:

➤ Writing in short sentences and short paragraphs.

➤ Eliminating any words or phrases that you would not use in day-to-day conversation. For example:

- Herein or wherein
- My responsibilities include, but are not limited to....
- In accordance with...
- The aforementioned...

➤ Replacing formulas with short verbal summaries.

➤ Defining technical terms, or replacing technical terms with everyday words, wherever possible. If you are like most professionals, you may be so fluent in the jargon of your field that you are desensitized to it; it may roll off your tongue and from your keyboard naturally, with hardly a thought. So scrutinize your application for terms or concepts that might alienate the uninitiated.

➤ Providing enough background information about technical concepts for a stranger to the situation to understand it.

➤ Refraining from naming forms, regulations, programs and laws solely by their identifying numbers: Instead, identify them by titles or words that define their functions. For example:

JARGON	PLAIN LANGUAGE
A-76	The competitive sourcing program, a high-priority federal program that will privatize some federal jobs
SF-52s	Personnel documents
ISO 14001	International Standard 14001, which is composed of voluntary standards addressing the environmental performance of manufacturing organizations

➤ Defining all acronyms and minimizing your use of acronyms, whenever possible.

➤ Eliminating abbreviations.

➤ Asking yourself whether your essays are harder to read than publications, such as *The Wall Street Journal*, *Newsweek* and *Time*, and whether nonspecialists would understand your KSAs.

➤ Soliciting feedback on your essays from nonspecialists.

To help convince you of the power of plain language, provided below are three hard-to-read excerpts from real life KSAs and their plain language rewrites.

HARD-TO-READ EXCERPT	PLAIN LANGUAGE REWRITE
The drop date of the numismatic product was delayed.	The new coin was released late.
In my prior role, several efforts were utilized in finding solutions to track all issues associated with the Mail Order and Catalog System (MACS) maintained by the ERP. PVCS tracker was used to identify System Problem Reports (SPRs) and System Change Requests (SCRs).	As an IT specialist at Amazon.com from 2002 to 2004, I recalibrated systems used to identify errors in the company's marketing database, which is known as the Mail Order and Catalog System (MACS). I thereby significantly boosted the accuracy of MACS.
SG&A is down. I'm a believer in TPM.	As Plant Manager, I solicited employee suggestions for reducing wasted raw materials by twenty percent.

11. **Strike redundant or extraneous information:** Instead of expecting harried hiring managers to look for a needle in the haystack, give them only the needle; eliminate the haystack. If you bury your best credentials in unnecessary information, you will dig your own grave.

Many applicants throw all of their ammunition against the wall, in the hope that something — anything — will stick. But that approach rarely works. Why not? Because the typical hiring manager has neither the time nor the will to sift through unnecessary information. Confronted with a thicket of rambling prose, a hiring manager is likely to presume that if the applicant couldn't identify which aspects of his/her own experience were relevant to the question, it won't be worth the hiring manager's efforts to try to do so either.

Also eliminate any unnecessary or redundant words and phrases. One important way to eliminate excess words and to inject vigor into your writing is to rebuild sentences that contain a version of the passive verb "to be" around more energetic verbs. The telltale signature of the verb "to be" is the presence of the words *am, is, are, was, be, been* and *were*. In particular, almost any sentence that contains the phrase "there are" can be restructured around a more energetic verb. Compare the following "before" and "after" versions.

BEFORE: PASSIVE AND WORDY	AFTER: ENERGETIC AND CONCISE
There are many ways in which the program was successful. WORD COUNT: 9	The program succeeded in many ways. WORD COUNT: 6
I was responsible for editing the Director of the Customer Care Center's outgoing correspondence sent out under her signature. WORD COUNT: 19	I formatted, proofread and fact-checked about 20 letters from the Director of the Customer Care Center per week. WORD COUNT: 18 [Notice how much more specific information this sentence contains than the "before" version.]
Following termination of the contract, there was a marginal incrementation in workload, and, at this moment of time, it would appear that there has been a significant degree of improvement in profit capacity. WORD COUNT: 33	When the contract ended, our office's workload increased, but our profits soared. WORD COUNT: 12

The "after" versions of the above examples are clearer and shorter than the "before" versions because they:

➤ Eliminate empty phrases, such as "at this moment in time."
➤ Replace wordy phrases with shorter ones.
➤ Use common words, such as "ended," instead of pompous words, such as "termination."

12. **Numbers:** Write out all numbers up to and including "nine." Use the numerical form of 10 to 999,999. Write out numbers that are in the millions and higher. For example, $2 million. Double check the accuracy of all numbers that you cite. (Wrong numbers serve as quick credibility busters.)

FORMATTING ESSAYS

Do you doubt the power of effective formatting? If so, compare the unformatted me-o-centric KSA on page 117 with any of the well formatted essays provided on pages 151 to 160. Don't the well formatted essays look more inviting, and don't they broadcast important credentials with more umph and emphasis than does the unformatted me-o-centric KSA? Aren't they faster to read and easier to skim?

The following features improve the readability of KSAs and ECQs:

➤ Bolded, enlarged headings.
➤ Short paragraphs.
➤ Bulleted or numbered lists: Instructions for creating bulleted and numbered lists in WORD are included in Appendix 3: Formatting Tips.

HOT • TIP

TO BULLET OR NOT TO BULLET?

One popular myth among applicants for federal jobs is that bulleted lists are, in the words of one applicant, "too informal for job applications." Nothing could be further from the truth!

Because bullets support skimming and fast reading, and because they break up text, most hiring managers savor every bulleted or numbered list that appears in a KSA or ECQ. As one hiring manager recently said, "The more bullets, the better. I like KSAs that fire off credentials with the rat-tat-tat of machine guns unloading their ammunition."

So be sure to bullet or number sequences of events or procedures and descriptions of activities.

These features improve the readability of KSAs and ECQs because:

➤ Long monotonous paragraphs without headings or bullets look suspiciously like a swamp that sucks in the unsuspecting, and then exhausts and fatally traps its prisoners. Harried, time-pressured hiring managers are about as likely to voluntarily submerge themselves in the morass of long, dense monotonous text as savvy hikers are to walk into bogs bearing warning signs for deadly quicksand. In other words: Not at all!

But by breaking up your essays with headings, bullets and short paragraphs, you will enhance their allure and thereby increase the likelihood that they will draw the focused attention of hiring managers. In addition, studies show that readers remember text that is broken up into smaller chunks much better than long-winded slabs of unbroken text. Therefore, by breaking up the text in your essays with bolded headings, bulleted lists and short paragraphs, you will encourage hiring managers to remember your application.

➤ Headings that highlight your results and positive feedback will emphasize your successes. This is important because **what stands out on the page is what stands out in the reader's mind.** So if you emphasize your results and positive feedback with headings, they will stand out in the hiring manager's mind. But if, on the other hand, such selling points remain camouflaged within a morass of monotonous, featureless text, they are likely to remain overlooked or quickly forgotten.

➤ Headings expose the logic of your document. When your document looks logical, you look logical.

➤ Headings make text easily skimmable.

Here are some other important formatting tips:

1. Print your name and the title of your target job at the top of each page.

2. Number your pages.

3. Answer your essays in the same order in which they appear on the application.

4. Repeat the question with each essay.

5. Use margins that are between one inch to one-and-a-half inches wide. Instructions for manipulating margins are provided in Appendix 3: Formatting Tips.

6. Limit each essay to about one page. If your essay runs over one page, fit it onto a single page by eliminating irrelevant information and unnecessary words and manipulating font sizes and margins. (But do not resort to minuscule margins.)

7. Use a font size of at least 9 or 10 points, so that your essays won't give hiring managers eyestrain.

8. Use plain fonts, such as Arial, Helvetica, Futura, Optima, Univers, Times New Roman, Palatino, New Century Schoolbook and Courier.

9. Print paper applications on only a single side of the page. That way, you won't risk losing half of the pages of your essay if the hiring agency duplicates your application with single-sided copying.

10. Do not print your application on odd-sized paper.

11. Print paper applications on white or off-white paper. Do not print your application on colored paper or include any other formatting gimmicks that will imply that you are eccentric.

12. Review Appendix 3: Formatting Tips for more ideas on how to attractively format paper essays, and for instructions on how to format essays in automated application systems.

EDITING

1. **Take breaks from working on your essays:** Each time that you return to your document after a break, you will bring a new perspective to your work that will help you recognize logical leaps that should be bridged, unnecessary information that can be eliminated, terms that should be defined, and important credentials that you may have omitted. In other words, your fresh perspective will show you what is *really* on the page rather than what you *think* is on the page.

BROTHERLY ADVICE FROM BILLIONAIRE WARREN BUFFET

Warren Buffet advises, "Write with a specific person in mind. When writing Berkshire Hathaway's annual report, I pretend that I'm talking to my sisters...Though highly intelligent, they are not experts in accounting or finance. They will understand plain English, but jargon may puzzle them.

No siblings to write to? Borrow mine: Just begin with 'Dear Doris and Berti.'"

2. **Run a spell checker on each essay.** Repeat the spell checker after making additional revisions. If you are writing an essay in an automated application system that does not have a spell checker, cut and paste your document into a WORD file. Then, spell check it, print, edit and revise your essay in WORD. When you are satisfied with your essay, cut-and-paste it into the automated application system.

3. **Proofread hard copy versions of your essays.** Many types of grammatical, spelling, punctuation and formatting mistakes are easier to identify in the hard copy documents than in their electronic versions. So don't rely exclusively on a spell checker for quality control. You must repeatedly proofread the hard copy of your draft to identify extra words, erroneous numbers and dates and misspellings that spell checkers don't detect, and substantive textual problems

4. **Read your essay out loud:** Check for:
    ➢ Logical leaps that should be bridged.
    ➢ Unnecessary information or words that should be eliminated.
    ➢ Generalities that should be described more specifically.

> ➤ Negativities that should be eliminated.
> ➤ Terms that should be defined.
> ➤ Grammatical errors.
> ➤ The accuracy of any numbers that you cite.

5. **Check that your essays are formatted attractively and consistently.**

6. **Solicit friendly fire on your essays.** Show your essays to colleagues, friends and relatives, and ask such editors to provide you with honest criticisms. And as one hiring manager put it, pick at least some editors "who don't love you, so that they will provide you with honest feedback without fawning over your application."

   Chances are that whatever flaws your editors find in your essays would also be noticed by hiring mangers. Why? Because remember that, as discussed in Chapter 5, hiring managers are in no way constitutionally or organically different from anyone else. So by seeking feedback on your essays from colleagues, friends and relatives, you will likely preview hiring managers' opinions of your essays.

   Don't be discouraged by your editors' suggestions. After all, every writer, including the finest, best-selling writers, has editors. This practice is so universal because all writers are just too biased by their own knowledge of their texts to accurately predict whether they will be understood by others. It takes nothing less than a fresh pair of eyes to tell a writer how their texts will be interpreted by a stranger.

   Collecting criticism is never easy. But it is much wiser to solicit friendly fire and use it to fix textual problems before judgment day than to submit a doomed application.

7. **See Chapter 10 for advice on making changes to an application that has already been submitted.**

THE MADDENING EDITING AND REVISING PROCESS

Many people wrongly believe that it takes less time and effort to write a short, easy-to-understand document than to write a long, technical document. Quite the opposite. As Blaise Pascal, a seventeenth century scientist said, "I have made this letter longer than usual because I lack the time to make it short."

Even expert writers must repeatedly revise in order to convey information clearly and concisely. For example, it took Pulitzer Prize winner Ernest Hemingway nothing less than a slavish devotion to the editing process to achieve his trademark simple, direct style. He rewrote the ending of the classic, *A Farewell to Arms,* almost 70 times!

Sadly, Hemingway ultimately killed himself. I suspect that the maddening editing process helped drive him to the edge! But fortunately, most of us can endure the necessary, though taxing, editing exercise without resorting to such extremes.

NO, THIS IS NOT A JOKE: THIS IS FROM A REAL LIFE KSA

Another Leadership role currently serving is President of the Bethesda Station Homeowners Association and representatives a community of more than 500 single-family dwellings. Leadership abilities involve frequent interaction with county managers, officials and politicians in an effort to improve the quality of life, promote growth and maintain harmonious relations amongst a very diversified which population is in excess of 5,500 people.

The many grammatical and logical errors in this KSA excerpt are not this book's mistakes. These mistakes were incorporated into a real life KSA. (Notice that according to the numbers provided in this excerpt, each home in the Bethesda Station Homeowners Association houses an average of more than 100 people: A tad crowded — wouldn't you say?)

But the real kicker is that the craven carelessness reflected in this KSA excerpt is NOT unusual. The federal government is literally flooded with applications that reflect as much sloppiness as the sample KSA paragraph provided here. It just goes to show that if you meticulously proofread your KSA over and over again until it is error-free, your KSA is virtually guaranteed to stand out from the pack for the right reasons.

TEN EXAMPLE ESSAYS

Ten example KSAs are provided in the following pages. These essays are based on real life, winning KSAs and ECQs (the names of employers, offices, dates and other details have been changed to disguise the identities of their writers.) Even if these example essays do not cover your field, they will give you ideas on how to describe your achievements and organize your essays; the organization of each essay is reflected in its headings.

Notice too that each essay identifies the applicant's title and employer — this information is critical to hiring managers. Moreover, these essays demonstrate various methods for quantifying activities, achievements and results, name-dropping and providing objective validation to an applicant's success as discussed in Chapter 6; they also incorporate effective story telling methods. For additional example essays, refer to the example stories provided on pages 124 to 134.

EXAMPLE ESSAY #1

<u>KSA for Customer Care Manager Position:</u>

Describe your communication skills.

MY CURRENT JOB

The United States Mint gives the best customer service in the federal government, according to the American Customer Survey Index (ACSI). As an award-winning Customer Care Representative at the Mint, I contribute to the Mint's number one position by providing fast, efficient and courteous service to Mint customers. I use my communication skills daily to:

- Process telephone orders for about $1,000 worth of coins, medals, jewelry and other collectibles per day.
- Resolve complaints about lost or broken merchandise. I am adept at calming angry customers by providing them with accurate information and extending extra services — such as free overnight delivery — as warranted.
- Research customers' questions about the history of U.S. coins and medals.
- Explain the Mint's products, billing procedures and shipping procedures to clients as I manage 50 on-going corporate/bulk order accounts.

Recognition: Since 2000, I earned three "Superior" evaluations on my annual performance reviews. I excel as a Customer Service Representative because I enjoy talking to people from all walks of life and all ages. This same trait would serve me well as a Customer Care Manager.

EXAMPLE ACHIEVEMENT

The anthrax mail contaminations of 2002 were more than just headlines for me. Why? Because they triggered a month-long suspension of mail deliveries to the US Mint's Customer Care Center. On the day that our mail deliveries resumed, the mailman delivered a mountain of mail that completely filled a 10 foot X 10 foot cubicle! I helped attack this mountain of mail by:

- Setting up a tracking system that flagged and gave priority to mail that was more than two weeks old.
- Drafting form letters to send out in response to low-priority, routine inquiries.
- Arranging for the hire of a temporary worker who helped process the backlog of mail.
- Working three hours of overtime every day for 21 business days.

Results: Within one month of the resumption of mail deliveries, the customer care center's huge backlog of mail was completely dissolved. Because of my pivotal role in this project, I received an On-The-Spot Award.

EARLY EXPERIENCE

From 1992 to 1997, I worked as an administrative assistant at the Department of Transportation. In this position, I answered about 20 controlled letters per week. My drafts for these letters were routinely approved by the Director of the Customer Care Center, without requiring any substantive changes.

EDUCATION AND TRAINING

- 24 hours of coursework from Fairfax Community College; Fairfax, Virginia (1990-1992)
- Five one-day courses in providing excellent customer service since 2000.

The structure of this essay would be adaptable to almost every job applicant's background. This essay structure would be particularly effective for an application's first essay, which should — for the sake of making the best possible "first" impression — include the applicant's most impressive achievements. In addition, this essay gets kudos for including a dramatic topic sentence; this applicant cleverly claims credit for the successes of her employer to which she contributed. This essay's other strengths include its success story that is particularly compelling because it was ripped from the headlines. In addition, the vivid imagery provided in the story adds to its punch. Also, this essay's "Recognition" paragraph tells why the applicant likes her job, and thereby conveys her enthusiastic, go-getter personality.

EXAMPLE ESSAY #2

<u>KSA for Executive Assistant position.</u>

Describe your ability to organize an office.

CAREER OVERVIEW

As an administrative assistant with 10 years of experience working for Chief Executive Officers, Chief Financial Officers, Senior Attorneys and Department Chiefs at General Electric (GE), Oracle and other large corporations, I have reveled in every opportunity to replace chaos with order.

I am an expert in developing and maintaining logical filing systems that enable the entire staff — from entry level professionals to executives — to quickly and easily access varied types of hard-copy and electronic documents, such as contracts, reports, personnel records, letters and memos, policy documents, forms and newsletters. My records management skills have frequently saved my employers large amounts of time and money.

EXAMPLE ACHIEVEMENT

BACKGROUND: As an Executive Assistant to General Electric's Chief Executive Officer (CEO) from 2000 to 2003, I frequently supported my supervisor as she negotiated multi-million dollar contracts.

PROBLEM: During the CEO's high-pressure negotiations with ABC Corporation in 2001 on the renewal of a $10 million dollar contract to supply GE with large quantities of plastic, a disagreement developed between GE and ABC Corporation over the existence of an addendum to our current contract, which had been signed three years before. This addendum verified the existence of current contract terms that were significantly more favorable to GE than were those proposed by ABC Corporation for the renewed contract. Unfortunately, however, ABC Corporation had no record of the addendum, and doubted its existence. Therefore, ABC Corporation would not agree to extend those favorable conditions to the renewed contract.

MY SOLUTION: Because I had maintained the original contract addendum in my files since it had been signed three years previously, I was able to immediately retrieve this document as soon as it was needed during the negotiations. The introduction of this document into the negotiations compelled ABC Corporation to sign a renewed contract that cost GE $50,000 less than the contract proposed by ABC Corporation would have cost.

POSITIVE FEEDBACK: While thanking me for swiftly producing the addendum, GE's CEO stated unequivocally that my solid record-keeping skills were solely responsible for the $50,000 in savings.

This applicant gets high points for name-dropping, in the very first sentence of her essay, the titles of her high-powered supervisors and the names of the corporate giants that employed her. In addition, this applicant tells a compelling, well organized story that offers money-saving punch.

EXAMPLE ESSAY #3

<u>**KSA for Administrative Assistant Position.**</u>

Describe your ability to arrange travel.

Federal travel management is currently being revolutionized by the Bush Administration's new e-travel initiative. As an expert in all aspects of the fast-changing federal travel arena, I would be able to smoothly steer your agency through this revolution.

EXPERIENCE IN TRAVEL MANAGEMENT

Under the title of Travel Manager, I serve as the "Travel and Shipping Go-To Person" for 200 employees at the Department of Interior. My typical travel projects involve the following tasks:

- Purchasing airline and train tickets, reserving hotel rooms and arranging car rentals.

- Preparing travel authorizations and issuing vouchers and itineraries under tight deadlines. I also ensure that all travel paperwork adheres to federal regulations, and is approved by the appropriate officials.

- Trouble-shooting through snags, such as lost tickets and cancelled flights, and accommodating last minute schedule changes, stop-overs, side trips and medical emergencies.

- Processing reimbursements of expenses quickly so that employees will not be delinquent on their credit cards.

REGULATORY AND E-EXPERTISE

Every year since 2000, I have attended the annual Federal Travel Conference, where I have participated in workshops on the new federal e-travel initiative, the federal SmartPay System, and the Travel and Transportation and Reform Act, among many other topics.

I am an expert in using the Internet and Gelco's Travel Manager software to electronically process all aspects of travel — from planning to processing reimbursements. In addition, I am thoroughly familiar with all federal websites that address credit card use, travel regulations, per diem rates, international travel and shipping, as well as airline, hotel and car rental websites.

RESULTS

- My paperwork and travel arrangements are — almost without exception — flawless, requiring no redundant efforts. Moreover, because of my efficiency and courteous manner with internal and external customers, I am known as an exceptionally efficient and congenial professional.

- I wrote my office's 20-page Travel Manual, which my office's 200 employees treat as a travel Bible.

- By using electronic travel procedures and by training other professionals in their use, I have helped streamline my office's travel processes and helped transform my office into a user-friendly, paperless environment.

By citing the factors that are changing her field and proving that she has the training and knowledge to adapt to them, this applicant creates the impression of a prepared and forward-thinking professional. If you want to use a similar approach in your essays but have trouble identifying some of the factors that are impacting your field, conduct some online literature searches in publications such as *Government Executive (govexec.com)* or conduct keyword searches in Internet search engines using keywords from your field.

EXAMPLE ESSAY #4

KSA for Engineering Position.

Describe your ability to work with diverse groups of people.

As Director of the National Financial Center's (NFC) Energy Conservation Program, I interact every day with professionals of all levels — from blue collar laborers to pin-stripped engineers and executives.

INTERNAL CUSTOMERS

The success of the NFC's Energy Conservation Program hinges, to a large degree, upon the contributions of plant managers, building engineers and the energy coordinators of each of NFC's five facilities. Even though I do not personally supervise these professionals, I have gained and maintained their cooperation by:

- Convincing them of the importance of energy conservation efforts.
- Quickly addressing their concerns and questions. Because I am fluent in Spanish, I am able to communicate directly with NFC's many Spanish speaking laborers whose activities effect energy efficiency.
- Keeping all energy coordinators updated of changes in policy or regulations by providing them with easy-to-understand fact sheets and checklists.
- Advising each facility's energy coordinator on the development of its individual energy plan. I provide site-specific guidance that addresses the unique climatic demands of each facility's location and the unique constraints of each facility's buildings.
- Keeping each facility's energy coordinator informed of approaching deadlines.
- Meeting personally at least once every six months with the plant manager, building engineer and energy coordinator of each facility. (Nothing beats personal contact!)

In addition, my annual plan for NFC's Energy Conservation Program has been enthusiastically approved each year by NFC's Director.

RESULTS: Under my leadership, during the last two years, NFC's Energy Conservation Program has:
- Saved well over a $1 million dollars in energy costs.
- Reduced energy consumption by more than two million BTU per year.
- Won two annual Department of Energy Water Management Awards. No other federal agency has ever won this award two years in a row.

EXTERNAL CUSTOMERS

Managing the NFC's Energy Conservation Program requires interacting with:
- Energy conservation experts at the Department of Energy. I participate in several DOE sponsored working groups, such as the Utility Partnership Working Group.
- Energy experts at monthly meetings of the Interagency Task Force on Energy Conservation.
- Representatives of utility companies with whom I negotiate utility contracts.

RESULTS: Evidence of my ability to effectively represent NFC includes my record in saving NFC more than $50,000 per year in negotiated utility contracts and managing the completion of five contract energy conservation projects on time and within budget during 2003.

Notice how this essay's first "Results" section quantifies and takes credit for accolades received by the employer, and the second "Results" section cites the applicant's record in completing projects on time and on budget — both excellent strategies.

EXAMPLE ESSAY #5

<u>KSA for Chief Financial Officer Position.</u>

Describe your problem-solving skills.

In December 2001, immediately after I became Chief Financial Officer of Global Electronics Corp. — an electronics distributor with annual earnings of more than $50 million, the company's CEO laid down the gauntlet by instructing me to "produce faster, more comprehensive and cleaner financial analyses than Global Electronics has ever produced before."

ACHIEVEMENT #1: FAST FINANCIAL ANALYSES

Global Electronics has historically updated its financial statements and closed its books about 19 days after the end of each financial reporting period. (Each fiscal year has 14 reporting periods.) Under my leadership, the Office of the Chief Financial Officer (OCFO) — which includes 10 Accountants and 10 Financial Planners — sped the processing of the company's financial statements by:

- Consolidating over 150 expense accounts into 50 accounts, and thereby reducing opportunities for reporting errors from these accounts.
- Providing training in automating accounting data to all 30 of Global Electronics Accountants.
- Grading each of Global Electronics' 15 offices on the accuracy of its accounting data, and providing intensive guidance to offices that earned low grades.

As a result of these activities, Global Electronics closed its books within three days of the close of the financial reporting period in May 2003. This was the company's the first three-day-close in the company's 20-year history. Global Electronics has closed out every subsequent reporting period with similar timeliness.

ACHIEVEMENT #2: COMPREHENSIVE FINANCIAL ANALYSES

Under my direction, OCFO initiated the production of new comprehensive reports of the company's financial/ operational performance at the end of each financial reporting period. These reports include features such as comparisons of actual financial activity vs. planned activity for individual offices as well as for the entire company.

By posting these reports on the company's Intranet, OCFO allows all company managers — from the highest level executives to front-line managers — to easily access the same financial information at the same time. My office thereby promotes consistent and informed decision-making throughout the company as well as more proactive, agile decision-making than had been possible before. For example, during FY 2003, OCFO's financial reports supported precedent-setting mid-quarter adjustments to spending that accommodated fast-changing economic conditions.

ACHIEVEMENT #3: CLEAN FINANCIAL ANALYSES

During each of the four years in which I have served as CFO, Global Electronics's financial statements have been approved by its independent auditors. By contrast, the company had never before received unqualified opinions from its auditors for two consecutive years.

EDUCATION

I earned a B.A. in Accounting from the University of Colorado, and a Masters in Business Administration from the University of Chicago.

This essay opens with an attention-getting lead and then cites several impressive "firsts" which just goes to show that even those of us who lead tamer lives than Edmund Hillary and Tenzing Norgay — the first climbers up Mt. Everest — can take credit for pioneering some admirable "firsts" (without even ever getting altitude sickness).

EXAMPLE ESSAY #6

<u>KSA for Program Manager Position.</u>

Describe your ability to work in teams.

WHAT MAKES AN EFFECTIVE TEAM?

An effective team is more than just a group. It is group of professionals who <u>each</u> take the initiative, transcend rigid divisions-of-labor to advise and help one another conquer glitches, work doggedly and jointly to pursue a common goal, and then share the credit for their joint achievement. Of course, a natural simpatico and shared sense of humor among team members can also help grease the wheels within any working work.

EXAMPLE TEAM PROJECT

As the Special Assistant to the Assistant Secretary of Labor, I served as one of three organizers of the Mine Safety and Health Administration's celebration in 2000 commemorating the 30th anniversary of passage of the Mine Safety and Health Act. (This law was among the most important worker safety laws ever passed.) We were given a mere two months to organize this historic event, which was attended by more than 500 miners, widows of miners, mine operators, union representatives, state and federal regulators, and reporters.

Our planning of this event involved:

- Selecting and inviting speakers, and advising speakers on what topics to cover in their talks. We infused the event with a human touch of mine safety by including on the speakers list several miners' widows.
- Generating an invitation list of more than 500 of the major players in the mine safety field.
- Designing the event's program brochure, which reviewed highpoints in the history of mine safety and featured eye-catching photographs of miners. We also managed the printing contract for production of the brochure.
- Constructing event displays, which included photographs, narrative texts and historical objects.
- Addressing a myriad of logistical challenges, including managing the event's limited budget, finding and reserving a suitable meeting hall and negotiating catering.

The two other event co-organizers and I met our tight deadline by demonstrating the principles of effective teamwork: We collaborated on each aspect of the project, kept one other informed of the progress of all tasks, and helped one another work through a myriad of logistical snags, such as computer programs that crashed at inconvenient times and speakers whose travel arrangements became problematic. In addition, <u>each</u> member of the event planning team carried more than his/her fair share of the load by working until at least 10:00 P.M. every workday and every weekend during the month before the event. Nevertheless, because all team members maintained good cheer throughout the high-pressure planning process, we maintained an enjoyable and productive esprit de corps.

RESULTS: Evidence of my team's success included:

- Positive coverage of the event in trade publications. For example, the event was described in *Mining Today* as an "evocative, moving tribute," and in *Worker Safety* as "a lively history lesson."
- The heart-felt standing ovations given to many of the speakers that were selected by the event organizing tine.
- A $1,000 Team Award that was given to each team member.

If you are asked about your team work in essay or interview question, include in your response — as this applicant did — any team awards that you have won.

EXAMPLE ESSAY #7

<u>KSA for Office Director Position.</u>

Describe your ability to achieve results.

BACKGROUND

I became the Director of the Office of Information Technology (OIT) of the National Regulatory Institute (NRI) on October 1, 1999 — only three months before the Y2K showdown of January 1, 2000. Talk about having to hit the ground running!

Without a moment to lose as the day of reckoning approached, I dove head-first into Y2K preparations on my first day on the job. And there was much to do. Like many other government organizations, NRI had received harsh criticism from the Government Accountability Office (GAO) because of its inadequate Y2K preparations. Moreover, most of OIT's 20-person staff lacked any recognition of the importance of systematically planning for Y2K.

ACTIONS

I put NRI's Y2K preparations on a fast track by:

- Arranging for all of OIT staffers to receive an immediate two-day training on the importance of Y2K planning, which reviewed preparation strategies adopted by Fortune 500 companies.

- Directing the cataloguing of more than 5,000 hardware items and 300 software applications used at NRI. This action was necessary because NRI's documentation of its systems was outdated.

- Working with NRI's Office of Procurement to hire a contractor to test, modify and then certify NRI's systems as Y2K compliant, and then working with contractor as it completed these tasks.

- Managing the development of IRD's first Business Continuity Contingency Plan, which provided comprehensive analyses of the potential impacts of various types of system failures on all of NRI's operations, and developed IRD's first Disaster Recovery Plan for restarting operations after experiencing system failures.

- Prepared OIT's staff to implement our Disaster Recovery Plan.

- Created a temporary command center at which the OIT staff monitored critical systems and coordinated activities with NRI's five field sites, as the clock rounded midnight on December 31, 1999.

RESULTS

Most importantly, under my leadership, OIT's Y2K preparations ensured that NRI's Information Technology systems experienced zero system failures on January 1, 2003. Moreover, the Business Contingency Plan and Disaster Recovery Plan that my staff developed in less than three months has been incorporated into NRI's contingency planning for terrorist attacks.

The writer of this essay promises to fulfill every employer's desire to hire an employee who can take charge from their first day on the job without needing coddling or hand-holding. This story's appeal is enhanced by its description of a high-impact problem (Y2K) that everyone can remember.

EXAMPLE ESSAY #8

<u>KSA for Program Manager Position.</u>

Describe how you have demonstrated creativity.

BACKGROUND

Recent budget cuts have forced me — like many managers — to find ways to do more with less. As the Director of the National Center for Strategic Development (NCSD), I enhanced the productivity of my 50-person office despite a 10 percent budget cut since 2002.

MY ACTIONS

Here is a sample of the innovative programs that I adopted during FY 2003:

- Initiated a formal program for soliciting anonymous employee suggestions. Employee suggestions submitted through this program inspired NCSD to develop a new monthly employee newsletter and to offer flexible work schedules to employees.

- Purchased and implemented an automated e-learning system that enables every employee to receive training in diverse topics, such as communicating, negotiating, accounting, database management and web development, on their computers. This system has enabled NCSD to provide more training to more employees while slashing its training budget by 20 percent per year. This program has also enhanced NCSD's ability to provide cross-training to employees so that they can be transferred to the areas in which they are most needed.

- Issued an agency-wide directive to increase the use of incentives-based service contracts. This type of contract benefits NCSD because they are designed to encourage contractors to exceed minimum requirements on timeliness and quality. Because of my directive, during FY 2003, 70 percent of our performance based contracts were incentives based, compared to 10 percent in FY 2002.

- Developed a program for rewarding high-performing employees by giving them extra days off.

- Developed a telecommuting program for high-performing employees. This program serves as a low cost incentives program and has allowed NCSD to reduce office space by 10 percent, and thereby save $2 million per year.

RESULTS

These innovative programs:
- Are currently producing a gross savings for NCSD of $5 million per year.
- Helped improve employee satisfaction by 20 percent, as measured by our annual employee satisfaction survey.
- Enabled NCSD to avoid a lay-off during FY 2003 that would have otherwise been necessary.

These results prove that, contrary to popular belief, smart innovations *don't* need to break the bank. In fact, they can benefit the bank.

Many applicants are intimidated by essay or interview questions about "creativity" because they wrongly believe that they are expected to reel off accomplishments that would be worthy of Leonardo da Vinci. Not so. The "creativity" question usually means exactly the same thing as the question, "Explain how you have demonstrated that you think out of the box." The essay answer provided here conveys a trait that every hiring manager wants: The ability to, like an alchemist, spin gold out of hay…or at least, stretch the hay.

EXAMPLE ESSAY #9

KSA for Writer/Editor Position.

Describe your communication skills.

I am a jack-of-all-trades communications expert who can write just about any type of document on varied topics. For example, I have prepared:

- **TECHNICAL MANUALS:** As a technical writer at Environmental Systems Research Institute from 1995 to 2000, I wrote four user manuals for computer mapping systems. Production of each manual required acquiring mastery of the associated software program, explaining its use in easy-to-understand instructions, and then meticulously testing these instructions for accuracy and usability. Each manual was distributed to more than 10,000 system users.

- **PRESS RELEASES:** As a communications officer at the Securities and Exchange Commission since 2000, I have written approximately 50 easy-to-understand press releases on complex issues involving corporate fraud, insider trading and tax policy. Please note these comments from my supervisor on my latest performance evaluation:

  What did we do before Nancy worked at this office? This oft-used phrase aptly describes how valuable Nancy is to this office. Multi-skilled, she brings unwavering energy and professionalism to an office that requires both in spades.

- **ARTICLES FOR THE POPULAR PRESS:** I have published more than 20 articles in national magazines and flight magazines on varied topics including energy and environmental issues, corporate finance and personal investing. Because of the high quality of my articles and my ability to meet tight deadlines, my editors often asked me to submit additional articles. (See the attached list of my publications.)

- **ORAL PRESENTATIONS:**
  - ❏ I have delivered presentations at the National Science Foundation's (NSF) annual meeting in Arlington, Virginia on science communication every year since 1995. (NSF keeps asking me back because of the positive evaluations that my presentations have generated from meeting participants.) My NSF presentations — spiced with lively, humorous anecdotes — provide practical instruction in how to convey technical and scientific information in plain English. Each of my presentations has drawn about 200 professional communicators and government scientists.

  - ❏ As a Program Analyst at the Environmental Protection Agency from 1998 to 2000, I delivered presentations on Clean Air Act requirements to members of the regulated community, which included some hostile audiences. These assignments tested my persuasive powers, as well as my ability for quick thinking, maintaining grace under pressure and anticipating audience questions.

  - ❏ I have been a volunteer at the National Zoo since 1998. In this position, I spend one weekend afternoon per month presenting lectures to large crowds of visitors that mix entertaining and factual information about wildlife.

  - ❏ I am an expert in using PowerPoint.

Education
I earned a B.A. in English Literature and an M.A. in Journalism with Distinction from Columbia University.

If you have provided stories in several of your essays, it is fine to provide one or two essays that do not tell stories. This is a good example of a nonstory essay that is nevertheless impressive and interesting because it is well organized with headings, cites specific examples, incorporates an attention-getting quote, quantifies achievements, and reflects body of accomplishments.

EXAMPLE ESSAY #10

<u>KSA for Writer/Editor Position.</u>

Describe your communication skills.

Eric Schrodinger, a Nobel Prize winner in physics, said: "If you cannot — in the long run — tell everyone what you have been doing, your doing has been worthless." As a scientist I share Schordinger's respect for the importance of communication skills. So while I earned a B.A. in biology from the University of Massachusetts, I participated in various academic and non-academic activities that improved my writing and speaking skills.

WRITING SKILLS

I demonstrated my effective writing skills by:

- Completing a three-credit independent project on the effects of growing deer populations and urbanization on Lyme disease in Massachusetts. This project involved summarizing the current literature; interviewing 15 wildlife biologists, epidemiologists and urban planners; documenting an increase in Lyme disease in three counties over the last 20 years from state records; and synthesizing this information into a 30-page report. I earned an A- on this project. In addition, my advisor repeatedly complemented my ability to strategically balance the need to work with minimal supervision against the need to solicit guidance as appropriate.

- Earning a B+ in English Composition and Advanced English Literature during my junior year.

- Writing a five-page report on the ecology of the Hudson River as an Intern at the Office of Technology Assessment (OTA) during the summer of 2003. Because of the logic, conciseness and accuracy of my writing, my supervisor, the Director of Natural Resources Programs, approved my report with few substantial edits, and offered me a position for the summer of 2004.

SPEAKING SKILLS

I demonstrated my effective speaking skills by:

- Giving a 90-minute presentation on Elephant Ecology to my Wildlife Biology class. Completing this project required determining the structure of my presentation; becoming an expert in elephant ecology by scouring the literature; delivering a lively and informative presentation; designing reader-friendly PowerPoint slides; and answering 20 minutes of questions from students. My professor described my presentation as "a tour-de-force."

- Providing two hours of one-on-one tutoring per week to freshmen taking Introductory Biology during my senior year.

- Serving as Co-Captain of the varsity basketball team during my junior and senior years. In this leadership role, I often contributed to decisions on team management, coached team members and counseled them on their personal problems.

This essay by a recent college graduate builds a compelling case by citing the writer's coursework, grades, summer jobs and extracurricular activities.

WHAT HIRING MANAGERS WANT
BY KATHY ALEJANDRO, FEDERAL MANAGER AND SUPERVISOR

As the Deputy Director of a 130-person office in a large federal agency, I have helped hire and promote many federal employees. What do federal hiring managers, like me, usually look for in job applicants?

The three qualities that impress me most in job applications are *experience, experience* and more *experience.* That's because if I have a staffing need, I want to fill it NOW. So I want to hire someone who can hit the ground running with minimal supervision and training. And applicants who are experienced in the same types of projects demanded by the job opening are most likely to be able to quickly and independently deliver.

I also want to hire professionals who:

- Are hard-working and conscientious.

- *Really* want the job, and go the extra mile to prove it.

- Are professionally reliable. (Yes, when you are screening strangers, the possibility of hiring an axe murderer is, shall we say, less than appealing.)

How can you, as a job applicant, show hiring mangers that you have these winning qualities? First and foremost, by loading your KSAs with specific examples of successes that relate to the opening. You will thereby prove that you would produce similar successes if you are hired for the job.

But if, on the other hand, you submit an application that omits required KSAs, you are virtually guaranteed to be rejected. Likewise, if you pump up your KSAs with generic or irrelevant information that lacks specifics, you will probably strike out. After all, you can't expect hiring managers to fill in the gaps and make sense out of *your* past. That's your job.

Among my pet peeves are KSAs that are filled with conclusionary statements about how qualified the applicant is and what the applicant can do without providing any examples of accomplishments that support these statements. I am similarly turned off by KSAs whose irrelevance to the vacancy announcement suggests that they were originally written for another purpose.

As someone who has written many KSAs for my own job applications, I sympathize with applicants who would rather not have to write KSAs. But by the same token, as a hiring manager, I weigh KSAs even more heavily than resumes. That's because KSAs invite applicants to provide thorough but concise descriptions of their relevant qualifications. By contrast, resumes are usually diluted by jobs, projects and training that have, in no way, prepared the applicant for the opening. Why should I sift through that if I can get exactly what I need from KSAs? Moreover, any applicant who squanders the opportunity to sell themselves and show how they are qualified for the job probably doesn't want it very much.

Here are some other pointers for preparing winning federal job applications:

- **Write for Nonspecialists:** Let me give you an example of why this is important: By training, I am an attorney. But I have served as the selecting official for jobs such as a contract specialist or safety and health specialist, in which I have no particular background. So it is hard for me to understand let alone be impressed by applications for such positions that are filled with abbreviations, acronyms and technical or agency-specific jargon. But I am likely to be bowled over by applications for such positions that cite success stories and other credentials that are free of such impenetrable obstacles.

- **Research Your Target Agency:** Surf through your target agency's website, read recent articles about the agency in newspapers and magazines and research your target agency through the online resources provided in Chapter 2 and Chapter 9 of this book. Reflect your resulting knowledge in your application. In interviews, mention how you have researched the agency, and then mention specific, relevant news items about the agency to prove it.

- **Proofread and Edit:** Typos, grammatical errors, missing words and misspellings on job applications are absolute no-nos. One of my favorite bloopers involved an applicant who mentioned that he had brought a project "to fruitarian" (instead of "to fruition"). On first blush, I though the applicant had brought the project to someone who studied fruit or was a vegan! Other applications have included sentences such as "I have letters of accommodation" (instead of "commendation"), and ironically, "I am an excellent profreader" (instead of "proofreader").

  Though such mistakes provide comic relief to hiring panels, they reflect poorly on the applicant's communication skills. But even worse, an error-filled or incomplete application that incorporates a sloppy, half-hearted approach bodes poorly for an applicant's on-the-job performance.

  Here is a tip that will be the gift that will keep on giving: Run each of your applications by at least one critical, articulate editor. Your editor will help you eliminate bloopers and sharpen the organization and clarity of your descriptions of your experience.

- **Use Inside Contacts:** Do you have inside contacts who will vouch for your professional reputation and reliability? An inside contact may be an employee of the hiring agency or a personal or professional associate of a hiring manager. If so, encourage your inside contact to sing your praises to the powers-that-be as soon as you submit your application.

- **Infuse Your Application and Interview With LIFE!** Unfortunately, many job seekers wrongly believe that just because they are applying for a federal job, their application should read as dryly as the *Federal Register*. NOT! An application or interview that reflects a high-energy individual who enjoys their job, whose personality fits their profession and who considers their job important and respects the mission of the agency will almost always stand out from the pack

CHAPTER 8:
WRITING IRRESISTIBLE RESUMES
fpmi

CHAPTER 8:
WRITING IRRESISTIBLE RESUMES

I'll read a concise, neat, deftly formatted resume immediately. Long, difficult-to-read clunkers or resumes that have mistakes immediately get buried in the bottom of the resume pile — perhaps never to be exhumed again.

— A Federal Hiring Manager

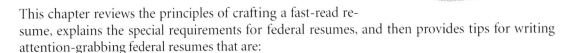

The typical time-pressured, harried hiring manager will only spend a few precious seconds skimming your resume before deciding whether to read on or move on to another application. Therefore, to be effective, your resume must serve as a verbal two-by-four that instantly knocks out hiring mangers. To do so, it must quickly prove that your previous triumphs qualify you to solve the hiring agency's current problems.

This chapter reviews the principles of crafting a fast-read resume, explains the special requirements for federal resumes, and then provides tips for writing attention-grabbing federal resumes that are:

- Interesting
- Concise
- Packed full of relevant, high level achievements
- Formatted to be eye-catching, and to support fast reading and skimming
- Easy-to-understand, and written for nonspecialists
- Error free

"*I see you've flown around the world in a plane, and settled revolutions in Spain. Around a golf course you're under par. Metro-Goldwyn has asked you to star. Very impressive, I must admit, but we're looking for someone with marketing experience.*"

THE TEST OF TIME

Compare the two resumes on the following pages.... Which is easier and faster to read?

Sam Eastman
1234 Yellow Brick Road
City, State Zip Code

Objective
To achieve my personal and professional goals by working on a management team where my education and experience in the graphic arts can be best utilized. Specifically, I can contribute in the areas of planning and achieving short and long range goals, team building, staff planning and development process improvement and profitability. My education, dedication, focus and diverse business experience provide the foundation for achieving these goals.

Education
M.A.S. Business - 1985
Johns Hopkins University, Baltimore, MD
B.S., A.S. Printing Management & Technology - 1975

Rochester Institute of Technology, Rochester, NY
A.A.S. Liberal Arts - 1973
Mitchell College, New London, CT

Experience
1999-Present
Desktop Operator-Jones Integrated Graphics, Silver Spring, MD
I joined Wallace while in the process of ceasing operations at the pre-press business I owned and operated until Dec. 1999. I provide Macintosh, PC and Scitex-based electronic pre-press services including scanning, preflight file preparation, RIPing, trapping, imposition, film output and digital proofing. Additional duties include conventional proofing and platemaking. I have continued to build my knowledge of electronic pre-press, network and digital asset management, which I feel are the key areas for me to stay abreast of in order to return to a formal management position.

1995-1999
Founder/Owner-Incredible Designs, Inc., Jessup, MD
Founded a pre-press service bureau based on my cumulative experience and education in the Baltimore/Washington graphic arts market. The business was targeted at providing more sophisticated Scitex-based pre-press services to the smaller design, publishing and printing buyers in the market, which was being contested by newly formed conglomerates and low-end service bureaus. Built the sales up to $250,000 with only several part-time employees and myself. I was responsible for all business operations.

1993-1995
Vice President Sales-Eagle Color, Forestville, MD
I joined the firm to try to revitalize falling sales, and have the opportunity to purchase an interest in the firm, which was privately owned. Developed and serviced new accounts, provided strategic planning and equipment upgrading plans. The owner's unexpected death forced the closing of operations and the return of leased equipment. My efforts to purchase the name and assets of the firm broke off when a closer inspection of the firm's financial and contract labor (union) obligations made it more logical to start with new equipment at a different location.

1980-1993
Vice President/Director-Harry W. King Co., Baltimore, MD
Originally joined the firm as a CSR/Planner. Promoted to Production Manager in four years; a shareholder and Vice-President of Production Operations in another two years, and elected to the Board of Directors in 1990. I reported directly to the President and the Board of Directors. Responsible for all printing operations including estimating, customer service, production planning, inventory control and contract labor relations.

Personal
Married 25 years, three children age 8, 17 and 20. My spouse owns and operates a successful music studio in Columbia, MD. My primary interests include motor sports and outdoor activities, although much of my spare time is devoted to assisting in the operation of the music studio and supporting our children's activities.

Can you identify the title of Sam Eastman's target opening and the titles of his previous positions within 10 seconds? If you cannot quickly do so, hiring managers won't be able to do so either. And slow-read resumes that try hiring managers' patience are usually destined for the circular file.

The most important principle of formatting documents is that WHAT STANDS OUT ON THE PAGE IS WHAT STANDS OUT IN THE READER'S MIND. But because nothing — not even Sam Eastman's job titles — is formatted to stand out, nothing stands out to the reader. Notice, for example, that Eastman's job titles are no more prominent than his ZIP code! Moreover, Eastman's job summaries are lackluster because they are wordy and because they are not achievement-oriented. (See Chapter 6 for instructions on describing achievements.)

What's more, this resume, which is based upon a real-life resume that was submitted for a public affairs job, provides no qualifications that fit the target job. No wonder the federal government rejected this resume's real-life counterpart.

JANE SMITH

1234 Yellow Brick Road • City, State, Zip Code
Work: (123) 123-4567 • Home: (123) 123-4567 • E-Mail: Jsmith@email.gov

Social Security Number: 000-00-0000   U.S. Citizen

OBJECTIVE

SENIOR CONTRACT SPECIALIST: GS-1102-13 (Announcement Number HF2129TL)

SUMMARY OF QUALIFICATIONS

- **Award-Winning Contract Manager:** Seven years of experience in managing multi-year, multi-million dollar contracts for large federal agencies.

- **Regulatory Expert:** Advise senior officials on federal regulations (including Federal Acquisition Regulations) for managing high-dollar contracts, and for procuring high-profile goods and services.

- **Warrant:** Authorized to award contracts worth up to $5 million without additional approvals.

- **B.A. in Economics**

PROFESSIONAL EXPERIENCE

US MINT

801 9th St NW Washington DC 20008

SENIOR CONTRACT SPECIALIST (1102 Series)   May 2000 - Present
Office of the Chief Information Officer

CONTRACT SPECIALIST (1102 Series)   May 1999 - May 2000
Office of Numismatics Strategic Business Unit

ACCOMPLISHMENTS AT THE MINT:
- Lead team of six Mint Contract Specialists who procure Information Technology (IT) support and services worth approximately $6 million annually.
- Develop streamlined procedures for conducting pre-award cost analyses, planning, negotiating and soliciting contracts, and for administrating and closing out contracts.
- Advise program managers on cradle-to-grave acquisition planning, including preparing Statement of Works and conducting market research of vendors.

Can you identify the title of Jane Smith's target opening and the titles of her previous position from the first page of her federal resume within 10 seconds? It is easy, isn't it?

Unlike Sam Eastman's resume on the previous page, Jane Smith's resume heeds the principle that WHAT STANDS OUT ON THE PAGE IS WHAT STANDS OUT ON THE READER'S MIND. Because the title of her target job and the titles of her previous jobs are bolded and capitalized, they leap off the page. This resume's other virtues include its Summary of Qualifications, which provides a fast overview of Jane Smith's best credentials, and the achievement-oriented bullets.

I have provided this resume format to countless numbers of successful applicants. A template for this format is included in the CD accompanying this book.

REQUIREMENTS FOR FEDERAL RESUMES

Resumes submitted for federal jobs must include considerably more persnickety details than resumes submitted to private sector or nonprofit employers. Many federal applicants wonder whether it is *really* necessary for them to include all of these required details in their resumes. The truth of the matter is that many federal hiring managers will not even notice, let alone care, if you submit a standard, nongovernment resume instead of a federal resume. If the truth be known, some hiring managers may even prefer if you submit a standard, nongovernment resume rather than a federal resume that is cluttered with useless details.

But, on the other hand, some federal hiring managers automatically reject any application that lacks required information. And because you probably cannot predict whether your resume will be reviewed by tolerant or nit-picking hiring managers, the safest strategy is to give the federal government exactly what it requires. Listed below are the types of information required in federal resumes:

INFORMATION ABOUT THE OPENING:

- ❑ Announcement number, title and grades

YOUR PERSONAL INFORMATION:

- ❑ Name, address with zip code, and day and evening telephone numbers
- ❑ Social Security number
- ❑ Country of citizenship
- ❑ Veterans preference
- ❑ Reinstatement eligibility
- ❑ Highest federal civilian grade held, including job series

EDUCATION:

- ❑ Names of each college or university
  - ☞ City, state and ZIP code if known
  - ☞ Major
  - ☞ Type and years of degrees received. If no degree, show total credits earned and whether semester or quarter hours

- ❑ Name of high school
  - ☞ City, state and ZIP code, if known
  - ☞ Date or diploma or GED

WORK EXPERIENCE (including relevant volunteer jobs):

For each job you held within the last 10 years or for earlier jobs that are relevant to the opening:
- ❏ Job title
- ❏ Accomplishments
- ❏ Employer's name and address
- ❏ Supervisor's name and telephone number: Indicate whether your current supervisor may be contacted
- ❏ Starting and ending dates (month and year)
- ❏ Hours worked per week
- ❏ Salary

OTHER QUALIFICATIONS

- ❏ Job-related training courses, including the title and year
- ❏ Job-related skills, including languages, computer software/hardware, tools, machinery, typing speed
- ❏ Current job-related certificates and licenses
- ❏ Job-related honors, awards and special accomplishments, including publications, public speaking credentials, performance awards (including dates), leadership activities, and memberships in professional or honor societies

RESUME FORMAT OPTIONS

Some federal agencies accept any and all resume formats, including electronic or paper resumes that may be formatted however the applicant chooses. But some federal agencies only accept resumes that are submitted via automated application systems that accommodate only minimal formatting. Several other federal agencies only accept electronic resumes that follow the format of a specified template.

Alternatively, some federal agencies allow applicants to choose between submitting automated resumes that accommodate minimal formatting or submitting paper or electronic resumes that can be attractively formatted. If your target job gives you such a choice, choose the latter option. Why? Because the overwhelming majority of federal hiring managers are more likely to read and remember an eye-catching, quick-read resume than a minimally formatted resume that is slow and difficult to read.

But no matter what format your resume takes, be sure to follow the tips on resume length, targeting your resume to the opening, and resume components that are provided in this chapter.

DESIGNING YOUR OWN RESUME FORMAT

You may design your own resume format by:

1. Customizing the resumes contained in the CD accompanying this book to your own background. These resumes are formatted for fast and memorable reading and adhere to all requirements for federal resumes.

    Note that the resumes in the accompanying CD incorporate two different approaches: One of these approaches involves including *all* information required in a federal resume in the body of the resume. Alternatively, the other approach involves crafting a standard, clutter-free resume, but providing the extra persnickety details required by the federal government in a Supplemental Resume Sheet. This approach is designed to appeal to EVERYONE: Hiring managers who prefer reading standard, nongovernment resumes as well as persnickety hiring managers who insist that federal resumes include all required information.

2. Designing your own resume layout. Review Appendix 3: Formatting Tips for ideas on how to format your resume.

DESIGNING AN AUTOMATED RESUME

If you submit your application via an automated application system that accommodates only minimal formatting:

☞ Use the formatting tips for "Formatting Text in Automated Application Systems" that are provided in Appendix 3: Formatting Tips.

☞ Review the resumes in the CD accompanying this book to get ideas on phrasing your accomplishments.

☞ Bring an attractively formatted resume with you to your interview. By doing so, you will draw attention to your resume, and guarantee that you will stand out from the pack.

USING RESUME BUILDERS

Most federal agencies accept resumes created on the Internet-based resume builder featured on USAJOBS. In addition, the websites of some federal agencies include resume builders that can be used by any job seeker to create and submit a resume. Nevertheless, the formatting accommodated by most federal resume builders is extremely limited. (Translation: The resumes produced by most of these resume builders look HORRIBLE.)

Moreover, keep in mind that no electronic resume builder or electronic repository of resumes is foolproof. A case in point: The server supporting the USAJOBS resume builder has experienced at least one recent crash that blew out large numbers of job-searchers' resumes. So always keep copies of resumes that you create on resume builders. And if you store your resume on an electronic resume repository, periodically check that it is, in fact, still there.

RESUME LENGTH

Because of their extra information requirements, federal resumes are usually longer than standard resumes; the "one page rule" does not apply to federal resumes.

But remember that hiring managers don't have time to sift through long-winded tomes. So rather than aiming for a specific resume length, aim to: 1) Keep your resume as short as possible. 2) Format your best credentials prominently and as close to the top of the document as possible. 3) Ruthlessly edit dated information and information that is irrelevant to your target job.

TARGET PRACTICE

No matter how you format your resume, make sure that this document (as well as the rest of your application) reflects the characteristics that the hiring agency is looking for. Target your resume to the opening by:

- Tailoring your objective to match the opening.

- Including a summary of qualifications that ticks off your best credentials and addresses the most important KSAs or ECQs of the job opening.

- Positioning your credentials that most closely match the demands of the opening as close to the top of your resume as possible.

- Phrasing your job summaries to reflect the demands of the opening; use keywords from the vacancy announcement.

- Eliminating information from the resume that does not relate to the opening.

RESUME COMPONENTS

Many of the tips for planning, writing and editing KSAs, which are provided in Chapter 7, apply to writing resumes as well. Here are some additional tips on writing resumes:

THE HEADER

- Include your name, address, telephone numbers and e-mail address.

- Encourage hiring managers to remember your name by writing it in large, bold letters. After all, you are the star of this show, so make your name stand out like the name of a movie star on the marquee of a movie theater.

- Consider giving yourself a title to help hiring managers immediately identify your profession. This strategy is used in some of the resumes included in the CD accompanying this book. If your current job title is not particularly flattering, or if you are currently unemployed, use the phrase "Expert in…." instead of a title.

- See Appendix 3 for instructions on how to insert special characters into your header, or how to insert a black line below your header.

- Create a header that is balanced on the page and does not create large, gaping holes on the page.

OBJECTIVE

Although an "Objective" is not required in federal resumes, you may include this optional feature in your resume to quickly identify your target job and/or concisely explain why you are qualified for the position. To be effective though, an objective — like all other resume features — must honor the principle that hiring managers care more about what applicants *offer* than what applicants *want*. Unfortunately, however, most federal resumes include abstract, long-winded objectives that violate this principle by citing everything the applicant would need to reach a state of professional Nirvana. (Such objectives might as well be relabeled as "the gimme section.")

Other resume objectives pile on meaningless information. Consider, for example, Sam Eastman's objective on page 166. Its opening — Eastman's stated desire to achieve his personal goals — is completely out of bounds for a resume. (Is Eastman looking for a job or a date?) Moreover, Eastman's stated desire to achieve his professional goals merely states the obvious. And the second sentence of Eastman's objective, which begins with the word "Specifically," includes everything but the kitchen sink. Sorry pal, the credibility meter just hit zero.

By contrast, Jane Smith's objective, which merely cites the name of Smith's target job, is specific, concise and informative. Alternatively, you may opt for another type of objective: One that provides a brief summary statement that names your target job and concisely defines how you would add value to the agency.

Here are some examples of effective objectives:

☞ *An administrative position using my eight years of experience organizing meetings, arranging travel and finalizing documents for senior executives.*

☞ *A marketing position where my advertising expertise will help boost the company's bottom line.*

☞ *A position on an IT Help Desk where my knowledge of large networks and trouble-shooting expertise will improve network efficiency.*

SUMMARY OF QUALIFICATIONS

Federal resumes are not required to include a "Summary of Qualifications." But by positioning a brief "Summary of Qualifications" near the beginning of your resume, you can:

☞ Quickly call attention to your best, most relevant selling points, including relevant degrees that you have already earned or degrees that you are currently working towards (along with your expected date of graduation). By doing so, you will help ensure that hiring managers who only skim your resume or who don't read your entire resume will still extract your best selling points.

☞ Underscore how you satisfy the KSAs of your target job. You can do this by addressing each KSA, or the most important KSAs, from your target job in a one sentence summary in your Summary of Qualifications. For example, an applicant targeting a job that included a KSA for "communication skills" would emphasize his/her communication skills by including the following bullet in his/her resume:

• **Polished Communicator:** *Experienced in researching and writing newsletters, fact sheets, and press releases, and delivering oral presentations to executives.*

☞ Emphasize older, but relevant and important qualifications from earlier jobs that might otherwise be overlooked because of their positioning deep in the document.

A "Summary of Qualifications" should consist of four or five quick-read bullets. Make sure that all selling points cited in this section are supported by information provided in the body of your resume.

Are you an applicant for a Senior Executive Service (SES) job who has been certified for the SES by the Qualifications Review Board? If so, your certification will give you an important advantage in your application. So be sure to broadcast this credential prominently in your resume; including it in your summary of qualifications is a good way to do this.

WORK EXPERIENCE

- In most resumes, the "Work Experience" section should precede the "Education" section. But if you are currently a student or a recent graduate or if your degree(s) is more relevant to your target job than your work experience, position your "Education" section before your "Work Experience" section.

- Sequence your job summaries in reverse chronological order (from your most recent job to your earliest job). In addition, devote more space to recent jobs than to earlier jobs, unless your earlier jobs are more relevant to your target job than you're your recent job.

- If you worked more than one job for a single employer, do not repeat the name and address of this employer over and over again. Notice, for example, how Jane Smith's resume identifies the United States Mint as an employer only once, even though Smith worked two Mint jobs. Smith achieved this concision by creating a heading for the Mint, listing both of her Mint jobs under her Mint heading, and consolidating her best achievements at the Mint into a single list of bullets. This strategy saved space. In addition, because it enabled Smith to position her titles directly on top of one another, it emphasized her rise within the organization. Alternatively, Smith could have positioned her achievements under each respective Mint job title.

- Either omit information about jobs that ended more than 10 or 15 years ago or list them under an "Early Experience" or "Other Experience" heading. Include only very brief descriptions of such jobs, or list only the titles of such jobs without providing any descriptions of them at all, unless they are directly relevant to your target job.

- Present each job summary on your resume as a list of snappy, quick-read bullets that is, at most, several lines long. Instructions for creating bullets are provided in Appendix 3: Formatting Tips.

- Convey in your job summaries your unique *achievements, accomplishments* and *home run triumphs.* Instructions on how to identify and phrase such successes are provided in Chapter 6. Do not include in your job summaries job descriptions — long laundry lists of responsibilities and day-to-day activities that could apply to hundreds of other employees.

- Begin each bullet with an energetic action verb. To access dozens of sites listing such action verbs, conduct a search on an Internet search engine using the phrase *action verbs for resumes.*

  Don't squander precious space in your job summaries by including the pronoun "I"; hiring managers already know that your resume describes *your* work history without your telling them so.

  Put the verb that begins each bullet in the first person; this is the verb form that would accompany the pronoun "I" if it were present. You can test for the first person by silently inserting the pronoun "I" in front of it.

WRONG	FIRST PERSON: CONTACT
Manages high-traffic website.	Manage high-traffic website.
Tracks congressional correspondence.	Track congressional correspondence.
Prepares exhibits for hearings and trials.	Prepare legal exhibits for hearings and trials.

✎ Omit wasted words, such as: *I had responsibility for…I was responsible for…My duties included…I served as…*

✎ Convey a unique, distinct accomplishment in each bullet; make sure that bullets do not provide overlapping information.

✎ Sequence your bullets in their order of importance. Position your most relevant, most impressive bullets before your less relevant, less impressive ones. Do so even if your most relevant, most impressive bullets did not account for the majority of your time.

✎ Limit each job description to a maximum of 15 bullets or fewer, if possible. Break up long lists of bullets into categories, as done in the sample resumes included in the CD accompanying this book.

✎ If a previous job(s) is more relevant to your target job than your current job, bring this previous experience closer to the top of your resume by creating various categories of work experience, and leading with the most relevant category. For example, suppose you were applying for a job as a Web Developer, and you worked as a Web Developer before you took your current position as a Press Officer. You could create one category of work experience for "Web Development Work Experience" and another category of work experience for "Press Relations Work Experience." Then, you could position your "Press Relations Work Experience" before your "Web Development Work Experience."

✎ Phrase descriptions of previous jobs in the past tense. As one hiring manager observes, "If I see sentences that are not in the first person, or in the wrong tense, I know that the applicant has simply cut and pasted sections of their resume from a job description. Such mistakes smack of laziness and carelessness."

✎ Briefly state a good reason for any significant gaps between employment dates, such as: *returned to school full-time, worked on consulting projects, became care-taker for seriously ill family member, or took sabbatical to manage family responsibilities.*

EDUCATION

- List academic credentials in reverse chronological order.

- If you are currently a student, indicate degree, university and expected date of graduation.

- If you are working towards a degree while holding down a job, or previously did so, mention this achievement. For example:

    Concurrent with full-time employment: JD, Howard University Law School, Washington DC 20008 (Expected in 2004)

- If you are currently a student or are a recent graduate, you may include your Grade Point Average if it is B plus or better.

OTHER HEADINGS

Your resume may include additional headings, such as:

- Awards and Honors
- Licenses and Certificates
- Public Speaking Experience
- Publications
- Systems and Software
- Foreign Languages
- Military Experience
- Community Service
- Programming Languages and Operating Systems

List credentials under such headings in reverse chronological order, as appropriate.

EXCLUDED INFORMATION

Your resume should not mention your marital status or whether you have children, because such information should not influence hiring decisions. Only provide your date of birth if the application for your target job specifically asks for it.

FORMATTING

Your resume should stand out — but not for the wrong reasons. A resume that is heavier than a sumo wrestler, has tiny margins, is hand-written in Olde Englishe calligraphy, printed on paper that is as bright as disco lights, and packaged in a big honkin' binder will generate attention without drawing an invitation for an interview.

What *will* impress hiring managers is an ultra neat, organized document that has wide margins, clean, conservative fonts (of at least nine or 10 points), prominent headings, job titles and employer names, and bullets that send a hiring manager's eyes flying down the page. So encourage hiring managers to read your resume by:

☞ Emphasizing important information by using capital letters, various font sizes, various font types, indents and bolding. Many of the tips for formatting KSAs, which are provided in Chapter 7 also apply to formatting resumes. (Again, use the formatting tips provided in Appendix 3: Formatting Tips.)

☞ Expressing subordination through formatting. That is, headings should be bolded and positioned to stand out, and information that follows headings should be formatted to reflect its subordinate status.

☞ Using white space to break up text and enhance its readability.

☞ Creating a balanced layout that sensibly distributes information throughout the page. In particular, do not create large holes in your resume. Remember that your resume, and particularly the first page of your resume, represents valuable acreage. Don't short sell yourself by wasting this prized real estate on empty space that does not sing your praises.

☞ Formatting your resume consistently. This means that once you pick a format, you should stick to it throughout your resume. For example, margin size, alignments, justifications, the size of the gap between each bullet and accompanying text, and the amount of space following headings and lines should be identical throughout the document. In addition, headings of comparable weight should be formatted identically.

☞ Printing out the hard copy version of your resume, repeatedly proofreading its content, and repeatedly eyeballing its format to make sure it is attractive and consistent. When you are satisfied with the content and format of your resume, check it again, and then show it to an objective editor. (The discussion on editing KSAs in Chapter 7 applies to editing resumes, as well.)

GAFFE-FEST: Can You Find The Gaffes In This Real-Life Resume Excerpt?

ANDREW SMITH

United States Citizen
(H) 123-123-4567
(W) 123-123-1234

1234 Yellow Brick Road
City, State ZIP Code
SSN: 000-00-0000

SUMMARY OF QUALIFICATIONS
- Eight years of Contracting experience with consistently increasing responsibilities in large dollar procurement, formal advertising, procurement planning, bid analysis, negotiations, and contract monitoring. Contracting Officer, Warrant amount $5,000,000.
- Three years of Marketing experience relating to managing office marketing environment, customer feedback evaluation, market research, and advertising.
- Proven ability to effectively communicate and coordinate with others at all levels, proficiency using standard office technology, and capability to manage multiple tasks and responsibilities simultaneously and effectively.

EDUCATION:
-**Master of Business Administration-Contract Mgmt** – Colorado Institute of Technology - Dec 1997
-**Bachelor of Science-Marketing** - Bowie State University - May 1991

PROFESSIONAL EXPERIENCE:

Contracting Officer: Office of Procurement, U.S. Army Corps of Engineers, 441 G Street, NW Washington DC 20314 (JUL 2000 - PRESENT) Supervisor - Harry Hopkins (202) 354-7611, 40 hours per week, GS-1102-13 - $66,229.
-Serves as Contracting Officer to the Office of Procurement.
-Handles all aspects of contracting transactions for pre-award and post-award functions including negotiation and administration of contracts for services, materials, and equipment.
-Works closely with the requesting office to analyze requirements, conduct market research, provide guidance on preparing statements of work and recommend revisions as necessary. Formulates the contracting approach to be taken that will best satisfy the requirement, including sourcing strategies.
-Reviews sole source justifications and obtains other required clearances, and prepares file documentation.
-Prepares solicitation documents incorporating the appropriate terms and conditions. Solicits proposals from prospective contractors analyzing proposals for conformance with the solicitation. Performs cost or price analysis to determine reasonableness. Coordinates technical evaluation of proposals, conducts pre-award surveys to establish contractor responsibility, and obtains audits and pricing reports as necessary to develop negotiation strategy. Negotiates with potential contractors and recommends award.
-Interprets contract provisions for contractors and for personnel of the Mint and provides advice and guidance and negotiates contract modifications and issues delivery orders as necessary.

DISCUSSION OF GAFFE-FEST

Where to begin? For starters, were you tempted to drive your SUV through the humongous hole located right smack in the center of the header? This hole wastes precious front-page space.

In addition, Smith's formatting gives prominence to some minor details, such as his citizenship and many of the details of his contracting officer job that should be de-emphasized with small, unbolded fonts. Notice, for example, that Smith's formatting gives the same weight to the name of his employer as to his bosses' phone number. Which do you think is more important?

Smith's resume is also riddled with consistency errors. For example, the itty bitty, poorly spaced bullets contained in the Contracting Officer job summary should be formatted exactly like the buxom bullets included in the "Summary of Qualifications." And how 'bout that box around the "Summary of Qualifications?" A little ungainly, wouldn't you say?

Notice also that:

- The verbs in the contracting officer job summary should be in the first person.

- The first bullet in the contracting officer job summary is redundant because Andrew Smith's job title and his office are identified before the bullets in his job summary.

- The rest of the bullets in this job summary are boring and unimpressive (yawn!) because they are not achievement-oriented, and do not cite objective validation of Smith's success. Moreover, Smith neglected to quantify his achievements by even citing the value of any of the contacts that he manages.

Which is not to say that Smith's resume lacks any redeeming features. For example, Smith should be congratulated for including a "Summary of Qualifications," and citing his eight years of contracting experience and his $5 million warrant.

PERSERVERANCE · SUCCESS · STORY

I GOT THE JOB!

BY ANDREW MCDONALD, ENGINEER

After working at the same federal agency for seven years as a mechanical engineer, I decided that it was time to move on and find other challenges. So, I started looking for a new job. Now, I am working for another federal agency, learning new things and earning a significantly higher salary.

I landed my promotion strictly through my own efforts; I had no contacts helping me. I did it by:

1. **Searching USAJOBS at Least Once a Week**

   I was diligent about regularly searching USAJOBS, because each job listed on the site has its own rolling window of opportunity. If I hadn't regularly checked the site, I might have missed the opportunity to apply for some great jobs.

   If I'm going to submit a package, I want it to reflect my best effort. So I spent about one week on each opening that really interested me. I never use the shotgun approach because I believe that it only produces more rejections. Who needs that?

2. **Using Keywords**

   I incorporated keywords from job descriptions in vacancy announcements into my resume and KSAs. For example, because the responsibilities for the job description for my current job included "blueprint reading" as an important responsibility, I included it in my resume and KSAs. Although I ordinarily wouldn't have mentioned such an obvious duty, I knew that doing so might improve my chances. Anything for a higher score! Also, I noticed that some vacancy announcements even list keywords that are desirable in applications. If you find such keywords listed in a vacancy announcement for a job that is similar to your target job, mention them throughout your application.

3. **Researching the Agency**

   I read through the website of each agency that I applied to. Based upon this research, I was able to specify in my cover letter how I would be able to contribute to the agency's goals.

4. **Telling Success Stories**

   My KSAs included examples of my projects that showed that I was qualified for the target job. I found it useful to put these stories into the format suggested by this book; for each story, I described necessary background information, my actions, evidence of results and objective validation of my success.

5. **Designing Graphically Pleasing Layouts**

   When I was on a selection panel for hiring another engineer, I learned what torture it is for hiring managers to trudge through the long, densely worded paragraphs. The experience made me appreciate easy-to-read, graphically pleasing layouts. So my goal was to design application documents that presented my credentials to hiring managers in an easy and efficient manner. I did this by:

   - "Bulletizing" my resumes and KSAs as much as possible.

   - Repeatedly examining the hard copy versions of my documents. Because the layout on a computer screen is subtley different from that of a hard copy, you have a greater chance of missing typos and column misalignments on the computer.

- Checking that headings stood out, information was distributed on the page in a balanced way, font sizes were easy to read and that I had used enough white space to break up the text without wasting space. I made sure that my layout was consistent (fonts, margins, etc.) throughout all of my documents.

- Using as few words as possible in order to make the best use of the precious seconds that the hiring manger spent on my application.

6. Working on My Resume and KSAs Only 15 Minutes Per Day

I found it much easier to attack these very difficult-to-write documents a little bit a time, and not to even try to finish them in a single session. This multi-session approach enabled me to improve my application by repeatedly reviewing and editing my answers.

When KSA ideas occurred to me when I am doing other things, I quickly jotted down these ideas and then incorporated them into my resume and KSAs during my next writing session. Because of such improvements, my answers were more thoughtful than they would have been had I whipped out my application in a single sitting.

7. Recruiting a Colleague To Provide Feedback

I recruited a colleague to provide me with objective feedback on my resume, KSAs and cover letters. This person helped me simplify passages that were too technical for non-engineers, edit unnecessary information, and add background information where it was needed. Seeking and using my colleague's feedback took extra time. But this time was well spent because, from my experience serving on a selection panel, I know that the quality of applicants' KSAs determines who gets the job.

8. Preparing For The Interview For My Current Job

I reviewed Internet sites that provided "how to" advice on interviewing and listed standard interview questions. Sure enough, many of those standard interview questions did pop up in my interview. But because I was prepared to answer these questions, I handled them with more confidence and speed and with less fumbling than I otherwise would have.

For example, when my interviewer asked me to discuss an on-the-job mistake that I had made, I could — because of my preparation — quickly cite a non-serious scheduling snag that had developed on one of the construction projects I was managing. I was careful not to say that I had messed up the project irreversibly. Instead, I emphasized how I quickly resolved the scheduling problem, reworked the schedule to prevent delays in the completion of the project, and learned from the experience how to avoid similar snags in the future.

During the interview, I also mentioned some specific information about the hiring agency's recent construction projects that I had read about on its website. I thereby showed my interviewers that I gone to the trouble to research its activities.

Shortly after the interview for my current job, I was offered and accepted the job. My new agency operates under a pay scale that is known as pay banding, which gives managers more flexibility in setting salaries than does the General Schedule system under which my previous job operated. Because of this difference and because my current boss was impressed with my qualifications, my new agency significantly beat my old salary. I didn't even have to negotiate for a promotion. Moreover, as I had hoped, I am now managing very different types of projects than I had managed at my previous job, and I am broadening my experience.

During my job search, which lasted over a year, I was rejected for a number of jobs. With some applications, I did not even get a response. But I didn't let the disappointments stop me. I expected this and persevered. I also found it helpful to keep reminding myself that if you put in the extra effort to create a concise, eye-catching, and verbally pleasing application, you will eventually be rewarded because, as the writer Silvana Clark said, "There is so little traffic on the extra mile."

RESUME PADDERS NEED NOT APPLY

If you lie on your application or interview for a federal job, you will likely end up having some splainin' to do, as Ricky Ricardo would say.

HOW THE MIGHTY HAVE FALLEN

Consider the cautionary tale of Laura Callahan. In April 2003, she landed a coveted position as the Deputy Chief Information Officer in the Department of Homeland Security. But when Callahan — who often used the title "Dr." — was screened for a top secret security clearance, investigators discovered in May 2003 that the B.A., masters degree and Ph.D. in computers listed on her resume were from a diploma mill that was located in a refurnished motel. Ouch!

"Oops! The padding just fell out of your résumé."

Callahan's troubles only snowballed when — in the wake of the brouhaha over the bogus degrees — many of her colleagues unleashed a torrent of allegations against her for other whopping ethical and managerial blunders made during her previous high-level stints at the White House and Department of Labor. After being suspended from her federal job, Callahan resigned in March 2004.

SOUR TOPPINGS

Although Callahan was evidently not qualified for her job, many professionals who do have enviable qualifications top them off with false degrees or phony experience. Too bad. The principle ignored by such embellishers is that, even ethical considerations aside, it is usually more effective to trumpet genuine achievements through the methods discussed in this book than to trump-up false achievements. In other words, spend your energy finessing descriptions of your finest qualifications rather than covering up phony toppings that can end up biting you back.

WHAT THIS MEANS FOR YOU

Now, in the wake of the high-profile Callahan scandal, federal job applications that include false or inflated credentials are more likely than ever to be discovered. Why? Because for the first time ever, the federal government is training hundreds of its human resource staffers how to spot such fabrications. Applicants who are busted for lying may be barred from reapplying to the federal government. And applicants who do manage to get hired under false claims may be fired, fined or even jailed.

Which does not mean that you must spotlight your weaknesses under klieg lights. But it does mean that you shouldn't invent degrees, titles or experience that you simply don't have, or cover gaps in your resume with whole cloth. Here's a litmus test: If you can't imagine a credential holding up under a background check, don't use it.

Reprinted from *Fortune* magazine: July 21, 1997

STUPID RESUME TRICKS
How to Avoid Getting Hired

By Anne Fisher

So there you are, busily recasting your resume — that crucial chronicle of just how much you have achieved and how indispensable you expect to be to the outfit that's thinking of adding you to the payroll — and you genuinely believe that everything on there makes perfect sense.

Think again. Better yet, ask somebody else (ideally, somebody smart who likes and admires you, but not overly much) to take a dispassionate look at the finished product. Then listen carefully while he or she points out just where you may have stepped off the pier into muddy water. Robert Half International, a worldwide executive-search firm based in Menlo Park, Calif., collects and publicizes bloopers like the ones listed below from real resumes — not to make anybody feel stupid but as a cautionary exercise. Here is a sampling of the kind of thing you don't want to send out.

- ✗ "I demand a salary commiserate with my extensive experience."

- ✗ "I have lurnt Word Perfect 6.0, computor and spreadsheat progroms."

- ✗ "Received a plague for Salesperson of the Year."

- ✗ "Reason for leaving last job: maturity leave."

- ✗ "Wholly responsible for two (2) failed financial institutions."

- ✗ "Failed bar exam with relatively high grades."

- ✗ "It's best for employers that I not work with people."

- ✗ "Let's meet, so you can 'ooh' and 'aah' over my experience."

- ✗ "You will want me to be Head Honcho in no time."

- ✗ "Am a perfectionist and rarely if if ever forget details."

- ✗ "I was working for my mom until she decided to move."

Continued from previous page...

✗ "Marital status: single. Unmarried. Unengaged. Uninvolved. No commitments."

✗ "I have an excellent track record, although I am not a horse."

✗ "I am loyal to my employer at all costs. ... Please feel free to respond to my resume on my office voice mail."

✗ "I have become completely paranoid, trusting completely no one and absolutely nothing."

✗ "My goal is to be a meteorologist. But since I possess no training in meteorology, I suppose I should try stock brokerage."

✗ "I procrastinate, especially when the task is unpleasant."

✗ "As indicted, I have over five years of analyzing investments."

✗ "Personal interests: donating blood. Fourteen gallons so far."

✗ "Instrumental in ruining entire operation for a Midwest chain store."

✗ "Note: Please don't misconstrue my 14 jobs as 'job-hopping.' I have never quit a job."

✗ "Marital status: often. Children: various."

✗ "Reason for leaving last job: They insisted that all employees get to work by 8:45 every morning. Could not work under those conditions."

✗ "The company made me a scapegoat, just like my three previous employers."

✗ "Finished eighth in my class of ten."

✗ "References: None. I've left a path of destruction behind me."

CHAPTER 9:
COVER LETTERS THAT OPEN DOORS
fpmi

CHAPTER 9:
COVER LETTERS THAT OPEN DOORS

You will automatically beat out 95 percent of your competition if you submit an error-free cover letter that concisely describes how you meet the requirements of the opening.

— A Federal Hiring Manager

Your cover letter will probably be the first part of your application that hiring managers will read. What's more, your cover letter may be the *only* part of your application that hiring managers will *really* read.

Why? Because while many hiring managers only skim lengthy federal resumes and pages and pages of Knowledge, Skills and Abilities (KSA) essays, virtually all hiring manager read one-page cover letters from top to bottom.

A skillfully crafted cover letter will get your potential employers panting with anticipation for the next page of your application, and thereby kick-open opportunities. Conversely a lousy cover letter can get your application kicked out of the running before the competition has even really begun. And even though federal job applications never require cover letters, naked applications lacking cover letters stand out for all of the wrong reasons; they might as well have the words, "I don't care enough about getting this job to write a damn cover letter," written across the top of them.

THE LAST SHALL BE FIRST

Even though an effective cover letter is key to making a good *first* impression with potential employers, most job seekers thoughtlessly dash off this important document in the *last* minute. Make sure that, no matter when you write a cover letter, you leave enough time to craft a first-rate document.

But despite the make-or-break importance of effective cover letters, many job-seekers completely omit them from their applications. Others submit typo-tarnished cover letters; long-winded cover letters that are the written equivalents of A&E Biographies; or terse cover letters that reveal only about as much information as captured soldiers disclose to the enemy: Name, rank and serial number. None of which make for compelling sales pitches.

In this chapter, you will learn about the multi-faceted powers of cover letters, review sample cover letters, and learn how to write cover letters that are:

☞ Interesting
☞ Concise
☞ Packed full of relevant, high level achievements
☞ Formatted to be eye-catching, and to support fast reading and skimming
☞ Easy-to-understand, and written for nonspecialists
☞ Error free

COVER ME: I'M GOING IN

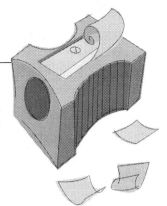

An effective cover letter works its magic by:

- Introducing the applicant by identifying the applicant's current title and the opening targeted by the application, and by stating whether the applicant is applying for a noncompetitive appointment.

- Conveying an enthusiastic attitude.

- Showcasing the applicant's knowledge of the organization.

- *Concisely* conveying the applicant's most relevant educational and professional credentials.

- Serving as a writing sample, a well written, strategically formatted cover letter provides tangible evidence of an applicant's communication skills.

- Naming a contact in the organization who can vouch for the applicant, if possible.

SCOPING OUT YOUR TARGET AGENCY

You can practically bet that the hiring agency for your target job will hire someone who is passionate about their organization and the issues that it addresses. Why? Because hiring manages are looking for reasons to reject applicants and because most applicants don't bother to research their target agency at all. Therefore, the applicant's knowledge of the organization provides a convenient screening criteria.

But more importantly, hiring managers operate on the theory that employees work hardest and put their hearts and souls into what they are passionate about. In other words, employees who really *care* about the organization will be loyal, self-motivated go-getters. (Look Ma! No cattle prodder!) This means that by demonstrating your knowledge of the organization and respect for its programs, achievements and culture, you will stand out from the pack and impress hiring managers.

Remember that federal agencies are as different from one another as are private companies. So in order to convey knowledge about an agency's goals, the issues that it address and its culture, you must research it. Start your research by debriefing any employees of your target agency who may be lurking within your network. In addition, research your target agency through the following free online resources that which will help make you an expert about your target agency:

- The website of your target agency: This is absolutely REQUIRED READING before writing an application and going to any interviews for a target job. Pay particular attention to the hiring agency's press releases, which will inform you of the agency's major programs. If, by chance, the agency's press releases are not posted on its website, call the agency's public affairs office, and ask for copies of recent press releases to be e-mailed or sent to you.

☞ The website of the Partnership for Public Service, a non-profit that promotes federal careers. See *ourpublicservice.org*. Check whether any information about your target agency is featured in the site's daily or quarterly newsletters, which you can access by clicking on the site's "Press Room" tab, the annual survey of best federal employers at *bestplacestowork.org*, or any of the agency profiles included in the "Analysis and Profiles" section or "Rankings" of *bestplacesto work.org*. If so, such information may provide particularly juicy grist for your cover letters and interviews.

☞ *Washingtonian* magazine at *Washingtonian.com*. Almost every year (usually in October or November), *Washingtonian* ranks the best places to work in Washington DC, including the best federal agencies. The blurbs accompanying *Washingtonian's* rankings often yield valuable insights about the culture of federal agencies. Rankings of federal agencies are posted on the magazine's website at *washingtonian.com/etc/business/great_places_to_work/govt.html* and *washingtonian. com/etc/business/great_places_to_work/agencies.html*. Find other listings by accessing the online archive of back issues.

☞ *FedNews™ OnLine* - a daily newsletter for federal employees that often includes short articles about hiring trends. Sign up for a subscription to this newsletter at *fpmisolutions.com*.

☞ The website of *Government Executive* at *GovExec.com*. Conduct a keyword search on your target agency using the site's search function. Also peruse monthly issues of *Government Executive*, which you can access by clicking on the magazine icon that appears on the upper right corner of the website's home page.

☞ The website of *Federal Times* at *federaltimes.com*. Pay special attention to the "Top News," "Career Info" and "Management Issues" sections of the website, which frequently post articles about hiring trends, federal recruitment drives and other personnel matters impacting job searchers.

☞ The website of the President's Management Agenda (PMA). See *results.gov*. Be sure to check the "New Management Scorecard," which will tell you how effectively your agency is implementing the PMA.

☞ The literature search function on your public library's website. The websites of many public libraries allow users to search and retrieve articles from magazines and newspapers from any computer. Usually, all you need to conduct such searches is the web address of your public library and a valid library card number.

COVER LETTER TONE

The tone of your cover letter should be friendly, energetic and efficient. And like all other documents included in your application, your cover letter should focus on your employer's needs. Remember that hiring managers care much more about what you offer and how you would solve their problems than about what you want.

In other words, ask not what the employer can do for you, but what you can do for the employer. Express your concern for the agency by citing your knowledge of its recent accomplishments, if possible, and by using words like "offer" and "contribute" rather than "growth potential" and "career opportunity."

OUTLINE OF EFFECTIVE COVER LETTER

Your Address
City, State, ZIP
Date

Name of Contact Person
Contact Person's' Title
Name of Agency
Address
City, State, ZIP

RE: Name and number of opening

Dear Name of Contact Person:

OPENER: AN ENERGETIC INTRODUCTION OF YOUR CREDENTIALS. MENTION A RECENT ACCOMPLISHMENT OF THE AGENCY, IF POSSIBLE.

MIDDLE: 1-4 SHORT PARAGRAPHS OF EMPLOYER-CENTERED INFO ON YOUR ACHIEVEMENTS/SKILLS.

CONCLUSION: THANKS AND LOOK FORWARD TO HEARING FROM YOU.

Sincerely,

Your Name

Enclosures: Resume and KSAs (if applicable).

Notice how this format is short and concise. Also notice how space is saved by the "RE" and "Enclosures" lines that eliminate the need to provide this information in full sentences.

COVER LETTER DISSECTION

THE SALUTATION

Address your cover letter to the contact name on the vacancy announcement for the opening. If the contact person's first name is gender neutral (such as Terry or Sandy), call the contact person to determine whether your cover letter should address them as Mr. or Ms. Be sure to spell the name of the contact person correctly.

If a contact person is not listed on the vacancy announcement, call the Human Resources office of the hiring agency to identify the proper recipient of your application. Alternatively, open your cover letter with "Dear Hiring Manager" or "Good Morning" rather than the more impersonal "To Whom It May Concern" or the sexist "Dear Sirs."

THE OPENER

Purge cliche phrases from your application, such as:

☞ Enclosed please find my application.

☞ Please accept the enclosed application.

☞ I am writing to….

☞ I am interested in…

☞ I am forwarding the enclosed resume for your consideration.

Instead, demonstrate your knowledge of the agency, and state how you could contribute to its success. Also, be sure to orient hiring managers by identifying your title right off the bat. For example:

☞ *Congratulations to the General Services Administration (GSA) for excelling in the "teamwork" category on GSA's annual employee satisfaction survey. As a logistics expert and a veteran of several award-winning workgroups, I share GSA's team-friendly work ethic. Please consider me for the logistics specialist opening.*

☞ *As a contract manager with an MBA and five years of experience in innovative contract management, I am qualified to contribute to the United States Mint's efforts to streamline procurement procedures, which were recently profiled in Fast Company.*

☞ *I couldn't be more excited about the recent announcement that NASA will return to the moon. I would welcome the opportunity to support NASA's many dynamic programs with my top-flight skills as an Administrative Assistant.*

Alternatively, if you cannot cite any relevant information about the hiring agency, simply state your credentials:

☞ *I am currently a senior attorney with Smith & Westlock, the largest firm in South Dakota. My qualifications match the qualifications that you seek for senior attorney.*

☞ *As an information technology analyst, I specialize in improving the efficiency of large networks used by federal agencies like yours.*

☞ *Does XYZ agency want to get more for less on its supply contracts? If so, I may be the right candidate for the contracts manager opening because, as a Procurement Specialist, I saved ABC organization $500,000 on its supply contracts last year. My credentials also include....*

☞ *Are you searching for a human resources manager who specializes in developing and managing programs that maximize workforce efficiency in large agencies like yours? I also offer particular expertise in training. My recent accomplishments include....*

One avant-guard method of spicing up a cover letter is to begin with a memorable quote either about success, problem-solving, efficiency or another topic relevant to the opening. You can obtain relevant quotes from quotation books or by conducting keywords searches on Internet search engines for websites that list witty quotations. (Use words like *quotations*, together with words like *goals*, *business* and *success* as your keywords.)

MIDDLE PARAGRAPHS

> **Purge your cover letter of presumptuous statements, such as, "I know that you will find that I am a perfect match for the position." Instead, describe how your credentials match the requirements of the opening, and let hiring managers decide for themselves that you're a perfect match for the position.**

☞ Emphasize your most relevant qualifications; do not repeat your entire resume.

☞ Address each Knowledge, Skills and Abilities (KSA) question with a one-sentence bullet, if possible.

☞ Use the techniques discussed in Chapter 6 to describe your accomplishments and achievements. Do not provide job descriptions that describe duties and responsibilities.

☞ Don't worry about restating credentials that are presented in your resume or KSAs...Remember: You are in sales...Take a page out of the advertisement industry's playbook: Repetition...repetition...repetition. (But change your wording when you repeat the same information.)

☞ State whether you have veterans preference or whether you want to be considered for a noncompetitive appointment.

☞ Explain any special situations presented by your application, such as your willingness to move to the job location from your current, distant location.

☞ Use active and conversational words, rather than stilted, pompous and bureaucratic words.

H O T • T I P

IF YOU HAVE YOUR OWN WEBSITE...
If you have your own website that showcases skills relevant to your target opening, consider directing hiring mangers to the site in your cover letter.

LAST PARAGRAPH: AU REVOIR

☞ Identify the best way to contact you. If your phone numbers and e-mail address are not on your letterhead, provide it in your closing.

☞ Express your availability for an interview.

☞ Say thanks for being considered.

FORMATTING AND LENGTH

☞ A cover letter should consist of three to six paragraphs. It should not exceed one page.

☞ Create a layout that is visually appealing and open. Margins should be 1.25 to 1.5 inches wide.

☞ Draw attention to your skills by using bold font, bullets, indented margins and columns.

SAVE TIME AND SPACE

☞ Identify your opening in a "RE:" line of a paper application or in the subject line of an e-mailed application.

☞ Identify enclosures in an "Enclosures" line of a paper application.

☞ Add a P.S. to emphasize an important fact, observation or credential. Why? Because studies show that a P.S. is the most read part of a letter. That's why so many fund-raising letters include part of their pitch in the P.S.

PROOFREADING

Proofread your cover letter fastidiously. Indeed, most hiring managers say that typos in an application can kill an applicant's changes. And when such typos appear on a cover letter, they invariably look as big as a barn!

Proofread your cover letter by:

☞ Running a spell check on it. But don't rely exclusively on spell checkers, which cannot recognize all mistakes. For example, spell checkers won't flag words that should be capitalized or tell you if you used the word "their" instead of "there."

☞ Printing out your letter. You will find errors in paper copies of documents that are easily missed on the screen. It is particularly important to print out e-mails…Never send an e-mail to a potential employer without first proofreading a paper copy of the document.

☞ Reading your letter out loud. Every time you make a correction, read the whole letter again.

☞ Asking yourself why you have positioned your sentences in their current order. If you don't have a good reason, rethink the order of your sentences.

☞ Getting distance from your letter, and then reading it again.

☞ Soliciting objective opinions of your letter, and using resulting feedback to improve your letter.

CAUTION: REMEMBER THAT YOU ARE APPLYING FOR A GOVERNMENT JOB

An application that has been churned out via an assembly line approach without being tailored to the hiring agency usually gives itself away sooner or later. For example, I have seen *many* cover letters submitted to federal agencies that profess the applicant's desire to "work for a company like yours," and objective statements on resumes that — believe it or not — identify the applicant's desire to work for a nonprofit company.

As one hiring manager explained, "if an applicant is that careless on an application for a job — something that he or she really cares about, that is in his or her direct interest, when they are supposed to be putting their best foot forward — I wouldn't trust them to work on projects that are not directly tied to their self-interest." In other words, nothing gets an application filed in the circular file faster than a careless mistake such as a pitch to the wrong type of organization.

See examples of cover letters on the following pages.

1234 Yellow Brick Road
City, State ZIP Code
January 31, 2004

Mr. Frank Howard
Personnel Analyst
Office of Human Resources
US Mint
801 9th St. NW
Washington DC 20220

Dear Ms. Howard:

Subject: Marketing Manager Position (#08-65-59)

Congratulations to the Mint for topping $150 million in on-line sales in 2003! As a Marketing Manager at Walmart since 1999, I have been tracking the Mint's record-breaking successes. I would like to help the Mint increase its sales even further.

A synopsis of my credentials:

YOUR NEEDS	MY CREDENTIALS
• Knowledge of business principles.	• B.A. in Business Administration from University of Maryland. Five years of experience as Marketing Manager at Walmart.
• Computer proficiency	• Expert in using PC Lotus, Ledger, Excel, PeopleSoft, PowerPoint, Word and various web creation programs.
• Negotiating skills	• Saved Walmart $500,000 since 2000 by negotiating pricing of advertising. Completed training courses in negotiating.
• Communication skills	• Experienced in creating and delivering PowerPoint presentations and written reports summarizing monthly marketing trends for senior managers.

I am eager to speak with you about the Marketing Manager position. My telephone numbers are (123) 123-4567(w) and (012) 123-4567(h), and my e-mail address is Jones@email.com. I do appreciate your consideration.

Sincerely,

Trudy Jones

Enclosure: Resume and KSAs

What's not to love about this letter? The opener demonstrates knowledge of the organization. But even more importantly, the letter's Your Needs/My Credentials columnar formatting broadcasts the applicant's suitability for the opening — even to hiring managers who may only skim the letter. This memorable formatting is guaranteed to stand out from the pack.

The Your Needs/My Credentials columns were created as a table without gridlines. Directions for creating such tables and for creating bullets are included in Appendix 3: Formatting Tips.

If you use this format, make sure that the "Your Needs" column reflects the requirements of the opening. If you don't fulfill one of the requirements of the opening, leave it out.

1234 Yellow Brick Road
City, State ZIP Code
February 12, 2004

Mr. Joe Smith
Human Resources Officer
Office of Human Resources
Bureau of Printing and Engraving
14th and C Streets SW
Washington DC 20228

RE: Customer Service Position (00-AA-45)

Dear Mr. Smith:

As a Telemarketer with five years of experience at Top-Sales Inc., I am eager to bring my skills and energy to the Bureau of Printing and Engraving (BEP). Here is what I offer:

Award-Winning Sales Record:
- Winner of the Employee-of-the-Month Award in May 2000 for selling $5,000 in jewelry at Top Sales in a single month.
- Developed and managed major commercial accounts worth $500,000 per month.

Record as Savvy Problem-Solver:
- Designed five major process overhauls that reduced customer complaints by 15 percent.

Excellent Customer Service Skills:
- Reputation for tactfully and effectively handling callers who are angry about lost/broken merchandise or over-charges.

It might be helpful for you to know that my former colleague, Mike Jenkins, who is currently a Marketing Associate in your Office of Sales and Marketing, would be pleased to vouch for my skills and dogged work ethic.

I would enjoy speaking with you about your needs and my qualifications. I can be reached at (123) 123-4567, and my e-mail address is sbrady@email.com. Thank you for your consideration.

Sincerely,

Scott Brady

P.S.   Congratulations on the favorable write-up given to the Bureau of Printing and Engraving in last month's issue of *Government Executive*!

Enclosures: Resume and KSAs

The formatting on this letter is second in effectiveness only to the Your Needs/My Credentials columnar formatting used on the letter on the previous page. If you use this format, make sure that your qualifications categories match the requirements of the job. Notice too how this letter skillfully uses numbers and mentions an inside contact. And the P.S. emphasizes the applicant's research of the organization.

LINDA WATSON
1234 Yellow Brick Road
City, State ZIP Code
Phone: (123) 123-4567 (w); (012) 123-4567 (h)
E-Mail: Linda.Watson@email.com

January 31, 2004

Ms. Jackie Harper
Personnel Officer
Office of Human Resources
U.S. Fish and Wildlife Service
3345 Wilson Blvd.
Arlington, VA 20456

Dear Ms. Harper:

Perhaps I am the "multi-talented Webmaster" that you seek (Position 123-WM-789). My credentials include:

- Seven years of experience as a Webmaster at the U.S. Environmental Protection Agency (EPA) designing and updating sites that broadcast scientific information in engaging screen formats. I also develop content for these sites by translating technical information about environmental regulations into plain language for general audiences and by obtaining approvals for content from subject matter experts.

- Earning superior performance awards for five out of the last seven years.

- An M.S. in Systems Administration from the University of Maryland.

- A B.A. in Graphic Arts from the University of Colorado.

I would also bring to the position my lifelong passion for conservation, which is reflected in all of my work experience, and my hobbies, which include bird watching and fishing, and reading publications, such as *Wildlife Conservation* and *National Geographic*.

Attached is my resume and KSAs. I would appreciate the opportunity to discuss the position with you further and show you my portfolio of web pages. Thank you for your consideration, and I look forward to hearing from you.

Sincerely,

Linda Watson

OK, I admit it; not everyone is going to research the hiring agency, or create a Your Needs/My Credentials Table. And not everyone really meets all the qualifications of the job. If these acknowledgments ring true to you, this type of letter may provide an appealing alternative for you. Notice that — even without agency research — this letter is enlivened by the applicant's mention of her lifelong passions. (Remember: Nonwork experience counts!)

SALLY BAKER
1234 Yellow Brick Road • City, State ZIP Code • 123-123-4567

December 15, 2003

Mr. John McCarthy
Personnel Analyst
Small Business Administration
Two Gateway Center
Newark, NJ 07102

Dear Mr. McCarthy: RE: Administrative Assistant (XX-AA-123)

PROBLEMS CANNOT BE SOLVED AT THE SAME LEVEL OF AWARENESS THAT CREATED THEM.
— ALBERT EINSTEIN

As an Administrative Assistant at Verizon, I continually strive — in the spirit of Albert Einstein's philosophy — to master new software and people skills that improve office organization. At Verizon, I am known as "the office fixer" and "the event fixer." I could similarly smooth the operations of your office.

I am an expert in:

- Organizing large events attended by dozens of high-level officials, including CEOs of telecommunications companies. Planning such events requires managing and troubleshooting conference room logistics, projection and microphone capabilities and catering. I also inform guests of the time and location of events, and maintain guest lists.

- Managing the busy schedules of executives using the latest e-mail, electronic calendar and palm pilot software.

- Creating and updating Word and spreadsheet files.

- Arranging conference calls and virtual meetings.

- Shepherding high-profile documents through the approval process.

- Establishing and maintaining electronic filing systems. During a pivotal point in my supervisor's recent contract negotiations with a contractor, I quickly retrieved an urgently needed legal document that compelled the contractor to agree to contract terms that saved Verizon $50,000.

I am methodical enough to comprehensively plan events and projects, and flexible enough to calmly confront the unexpected.

I would be happy to meet with you to discuss your needs and my skills further. Please call me at the phone number on my letterhead, or e-mail me at Sally.Baker@email.com. I do appreciate your consideration.

Sincerely,

Sally Baker

Enclosures: Resume and KSAs

Effective use of the quote method. Notice how this applicant has skillfully tied the quote into her own on-the-job approach. Also notice how this applicant's credentials are crafted to sound impressive even without mention of awards or performance evaluations.

1234 Yellow Brick Road
City, State ZIP Code
January 31, 2004

Ms. Jackie Harper
Personnel Officer
Office of Human Resources
National Science Foundation
4201 Wilson Boulevard
Arlington, Virginia 22230

RE: Program Analyst Position (111—PM-45)

Dear Ms. Jackie Harper:

Congratulations for winning the 2003 Presidential Award for Management Excellence! As a recent college graduate who is knowledgeable about the latest performance-based management techniques, I would like to help the National Science Foundation further improve upon its outstanding management record.

My qualifications include:

➠ **A BA in Business Administration from Northwestern University.**

➠ **Polished communication skills:** All of my classes in my major required papers or oral presentations. My GPA in my major was 3.50, and I graduated with Departmental Honors in my major.

➠ **A proven record as a self-starter and team-player:** As an undergraduate, I juggled a heavy academic course-load along with a 15 hour-per-week campus job and my responsibilities as co-captain of the lacrosse team.

I would be happy to provide any additional information about my background that might be helpful. I will be moving to the Washington DC area within the next two months. I can be reached on my cell phone at (012) 123-4567 before or after I move to Washington DC. My e-mail address is Linda.Watson@email.com. Many thanks for your consideration, and I hope to hear from you soon.

Sincerely,

Linda Watson

Enclosures: Resume and KSAs

An exemplary letter from a recent graduate. Notice how the applicant demonstrates knowledge of the National Science Foundation by referring to its recent management award, which was posted on *results.gov*. The applicant also cites her own grades as objective validation of her skills, and mentions her extracurricular activities as evidence of her work ethic and team-friendly credentials.

CHAPTER 10:
SUBMITTING YOUR APPLICATION

So you have finished writing your application for a federal job. Hooray for you! Oh, the satisfaction of a job well done! But before you gleefully pop your paper application into the mail or hit the "send" button on your automated application, you must still tie up a few loose ends.

KEEP A COPY

YOUR APPLICATION

Before you submit your application, make a copy of it for your files. Why? Because you will need a copy of your application if you:

✓ Must resubmit your application if your original submission doesn't reach the hiring agency.

✓ Are invited to interview for the opening; you should review your application before the interview.

✓ Can incorporate sections of your application into other applications for similar jobs.

VACANCY ANNOUNCEMENTS

You may need information contained on vacancy announcements in order to check the status of your applications. Moreover, you will want to review the vacancy announcement before any interviews you have for the opening.

But vacancy announcements for openings are removed from federal websites after their closing dates. So you should keep copies of any vacancy announcements to which you apply.

LET IT RIP!

Submit paper applications to hiring agencies via priority, certified mail. That way, you will receive a receipt after each application arrives at its destination.

If you submit an application via an automated hiring system, the system might send you back an e-mail verifying that your application has been sent. But beware that no system — not even an electronic application system — is glitch-proof. Believe it or not, verification that your application has been electronically sent does not guarantee the agency's receipt of your application. I have heard the sorrowful tales of a number of applicants who missed out on being considered for federal jobs because they found out after their target job's closing date that their application never reached the hiring agency — even though these applicants had received e-mails verifying that their applications had been submitted to their hiring agencies.

HOT • TIP

OH THAT SINKING FEELING!

Once you click the "submit" or "send" button on an automated application, it is gone — forever beyond your grasp. There is no way to unsend it.

So what should you do if, after you click the submit button, you realize that your application contains a mistake, or that you want to change an answer?

No problem: Just submit another application for the same job before the job closes. If you submit another application while the position is still open, your latest submission will automatically override your previously sent application.

If you want to make an important change on a paper application that you have already submitted, ask the contact person on the opening's vacancy announcement if you can replace your previously submitted application with another application.

So whether you submit a paper or electronic application, call the contact person on the vacancy announcement of your target job to confirm your application's arrival. And do so far enough in advance of the closing date to allow sufficient time to resubmit your application, if such action is necessary.

CHECKING THE STATUS OF YOUR APPLICATION

How long do federal agencies usually take to process applications? It varies. Some hiring agencies make a selection within a month or so of the closing date of an opening; others take several months to do so. (The federal government is currently streamlining the application process down to 45 days.)

If your application is screened by an automated hiring system, you may be e-mailed a status update of your application, or be directed to a website that informs applicants on the outcomes of major milestones in the selection process.

Alternatively, the hiring agency may snail mail you updates of the status of your application: Some agencies inform applicants how they faired in the screening for basic qualifications. Others only send out rejection letters when a final selection has been made.

Unfortunately, however, some agencies do not bother to communicate with applicants at any time during the selection process. Believe it or not, some agencies don't even send out rejection letters. So if you have any questions about the status of an application that you submitted more than about six weeks ago, contact the contact person identified on the job's vacancy announcement for a status update.

If more than 10 days or two weeks have elapsed since you were interviewed and the hiring agency still hasn't contacted you, ask your interviewer for the status of your application. But don't call too frequently. As one hiring manager says, "there is a fine line for job applicants between getting credit for being persistent and for getting a reputation for being a persistent pest."

If you are rejected from a job, go ahead and ask the interviewer for some helpful feedback. After all, what have you got to lose? And particularly if you have sent the interviewer a post-interview thank you letter, s/he may provide you with some additional leads or hot contacts.

CAUTION: DO NOT USE THE STATIONARY OF YOUR CURRENT EMPLOYER IN YOUR APPLICATION

If you are currently a federal employee, do not use the stationary or envelopes of the agency that employs you in your application. Doing so is a flagrant violation of federal regulations and will almost certainly get you kicked out of the competition.

SECTION III: THE TALKING STAGE INTERVIEWING AND NEGOTIATING SALARY

fpmi

CHAPTER 11:
INTERVIEWS THAT NAIL THE JOB
fpmi

CHAPTER 11: INTERVIEWS THAT NAIL THE JOB

Forget gimmicks like echoing the body language of your interviewer. Any intelligent interviewer sees right through that. What I look for is evidence that the applicant understands my agency and its goals, and is going to work like the dickens.

— **Howard Hyman, Federal Hiring Manager**

Congratulations! The powers-that-be were so impressed by your written sales pitch that they have summoned you for an interview. This means that you probably beat out dozens, if not hundreds, of job applicants to rank among the chosen few who will be interviewed. You may now officially consider yourself among the best and the brightest. So go ahead: Savor your victory… Crank up the sound track of *Rocky*, and do a few victory laps around your desk.

But once you settle back down, it's time to start preparing for your interview. That's right, you must *prepare* for your interview: Just as crafting your written application demanded time and thought, so too

"*O.K., which cup is your job under now?*"

does crafting your verbal sales pitch. And just as you targeted your written application to the hiring agency's needs, so too should you direct your verbal sales pitch to the hiring agency's priorities. That's because the hiring agency *still* doesn't care why you want the job; it still *only* cares about its own priorities. (Yes, the selection process is very agency-o-centric.)

What are the hiring agency's priorities at this stage of the selection process? The hiring agency probably wants to hire the Perfect Employee, who:

➤ Is knowledgeable about the agency.
➤ Has technical skills that will solve its problems.
➤ Gets along well with others.
➤ Works hard to meet deadlines.
➤ Is positive and upbeat.

By thoroughly preparing for the interview, applying strategic interview techniques and delivering proper post-interview follow-through as instructed by this chapter, you will prove that you are the Perfect Employee who deserves to be hired into your target job.

INTERVIEW PREPARATION

Thoroughly prepare for your interview by researching the hiring agency, crafting answers to expected questions and preparing questions to ask your interviewer.

RESEARCH THE HIRING AGENCY

Time and time again, hiring managers have told me that "knowledge of the agency" is among the most important traits that they look for in job applicants during interviews. So before your next job interview, be sure to follow tips on researching federal agencies that are covered in Chapter 2 and Chapter 9. Also prepare yourself to intelligently discuss trends in the industry addressed by your target agency.

Your interview may also be strengthened by some well-placed knowledge about your interviewer. So you would be wise to do an Internet search on your interviewer's name. Also, run searches of your interviewer via online resources that are covered in Chapter 9.

By all means, mention your research and demonstrate your knowledge of the hiring agency during the interview. Your insights may, in particular, provide fodder for pre-questioning patter, and help loosen up you and the interviewer.

Nevertheless, it is generally unwise to let on during an interview that you had been cyber-stalking your interviewer. Moreover, if your research reveals that the hiring agency is mired in scandal or that your interviewer has been tainted by "youthful indiscretions," well…um…er…the less said about such unpleasantries during the interview, the better.

PRACTICE YOUR ANSWERS

It usually takes more than three weeks to prepare a good impromptu speech.
— Mark Twain

Ironically, the more your rehearse for interviews, the more free-flowing and spontaneous your answers will sound. Start your rehearsal session by reviewing your resume, KSAs, Chapter 6 and Chapter 7.

As you craft answers to interview questions, consider that the real question behind many interview questions about your previous jobs, strengths and achievements is, "Why should we hire you?"

In other words, if you are asked about your past, it's not because the interviewer really _cares_ about you. It's because interviewers usually operate on the premise that the best predictor of an applicant's future on-the-job behavior is their past behavior; hiring managers generally regard the past as prologue. So craft answers to "Why should we hire you?" type questions that underscore the parallels between the demands of your previous jobs and the demands of your target opening. Show hiring managers that you can do the job because you have _already_ done it in the past.

Common types of "Why should we hire you?" questions include:

➤ The standard "tell me about yourself" open-ended opener. You might begin your answer with a summary line such as:

- "I am an expert in..."
- "I pride myself on being a professional who..."
- "My orientation is..."

Then follow with a logically-sequenced "greatest hits" summary of your top educational and professional qualifications that relate to the job. Also, cite objective validation of your successes and mention your team-friendly personality and work ethic. Cap off your answer with something like, "I have accomplished A, B and C at X, Y and Z organizations; I could do the same at this agency." You should provide about one-and-a-half minutes to two minutes worth of information; no need to filibuster with your entire life story.

➤ "Why do you want to work here?"; "What do you know about our organization?" or "What are you looking for in a job?" Base your answers to such questions upon your research of the organization. Present yourself as a problem-solver who really cares about the organization and wants to help advance its goals.

➤ "What would others say about you?" Respond by citing your plays-well-with-others credentials and exemplary performance evaluations. No need to invent or quote negative hearsay about yourself.

Another type of common question-behind-the-question is, "Why *shouldn't* we hire you?" By hiding this question beneath other questions, the interviewer hopes to compel you into revealing why you might be a burden to the office.

But fifth amendment rights against self incrimination don't operate in job interviews! Any potential problems that you give away about yourself through word or deed during an interview can and will be held against you. Remember that your interviewer wants to hire a problem-solver, not a problem.

The "why shouldn't we hire you?" type question commonly takes the form of:

➤ "What are your weaknesses?" Cite a weakness that would not interfere with your ability to perform the job. For example, if you are an accountant, it's OK to say that your strength is not in the graphic arts. If you are an artist, it's OK to say that you wish you could speak a second language. If the interviewer pressures you to reveal a weakness that is more self-incriminating, cite something that is as trivial and has as little bearing on the demands of the opening as possible.

HOT • TIP

BLOW AWAY YOUR INTERVIEW COMPETITION

I know a federal Human Resources Specialist who was delighted to make the final cut for a senior level position that she *really* wanted. But when she was invited to her first interview for the job, she was warned that she still faced fierce competition in the selection. So during her interview, the Human Resources Specialist searched for an opportunity to make a stand-out impression. Finally, she recognized one: The interviewer casually mentioned that the agency was having trouble motivating senior employees who lacked promotion potential.

Even though the interviewer did not solicit a solution to the problem from the Human Resources Specialist, she developed a creative problem-solving plan after the interview, and then presented her plan during a follow-up interview. The result: Even before the Human Resources Specialist got home from her follow-up interview, the hiring agency had called to offer her the job.

Moreover, the interviewer eventually told the Human Resources Specialist that she had not even been the favorite applicant before her follow-up interview. Nevertheless, by volunteering a creative solution that reflected comprehensive knowledge of federal personnel programs, she vaulted over her competitors — all of whom had either ignored the hiring office's problem altogether or proposed pat, obvious solutions.

If you want to stand out of the pack, you can go even one step further than the successful Human Resources Specialist: Ask your interviewer to identify some of the pressing problems or important goals facing the hiring office. If you can provide a thoughtful solution right away, do so. Otherwise, complete some problem-solving research after the interview, and then briefly sketch out your approach in your post-interview thank you letter and your next round of interviews.

➤ "What are your on-the-job failures?" Cite something that happened a long time ago, was relatively trivial, and has no bearing on the demands on the opening. Emphasize how you learned from your mistakes, and how you would handle the situation differently now.

➤ "What did you like least about your past job or past boss?" Whatever you do, refuse to criticize a previous boss or job. Why? Because whenever you trash a person or job, you invariably raise doubts about whether the problem was with you or the trashee — no matter how blameless you may really be. If you have no other alternative explanation, say you are leaving your current job because you need more room for growth. Or better yet, cite your desire to focus on whatever issues are addressed by your target agency.

➤ "What is your five year plan?" type of question. Reassure the employer that you are goal-oriented professional who is committed to patiently working your way up the career ladder. That is, you are not a job-hopping flake, nor do have delusions of effortlessly rocketing into executive management. Your answer may also include a question such as, "What are some of the career paths for this position?" You may also cite additional training or education that you would like to pursue, or mention that you recognize the possibility that you may confront opportunities in the coming years that you can't forsee right now.

During your interview, at all cost, avoid deriding anything or anyone — including yourself, past present or future bosses, jobs or colleagues and your family. Don't so much as hint that you have personality defects, family problems that might interfere with work, questionable judgment or any other characteristics inconsistent with the Perfect Employee.

Your interview may also include some "what would you do in this situation?" type of questions. You can usually tackle such questions by suggesting some variation of the following steps:

1. Research, including consultation with experts and collection of data
2. Consideration of ethical and legal constraints
3. Consideration of costs/benefits of various approaches
4. Obtaining approval from necessary superiors
5. Getting buy-in of stakeholders
6. Taking action

PREPARE QUESTIONS

Even if you already know way more than you ever wanted to know about the hiring agency, prepare questions to ask during the interview. The more insight and the more depth reflected in your questions, the better. Save your questions about salary and benefits until after you receive an offer.

If you fail to ask questions during the interview, you will give the impression — wrong though it may be — that you are lifeless and disinterested. A hiring manager recently explained to me, "Nothing sounds worse than if I ask an applicant for questions, and only the sound of dead air follows."

Here are some potential questions to ask your interviewer, as appropriate:

➤ What are the most essential qualifications or skills that should be possessed by the person filling this position?

➤ What are the biggest challenges currently facing this organization and/or industry? Alternatively, if you understand these challenges, you may suggest or emphasize ways in which your skills would help address those challenges.

➤ Where are the biggest weaknesses on your team? (Then, suggest ways that you could help plug them.)

➤ How are you trying to change this organization or encourage it to evolve? (Then, suggest ways that you could support this effort.)

➤ What do you find stimulating about working here? Why did you choose to work here?

➤ I read X, Y and Z about this agency's organizational culture in *Washingtonian* magazine or on the Partnership of Public Service's website? Do you agree with that assessment?

➤ I understand from my reading, that your industry is showing a trend in X. How is this affecting your agency?

➤ I understand that government agencies are as different from one another as are private organizations. I read in *Washingtonian* magazine that the organizational culture at EPA is characterized by A, B and C…Is your agency similar in any way?

➤ How would you describe your managerial style? (Then, explain that you would work well under that style. Provide examples when you have done so in the past.)

➤ How has the new agency director's emphasis on X impacted this office?

➤ What would be my first projects on this job?

➤ I noticed on the *results.gov* site that your agency scores high in X, Y and Z, but not so well in A, B and C. May I explain how my background would support the agency's efforts to improve its scores in A, B and C?

➤ Do you have any general impressions of my strengths and weaknesses? Is there any additional information about my background that I could provide that would help prove to you that I could do this job?

You might also ask your interviewer about the agency's working relationship with other agencies whose missions are related, or with various stakeholder groups. You may also raise questions about recent news items affecting your agency, an issue addressed by your agency or the federal government in general.

DURING THE INTERVIEW

During your interview, prove that you are the Perfect Employee by using your prepared answers to questions, and by following this section's dos and donts, guerilla interviewing tactics, and instructions for sidestepping employers' secret fears.

DOs

➤ Review the vacancy announcement for the job as well as your resume, application essays and Chapter 6 shortly before the interview. Also, make sure that you are up to date on the latest development in your field.

➤ Prepare for "Tell me about a time when…" questions by identifying instances when you have successfully managed conflicts or disagreements with superiors or colleagues; gone the extra mile; met goals; worked independently and demonstrated good judgment; worked well in teams; demonstrated leadership or persuasive powers; provided superior customer service; handled team members who were not pulling their weight; missed a deadline; dealt with an angry customer; and worked on a project that did not go as planned.

HOT • TIP

INTERVIEWS: WHAT WORKS; WHAT DOESN'T WORK

According to a survey of 300 recruiters by Korn/Ferry International, "The strongest candidates effectively correlate their experience in a concise and compelling manner."

Survey results also indicate that about 33 percent of interviewees are unprepared, 24 percent show over-inflated egos, and large percentages strike out because they talk too much, show bad hygiene or are poorly dressed.

Also, expect to be asked questions such as: What is your proudest achievement? What is your greatest disappointment? How do you deal with stress? What did you learn on any training programs you recently completed? What type of work environment suits you best? What makes a good supervisor?

If you are asked how you handled a certain situation that you have never encountered, describe how you *would* handle that situation.

➤ If your interview is by telephone, treat it just as seriously as you would treat an in-person interview. Suspend call waiting and hermetically seal yourself inside your telephone room: Keep out all pets and other people. Strategically position your resume, application essays, Chapter 6 and a pad and paper in front of you for easy access during the interview.

➤ If your interview is in person, dress conservatively. It is impossible to dress too professionally or too formally for an interview. Make sure that all aspects of your personal hygiene, including your nails, are in tip-top shape.

➤ Plan to arrive at the interview office about 10 minutes early. Build extra travel time into your schedule to accommodate navigational or traffic problems. Also be aware that since September 11th, it can take an extra 20 minutes or so to be admitted into federal garages and office buildings. Moreover, some federal buildings are large labyrinths; it may take a significant amount of time for you to find your interview office. Also leave time for some pre-interviewing primping and de-jittering.

➤ Bring with you a professional briefcase that holds several copies of your resume and your application, several business cards, and a pad and paper for note-taking. If you landed the interview by submitting an electronic application, provide your interview with a hard-copy, well formatted resume.

➤ If you are a recent graduate, emphasize your knowledge of the latest development and methods in your field.

➤ Bring to the interview show-and-tell material such as:

- Explanatory maps, charts and photographs.
- Project summaries.
- Printouts of PowerPoint presentations.
- Writing samples such as handbooks, press releases, press clips, manuals and published articles.
- Samples of artwork, manufactured products, catalogues or packaging that you have designed.
- Justifications for major awards.
- Praising or thank you e-mails and letters from superiors, colleagues or staffers, and superior performance evaluations that include glowing comments.
- If you are a recent graduate, emphasize your knowledge of the latest developments and methods in your field.

In addition, if you are a college graduate lacking professional experience, bring copies of your relevant papers or a list of your papers that received high grades.

As you discuss your achievements, introduce and show your show-and-tell items. You might introduce these items with a light joke. For example, "I happen to have my Ph.D. dissertation with me; I never leave home without it." When possible, leave copies of materials with your interviewer. Even if the employer doesn't inspect all of your show-and-tell materials, they may leave a vivid, even indelible impression distinguishing you from less equipped candidates.

➤ Be positive and energetic. Express enthusiasm about the opening and the organization. Describe what about your field inspires you. In short, show your fire in the belly. (Even if you are regularly tossing back fistfuls of anti-depressants, act cheerful during the interview. Nobody wants to hire a sourpuss.)

➤ Be friendly and easy-going.

➤ Exude confidence without acting cocky or superior.

➤ Congratulate the interviewer for any major awards or recent major accomplishments that the hiring agency or the hiring office has achieved, as indicated by your pre-interview research.

➤ Exploit any common ground that you share with your interviewer. Why? It may sound hokey, but it's true: People tend to like people with whom they share something in common, whether it is the same home town, favorite vacation spot, alma mater, past employer, former colleague, mutual friend or unbridled passion for Tibetan dance. This phenomenon was recently brought home to me by a hiring manager when she described her impressions of an applicant whom she had just interviewed, "I really liked Barry," the interviewer said. "We are both from Georgia, so we had a lot to talk about."

You may find some common ground between you and your interviewer through your pre-interview research or by glancing around at the memorabilia and photographs in your interviewer's office, or even by asking the interviewer about his/her own career path, if appropriate.

➤ Take notes during the interview, if you want to. You may also check your list of questions, when appropriate.

➤ If the interviewer fesses to the fact that s/he hasn't read your resume, offer to summarize some highlights.

➤ Answer questions by repeating credentials and success stories that are included in your resume and KSAs; don't worry about being repetitious. Remember: Even if your best credentials are highlighted on your resume or KSAs by blinking disco lights, the interviewer will not necessarily remember them during the interview. And in any case, it never hurts to emphasize your best selling points.

➤ Reflect your knowledge of the hiring agency in your answers. Even big organizations love to be loved. And by showing that you have researched the agency, you will prove that you have a burning desire to work there.

➤ Pause briefly before answering a question if you need to think it over. You may also conclude an answer by saying, "Is there any other information that I could provide that might be helpful?" or "Have I answered that completely?"

➤ If you have a panel interview, focus on each interviewer as s/he asks a question, and keep focused on the questioner for 30 seconds or so. Then, give eye contact to each member of the panel.

➤ If you are asked about a skill or type of experience that you do not have, admit it; don't try to fake it. I know many people who have been told by employers that their honesty in interviews — rather than hurting their chances — helped them land their jobs. Likewise, many hiring managers have told me that they are turned off by applicants who ignore their question and prattle on about irrelevant information; they see right through such fluff.

After you acknowledge your lack of a credential, quickly mention a similar credential that you do offer For example, an Environmental Planner was recently asked in an interview whether she had ever prepared a certain type of technical document. In response, she acknowledged that she had never done so, but that she had supervised people who had prepared that type of document; she also described some of the other types of technical documents that she had prepared. That was enough to get her the job.

When you must acknowledge your lack of a credential, you may also express your willingness to devote your own time to getting up to speed in a particular area. You may also emphasize that you are fast learner, cite instances where you undertook self-study and provide examples of instances when you have quickly acquired new expertise. Also mention the positive results that such efforts produced. As one hiring manager advises, "Don't just say that you haven't done X and leave it at that. Give me something to work with…some reason to think that you will be able and willing to rise to the occasion."

➤ Collect the business card of everyone who interviews you.

➤ As the interview winds up, offer a parting salvo that summarizes the most important requirements for the opening, and how your background meets those requirements. For example:

Ms. Harris: I just want to emphasize what I offer before I leave. Based upon what we've discussed today, I understand that the [name of opening] requires an A degree and B and C types of experience. I have an A degree from [name of University]. I have B experience from [Name of organization] and C experience from [Name of organization.] Does that help you understand the similarities between the requirements of the position and my credentials?

➤ At the end of the interview, say point blank, " I'd like to work here." Such reassurance may be important to the interviewer who may doubt whether you are still interested in the position. What's more, even interviewers like positive feedback; flattery frequently works.

➤ Ask about the next steps in the selection process, if the interviewer doesn't mention them.

DONTs

➤ Don't be late for an interview.

➤ Don't act desperate. I even heard about a victim of a layoff who needed a job so badly that she came close to tears during an interview. Although the applicant's plight understandably tugged at the interview panel's collective heartstrings, she was deemed too emotionally frail for the high-pressure opening for which she had interviewed.

➤ Don't slam the job opening or the selection process. Believe it or not, applicants commonly do this during interviews. Some even express doubt in the interview over whether they would take the job, if given the choice. Of course, such applicants never get the choice.

➤ Don't criticize your former bosses, employers or jobs. Complain about former positions to your friends or relatives — not to potential employers who will dismiss you out of suspicion that you would be a problem employee or that you would also badmouth them.

➤ Don't use profanity.

➤ Don't act annoyed if the interviewer is delayed or interrupted. Show how easy-to-get-along-with you are by rolling with the punches.

➤ Don't contradict yourself in an interview. For example, a friend of mine recently interviewed someone of Saudi Arabian descent for a security-related job. At the beginning of the interview, the applicant stated that neither he nor his family currently had any financial interests in Saudi Arabia. But the applicant dug his own grave a few minutes later when he slipped by referring to his family's huge property holdings in Saudi Arabia.

➤ Don't mention your religious or political beliefs because they may offend the interviewer.

➤ Don't try to fake skills that you don't have. For example, an applicant whose resume boasted of fluent French recently lost out on an overseas job because she responded with a deer-in-head-lights stare to a basic interview question that was conveyed in French.

➤ Don't forget to listen. In other words, don't talk too much. As one hiring manager put it, "When I interview people, I ask myself whether I would want to work with this person." No one wants to be locked in meetings with an unstoppable yacker.

➤ Don't reveal that you are a loose canon by admitting to breaking rules in previous jobs.

➤ Don't ask about salary, benefits or work schedules until you are offered the job. If you discuss these issues prematurely, you may give your interviewer reason to eliminate you or you may sacrifice grist for your salary negotiations. See Chapter 12 for more information about salary negotiations.

➤ Don't give the interviewer any reason to believe that you will be dissatisfied with the position.

➤ Don't challenge the judgment of the interviewer. I know, for example, of a serious contender for a job who wiped out by insisting that the interviewer had wrongly interpreted the hiring agency's rules on training.

➤ Don't answer hypothetical questions with empty responses, such as "that is a tough one" or with mere "yes" or "no" answers. If an answer doesn't occur to you right away, pause for a moment and think about your response. If you need clarification of the question, ask for it.

➤ Don't bring friends or significant others with you to the interview. In fact, the blooper of the century award goes to an applicant for a government job who brought her mother with her to the interview. When the interviewer asked the applicant to identify her goals, the applicant responded, "to move out of my mother's house." (I suspect that the applicant's mother shared that same goal!)

➤ Be courteous to everyone you meet at the hiring agency, including the receptionist.

➤ No matter how chummy your interviewer may act or how comfortable s/he may make you feel, don't let yourself get lulled into a false sense of friendship with your interviewer. Don't spill any information about yourself that you wouldn't print on your resume.

➤ Don't ask the interviewer to give you an on-the-spot answer of whether or not you will be offered the job.

➤ Don't use sexist language. One federal applicant recently nixed his chances by referring to his female interviewers as "you gals."

GUERILLA INTERVIEWING TACTICS

Most interviewers are not professional interviewers; they are primarily something else besides an interviewer. And sadly, in many cases, their lack of expertise in interviewing shows.

Some interviewers, for example, will not have even found, let alone have read, your resume before the interview. During the interview, some interviewers will prattle about their own rise to the top without asking you about your credentials. Others may ask irrelevant questions that recall the Barbara Walter's "what type of tree would you like to be?" school of interviewing.

If you don't seize control of such lousy interviews, the interviewer will — through no fault of your own — be left without a clear, let alone a favorable, impression of your credentials. How can you rescue a wayward interview? Here are several strategies for setting the stage for your break-out performance:

➤ If the interviewer happens to mention any of the types of "show and tell" materials that are in your portfolio, segue into a discussion of your work. For example, if the interviewer discusses some of the department's press releases, mention that you have some of your press releases with you and would like to show them to the interviewer.

➤ Say something like, "If I understand the position correctly based upon the vacancy announcement and my research of the agency, you are looking for X, Y and Z skills and a familiarity with A, B and C issues. May I illustrate how my background reflects these requirements?"

➤ Break up the conversation with a pointed suggestion, "Ms. Scott, may I be so bold to ask you a question? I've noticed that the Department of X tends to take an Y-based approach. I wonder if you would be interested in taking an alternative approach? Let me explain why I am suggesting this approach…"

➤ At the end of the interview, say, "I just want to mention before I leave that there are three main reasons why I am confident that I could make significant contributions to this organization…"

➤ When the interviewer asks you whether you have any questions, say: "Yes, I do have several questions. But first, if you don't mind, I would like to take this chance to tell you a little about some of my important qualifications that we haven't yet covered."

A JOB INTERVIEW THAT HELPED DECIDE A PRESIDENTIAL ELECTION

Know what sunk Senator Edward Kennedy's presidential aspirations? Not Kennedy's fatal car accident at Chappaquiddick. Rather, what doomed Kennedy's presidential bid was an interview that he gave during his campaign for the 1980 democratic nomination during which he was asked why he wanted to be president — the political equivalent of the "why should we hire you?" job interview question. In response, Kennedy fumbled, stammered and then petered out altogether. Kennedy's unpersuasive answer is widely cited as the last nail in his presidential possibilities.

If you are ever similarly stricken by hoof-in-mouth disease during a job interview, you can at least be grateful that your performance will not be replayed over and over and over again on national television.

THE FEAR FACTOR: SIDESTEPPING EMPLOYERS' SECRET FEARS

So you think that *looking* for a job is scary? Well, here's a shocker: Many hiring managers are just as scared as you of the hiring process.

So what are hiring managers so terrified of? The possibility of making bad hiring decisions — bad hiring decisions that they will have to live with for a loooooooooong time.

The fear of selecting the wrong job applicant is especially strong in the federal government, where it is particularly hard to fire employees; federal hiring managers may literally have to live with their bad hires until death do they part. This principle was recently underscored to me by a federal executive after I asked him whether he had ever made any bad hiring decisions during his 20 plus years in government. He responded to my question by offering to introduce me to his staffing mistakes, "They all work right over there," he said, pointing to a cubicle farm that encircles his office.

Like romantic commitment-phobes, some risk-averse selecting officials are ruled more by their fears of disaster than by their hopes for creating productive relationships. These risk-averse types usually reject even the worthiest applicants who inadvertently set-off their invisible fear sensors.

But pivotal though a hiring manager's fears may be, they are almost never openly acknowledged during the selection process. Indeed, the hiring manager's secret insecurities are like the proverbial elephant in the closet — the huge, dominating presence that is never discussed.

But even though you probably won't be given an opportunity to directly address hiring managers' fears, you can still head them off. Provided in the following table are profiles of the five most common types of problem employees and strategies for reassuring hiring managers that you represent the antithesis of each profile.

HOT • TIP

DEFUSING AGE DISCRIMINATION

Age discrimination is generally less prevalent in the federal government than in other types of organizations that are not required to follow federal diversity regulations. Nevertheless, age discrimination does occasionally rear its unwelcome head even in the federal government. So what should you do if you are an experienced professional who is interviewed by someone who is significantly younger than you?

Beware of your interviewer's secret, unspoken fears. S/he may be intimidated by your experience. S/he may decide not to hire you only to avoid the awkwardness of correcting, overruling and supervising an elder. So consider reassuring your interviewer by saying something like:

You may think that, because I have a significant amount of experience, that I might be rigid and might not take direction well. But I want to reassure you that I understand that you would be my supervisor, and that it would be my obligation to support you.

I also want to emphasize that I am energetic, flexible and take direction well. I am certainly prepared to accommodate and profit by any approaches that you may suggest.

If appropriate, provide a few examples that testify to your zest, flexibility and ability to take direction.

Also, make sure that your grooming and dress don't reinforce negative stereotypes and prejudices; dress neatly and in contemporary professional styles.

PROVING THAT YOU ARE A PRODUCER — NOT A PROBLEM

PROFILE OF PROBLEM EMPLOYEE	HOW TO PROVE THAT YOU DO NOT FIT THE PROFILE
The Wolf in Sheep's Clothing: This type of employee looks great on paper, interviews well and appears well-adjusted. But lurking beneath a presentable veneer is a sociopath who lies, cheats or steals, or behaves otherwise unstably or unreliably. Because of hiring managers' deep fears of saddling themselves with a wolf in sheep's clothing, objective validation of an applicant's mental stability may even trump impressive professional qualifications. I have heard hiring managers underscore this principle by stating preferences such as, "I would rather hire someone who is technically mediocre but who I know is sane and reliable than an off-the-street applicant who has first-rate technical qualifications but whose personality is an unknown quantity."	1. If you have any inside contacts, and I mean any inside contacts — even just an acquaintance who works in your target agency and can vouch for your character, mention your inside contact in your cover letter or body of your application. 2. Arrange for your inside contact to vouch for you as early in the selection process as possible — even before you are asked for your references. An early endorsement of your application by an inside contact will help keep your application in the competition. (I have heard many hiring managers profess regret that an inside contact endorsed a candidate too late — after the candidate's application had already been rejected.) 3. Even if you do not have inside contacts, during your interviews, mention the names and titles of people who will provide you with exemplary references. 4. See this chapter's "Prepping Your References" section for advice on choosing references.
The Team Wrecker: In government, few people work alone; most projects are either entirely team-based or involve major collaborative components. Therefore, a government employee who can't work well with others is usually an employee who doesn't work out at all. In the words of one hiring manager. "When I hire someone, I want to know that they are not going to run out of the office crying because someone looked at them the wrong way and leave me in the lurch right before a critical deadline."	Cite in your resume, KSAs and interview examples of your team and leadership successes, including your team awards, contributions to important workgroups, and elected positions that you have held in professional organizations. Bring to the interview any tangible evidence that you have of team successes, including thank you letters or e-mails mentioning your team successes, leadership skills or team contributions from supervisors, staffers, customers or stakeholders. You may also cite your contributions to nonwork teams in community, charity and PTA organizations. Also mention that you take suggestions/criticism well. If you are a student without any work experience, cite your contributions to group academic projects, team sports, musical groups, theater projects, school newspapers, and community or volunteer organization or your participation in Outward Bound type programs. You may also mention how your experience as a member of a large family taught you how to work with varied personalities or how traveling abroad increased your cultural sensitivity.
The Outshiner: Virtually every hiring supervisor wants to hire staffers who will help improve their stature without outshining them. This cardinal principle is violated by The Outshiner who diminishes the stature of supervisors by hogging the limelight and/or going over supervisors' heads.	If the opportunity presents itself during your interview, mention your recognition: 1. That your first loyalty is to your supervisor, and that one of your primary responsibilities is to keep him/her informed of important developments. 2. Of the importance of achieving a broad conceptual understanding of projects that will help you recognize emerging facts and issues that warrant your supervisor's attention. Cite examples of how you have flagged hot-button issues in a timely manner for your previous supervisors, if possible.

PROFILE OF PROBLEM EMPLOYEE	HOW TO PROVE THAT YOU DO NOT FIT THE PROFILE

The Lazy Bones: This type of employee needs constant nagging, hand-holding and prodding to get anything done. In short, such employees are more trouble than they are worth.

Convince potential employers of your dogged work ethic in interviews by:

1. Citing your work ethic if you are asked about your strengths or what you are proud of. Impress hiring managers by saying something like, "I consider myself reasonably smart, though I am not the smartest person in the world. But I won't let anyone outwork me. I am the employee who will be here until 10:00 at night, if necessary. And I have a stellar record for reliability. I am the Cal Ripken of my current office."

2. Citing projects that you have completed with little supervision and instances when you have gone the extra mile by taking the initiative, putting in long hours, and doing whatever was required to get the job done…no matter what.

3. Citing your record of meeting tight deadlines, and simultaneously juggling demanding projects.

4. Ask the hiring manger to consider hiring you as a temporary employee for an initial 90-day trial period, and then at the end of this trial period, converting you into a permanent employee if you demonstrate that you are a producer. (Federal agencies can accomplish such conversions relatively easily.) This suggestion will demonstrate your confidence in your abilities and your knowledge of federal hiring procedures. It will also provide employers with a no-risk option for evaluating your abilities. Moreover, because you will probably be the sole candidate to propose a trial period, your suggestion will virtually guarantee that you will stand out from the pack.

5. If you are student or a recent graduate, cite the independent projects that you completed or the demanding electives that you took. Also cite your record of working towards a degree and managing a grueling work schedule at the same time, if appropriate.

The Pointy Headed Pontificator: This type of employee might as well wear a sign across their forehead that reads, "I don't do projects."

The Pointy Headed Pontificator has no particular specialized knowledge, contributes little or nothing to tangible work products, and fancies himself or herself as decision-making management material: A thinker, not a doer. Though most government managers do value the critical thinking skills of employees, their main, burning desire is to hire professionals who can, above all else, get things done.

Don't make condescending remarks about the opening, or describe yourself as a "big picture generalist" who is above getting your hands dirty. Instead, in your cover letter, KSAs and interviews:

• Bill yourself as the "go-to person," the super charged, indispensable, unflappable professional who managers consult when they need a question answered, a problem solved, a customer satisfied — immediately.

• Express enthusiasm and recognition of the importance of the opening and your previous jobs.

• Cite your biggest, most impressive, concrete accomplishments, and the feedback that you received on them, as instructed in Chapter 6.

I N T E R V I E W · S U C C E S S · S T O R Y

I GOT THE JOB!

BY HEIDI MCALLISTER, ENVIRONMENTAL EDUCATOR

While living in Mexico, Heidi McAllister, a U.S. citizen, nailed a federal job in Washington DC solely through her resume, application and a phone interview; she never even had a face-to-face interview with a hiring manager. Heidi explains here how she learned how to give a killer phone interview.

I had been living near Mexico City and working as a consultant in environmental education mostly to the Mexican government for about 13 years when I started applying for jobs back in the U.S.

Soon after beginning my job search, I had about six phone interviews. All of these interviews seemed to go smoothly. But none of them lead to a job offer. As the rejection letters rolled in, I realized that something was wrong with the way I was presenting myself. In light of the fact that my resume and application had apparently been good enough to generate interviews, but my interviews apparently hadn't been good enough to generate job offers, I reasoned that the problem lay somewhere in my interviewing skills.

So I read up on interviewing strategies, and soon pinpointed the flaw in my interviewing strategy: I hadn't been selling myself enough. I know why I had been holding back: I have a self-deprecating style; I like to poke fun at myself. So tooting my own horn doesn't come naturally to me.

But my research on interviewing showed me how I could sell myself without coming off as egocentric. All I had to do was cite concrete examples of my previous achievements that matched the requirements of my target job. No need to sound pompous, haughty or conceited; I just had to be factual and specific.

I used this technique for the first time during my phone interview for a federal job as an Environment Program and Training Specialist. For example, one of the interview questions was, "What are the necessary components of an environmental education program?" In the old days, I would have answered this question by naming the essential components of an environmental education program, exactly as the question requests. Though technically correct, such an answer would not have proven that I can apply my knowledge and skillfully complete the varied tasks involved in designing and establishing an environmental education program, and that my program designs are good enough for government agencies to invest in.

So, inspired by my research on interviewing techniques, I answered this question by ticking off the countries where I had helped design environmental programs, naming the program sponsors, describing the target audiences, explaining the components of each program, and citing positive feedback earned by these programs. I think that the adage "actions speak louder than words" applies here. By showing that I had taken action — that is, set up successful environmental education programs, I impressed my interviewers more than if I had merely talked about what an environmental education should be.

Likewise, I incorporated into many of my other interview answers specific examples of my achievements well as objective evidence of my success. I was able to quickly identify these examples because I had studied my resume just before the phone interview began and because I could quickly glance at my resume, which was strategically positioned in front of me throughout the session. I know that my interviewing strategy worked because, within several weeks, I was offered the job, which I enthusiastically accepted.

PREPPING YOUR REFERENCES

Be prepared to provide your interviewer with a list of at least three references. Neatly print your list of references on your letterhead, and specify each reference's name, title, address, telephone number(s), e-mail address and relationship to you. In addition, you can give your reference list extra zing by specifying which of your achievements, projects or skills each reference will verify.

To ensure that your references sing your praises loud and clear, select references who are:

➤ **Respected:** Choose references who hold positions of authority in the business, nonprofit, government or academic sectors. Don't use friends as references.

➤ **Articulate:** Choose references who thoroughly familiar with your credentials and can describe them articulately.

➤ **Enthusiastic:** Before you ask a contact to serve a reference, ask whether s/he can give you an enthusiastic endorsement. If your contact expresses *any* reluctance or hedging, don't use that person as a reference. After all, if you detect ambivalence from the contact, so will hiring managers. And any reference that is less than hardy can doom an application. One hiring manager described how a reference's ambivalence can express itself: "When I call the former employer of a job applicant, I always ask them if they would hire the applicant again. If the reference pauses at all before responding, I know what their true answer is, and I won't hire the applicant."

➤ **Prepared:** Review your qualifications with your references and provide them with your resume. You may also remind your references of specific projects that you completed for them and positive feedback that they have given you. Don't assume that references necessarily even remember praise that they have given you in the past; feel free to remind them of it, or show them praising written documents that they provided you in the past.

Also describe to references the position that you are applying for, and which aspects of your background you would like them to emphasize.

➤ **Easily Reachable:** Don't use references who are likely to be on vacation or otherwise unreachable when your potential employers may try to contact them. Provide the hiring agency with all possible contact information for your references including their title, home and work telephone numbers and e-mail address. I have heard of finalists not making the final cut simply because the selecting official reached the references of another, equally worthy applicant first.

POST-INTERVIEW THANK YOUS

QUESTION: What is the first thing you should do when you get home from an interview (after you rip off your uncomfortable interview outfit and pour yourself a stiff, cold drink)?

ANSWER: Write a thank-you letter to everyone who interviewed you.

It may seem unfair that you are obliged to thank an interviewer(s) who hasn't really done anything for you. Indeed, if you are like most job applicants, you probably think that your interviewer(s) should thank *you* for trucking down to *their* office, submitting to the Spanish Inquisition and perhaps even graciously agreeing to itemize some of your weaknesses.

But, like it or not, your fate hinges on the decision of your interviewer(s). And sending a thank you letter to everyone who interviewed you is one of the easiest and most important things you can do to win over those decision-maker(s). Indeed, according to many formal studies as well as my own interviews with dozens and dozens of hiring managers, a post-interview thank you letter can make or break your application. Why? Because:

➤ Very few applicants bother to write thank you letters. Therefore, if you write one, you are virtually guaranteed to stand out from the pack.

➤ An effective thank you letter will remind the interviewer of your strengths. As one hiring manager put it, "If a letter is right in front of me, it is a tangible nudge that forces me to think about the candidate again." This is important because an interviewer who screens many candidates can, soon after the interview, easily forget the credentials of even an outstanding candidate.

➤ By sending a thank you letter to your interviewer, you will demonstrate that you are a polite, conscientious candidate who follows-through and who really wants the job — all rare traits that are valued by employers.

CONTENT AND FORMAT

A thank you letter should be brief and zippy; no more than several paragraphs. It should:

➤ Thank the interviewer for their time and trouble.
➤ Summarize what you discussed in the interview.
➤ Reaffirm your interest in the position.
➤ Concisely summarize your most relevant value-adding qualifications.
➤ Briefly review why the job appeals to you.
➤ Add any information that you forgot to mention during the interview or correct any misinformation that you provided during the interview.

It's fine to send a quick e-mail immediately after your interview. But don't let an e-mail be your last word. Within 24 hours of your interview, follow-up with a printed business letter or a hand-written card that demonstrates neurotically neat penmanship. If you are applying for a position as a graphic artist, consider designing your own thank you card.

Send your thank you letter overnight delivery. (Yes, a thank you letter that arrives right away will score more points than one that arrives even one day later.)

PROOFREAD

Don't let careless errors on a thank you letter or e-mail nix your application. So call the hiring office if you need to check the spellings of any names or titles of interviewers.

Also proofread for grammar, punctuation and spelling. E-mails are particularly prone to typos; so spell check and read hard copy versions of all e-mails before sending them.

SAMPLE THANK YOU LETTER: BUSINESS FORMAT

Sam Murphy
ABC Lane
Washington DC 20008
January 1, 2004

Mr. John Harris
Director
Public Affairs
US Department of Labor
401 Wilson Blvd
Arlington, VA 20220

Dear Mr. Harris:

It was a pleasure chatting with you about the opening for a Public Affairs Officer and meeting Jack and Cindy. Your energetic presentation, your office's congenial atmosphere and your office's many new dynamic programs added to my enthusiasm for the opening.

As I mentioned when we talked, I won three on-the-spot awards at the Department of Energy for developing exactly the type of employee newsletter that Public Affairs will soon launch. In addition, my editorial experience at ABC News and my writing experience at MSNBC.com would allow me to contribute to your multi-media outreach campaign.

Again, I would welcome the opportunity to join your team. My telephone number is (123) 123-4567, and my e-mail is JHarris@email.com. I look forward to hearing from you.

Sincerely,

Sam Murphy

TEXT OF SAMPLE HAND-WRITTEN THANK YOU CARD

Dear Mr. Franks:

Thank you for spending so much quality time with me this afternoon. I am particularly excited about the Benefits Manager position because it would combine my dual interests in managing health insurance benefits and payroll records.

In light of my 15 years of experience in managing payroll and benefits programs for 500 corporate employees, I am certain that I would be able to hit the ground running and make immediate contributions to the Office of Personnel Management's benefit programs.

One achievement that I neglected to mention when we talked: As a Benefits Manager at British Petroleum, I identified, researched and recommended a life insurance program that cut company costs by 10 percent and improved employee satisfaction by 20 percent. I am confident that I could produce similar results for the Office of Personnel Management.

I can be reached at (123) 123-4567, and my e-mail address is JBrown@email.com.

Thanks again for your personal attention. I hope I will have the opportunity to contribute to the Office of Personnel Management, and I do appreciate your consideration.

Sincerely,

Jack Brown

CHAPTER 12: COMMANDING A TOP DOLLAR SALARY

By not negotiating a first salary, an individual stands to lose more than $500,000 by age 60.

— From *Women Don't Ask: Negotiation and the Gender Divide* by Linda Babcock and Sara Laschever

So you've received a job offer from a federal agency. As Sally Field might say, "They like you! They really like you!"

The mere utterance of an offer from a hiring manager may flush your nervous system with happy hormones and send you into a rapture of relief. But don't let the thrill of your victory compel you to accept an unacceptable salary. Remember: An employer in any sector — including the federal sector — may offer a new hire the lowest possible salary that they can get away with. That's simply how the game is frequently played.

But the federal government has even more leverage over most new recruits than do other types of employers. How come? Because the typical federal job-seeker wrongly believes that federal salaries are nonnegotiable. Such unfortunates almost always cave to lowball salaries with nary a question, such as, "Is this salary negotiable?" They may thereby unwittingly sacrifice earning potential that may be worth hundreds of thousands of dollars over the course of a career.

DON'T BUY INTO THE MYTH OF THE NON-NEGOTIABLE FEDERAL SALARY. The real deal is that salaries for many full-time permanent federal jobs — like those for jobs in other sectors — *are* flexible. But the raw reality is that you are unlikely to ever receive more money without asking for it. Even if the meek *shall* inherit the earth, they shan't get a decent salary without negotiating one.

In order to counter the ongoing federal retirement wave, many federal agencies have adopted new flexibilities on pay and benefits. This means that the bargaining power of applicants who receive job offers from federal agencies is currently at an all-time high.

This chapter introduces the various pay scales used by federal agencies, and then reviews tried-and-true methods for negotiating for top dollar salaries. I know that these negotiating methods work because I have personally used them many times, as have job-seekers whom I have advised. Believe me, these strategies are worth money in your pocket.

H O T ● T I P

EASY MONEY FOR CURRENT FEDS

If you are already a federal employee, you may be able to land a big bonus just for staying put at your current job. In government lingo, this type of prize is called "a retention bonus." The cap for a retention bonus is 100 percent of an employee's pay. To be eligible, you must:

- Have unusually high or unique qualifications, or your agency must have a special need for your services.

- Be considered likely without a retention bonus to leave the federal government for any reason, including retirement.

You may be particularly primed for retention bonus if you are currently playing a pivotal role in an ongoing-project, such as the implementation of a new program or regulation. Note that one way to prove that you would be likely to leave the federal government is to land an offer from another employer.

For more information about retention bonuses, go to *opm.gov,* then click on the following sequence of links: "Employment & Benefits"..."Pay and Performance"..."Allowances & Bonuses" and finally "Retention Allowances."

You are eligible for an "extended assignment incentive" if you are an overseas federal employee *and* you meet the following conditions:

- You work in a territory or possession of the United States, Puerto Rico or the Northern Mariana Islands, and you have two years of continuous civil service experience in the covered area.

- It would be difficult to replace you.

- The agency determines that it is in the government's best interest to keep you for a specified amount of time.

An extended assignment incentive may be worth up to $15,000 or one-fourth of the employee's annual basic pay times the number of years that the employee agrees to stay on the job — up to five years. For more information about extended assignment incentives, see *opm.gov/oca/pay/HTML/EAIFacts.asp.*

SHOW ME THE MONEY: FEDERAL PAY SCALES

A variety of pay scales operate within the federal government. Most of these pay scales incorporate annual cost of living increases of about two to five percent. In addition, many federal agencies give annual bonuses to their employees. But, before you start drooling, be aware that such bonuses are usually considerably less than those given to employees in private industry; the typical federal bonus equals about 1.6 percent of annual salary.

Listed on the following page are the most common federal pay scales. To access salary tables for these pay scales, go to *opm.gov*, and then click on the following sequence of links: "Career Opportunities"…"Salaries and Wages."

➻ **GENERAL SCHEDULE SYSTEM:** General Schedule jobs are graded from GS-1 to GS-15. Each GS grade has 10 steps. Salaries increase with each increase in grade and step. **Generally speaking, under the General Schedule (GS) pay system, entry-level jobs are graded through GS-9; mid-career jobs are graded from GS-11 through GS-13; senior level jobs are graded from GS-14 through GS-15 and also include all jobs in the Senior Executive Service.**

"We reward top executives at the agency with a unique incentive program. Money."

Federal employees who live in cities where the cost of living is particularly high receive locality pay, which can boost pay by as much as 12 percent over base pay rates.

Under the GS system, federal employees usually automatically receive a step increase every one, two or three years, depending upon the employee's position on the career ladder. The following rules govern merit promotions based upon performance:

- An employee must usually remain in each grade and step for at least one year before being promoted to the next highest grade or step.

- Employees cannot skip any grades as they advance up the federal career ladder.

These regulations generally act as speed bumps on federal careers in the GS system. Moreover, employees are not necessarily given merit-based promotions upon completing their time-in-grade or time-in-step requirements; they must frequently wait longer than minimum waiting periods for non-automatic promotions that are based on merit.

Although the GS pay system is the most common pay system for white-collar employees, more and more federal agencies are currently abandoning it in favor of pay systems that offer more flexibility.

➤ **PAY BANDING SYSTEMS:** In order to gain more discretion in setting pay, more and more agencies have either already opted out of the GS system or are currently in the process of doing so. These agencies include the Congressional Budget Office, the Department of Defense, the Department of Homeland Security, the Federal Aviation Administration, the Government Accountability Office, NASA and the Security and Exchange Commission, among other agencies.

The most common alternatives to the GS system are systems based upon "pay banding'" in which grades are combined. Systems based upon pay banding sometimes enable agencies to set higher starting salaries, and are designed to reward employees for good performance and new academic degrees. However, the Bush administration is working to remove automatic step increases under these systems. In addition, it may be easier to fire employees under pay banding systems than under the GS system.

➤ **HIGH-DEMAND PROFESSIONALS:** Special salary rates are given to some types of high-demand professionals, including some Information Technology (IT) specialists, medical specialists, scientists and engineers.

➤ **SENIOR EXECUTIVE SERVICE:** The federal government is currently adopting a new performance-based system for the Senior Executive Service that rewards high performers with raises but eliminates automatic annual pay raises. Agencies that have been certified by the Office of Personnel Management for adopting performance-based appraisal systems for SESers can pay higher SES salaries than can uncertified agencies.

If you are just entering the SES, your hiring agency should top your previous salary. Some agencies base offers for new SESers on a certain percentage increase over his or her previous salary. But other agencies are not guided by such percentages.

➤ **LAW ENFORCEMENT EMPLOYEES:** A patchwork of laws and rules have created differences in basic pay, overtime pay and retirement benefits for federal law enforcers across the federal government. Many law enforcement officers are covered by the General Schedule (GS) system's special law enforcement salary rates. These rates are posted at *opm.gov/oca/04tables/index.asp*. But many other law enforcement officers are covered by alternative pay systems.

Organizations that pay their law enforcement officers particularly well include the Border Patrol, the Bureau of Engraving and Printing, the Capitol Police, the Defense Department's Protective Service Police, the FBI, the Government Printing Office, the Mint, the Secret Service Uniformed Division, the Park Police, the Supreme Court Police and the Transportation Security Administration. The Department of Defense and the Department of Homeland Security will soon establish pay banding systems for their law enforcement officers.

It is also important to understand that the types of jobs that are classified as law enforcement officers vary inconsistently across the federal government. Therefore, some security professionals who do law enforcement work are not officially classified as law enforcement officers. At press time, the federal government was considering creating a single pay scale for all federal law enforcers.

➤ **BLUE-COLLAR WORKERS:** Blue collar workers are covered by the Federal Wage System, which has 15 grades of five steps each.

➤ **CONGRESSIONAL STAFFERS:** Generally, jobs in Congress pay much less and offer much less job security than do comparable jobs in federal agencies. Moreover, Congressional staff jobs usually require longer hours than do agency jobs. But by the same token, Congressional staff jobs frequently offer unique intangible perks — such as opportunities to work closely with members of Congress and to contribute to national legislation, and perhaps even to occasionally ride on Air Force One.

A few more rules of thumb: 1) Jobs on Congressional committees usually pay better than jobs on the staffs of members of Congress. 2) Jobs on Senate staffs tend to pay better than jobs on the staffs of members of the House of Representatives.

NEGOTIATING BASICS

THE BASIS OF YOUR OFFER

Virtually every vacancy announcement posted on USAJOBS identifies a salary range for the opening. How does a hiring agency determine what salary to offer you? Probably largely based upon your salary history. As very general guidance, it may be helpful to know that:

➤ **If you are currently employed,** the hiring agency will, in many cases, match or best your current salary or a current and reasonable competing offer. A professional who transfers from a non-profit organization or another organization that pays significantly less than federal agencies may even receive a considerable bump in salary when s/he moves into the federal government. But conversely, a professional who transfers from a corporation that pays extravagant salaries may not fare quite as well.

➤ **If you are currently unemployed,** the hiring agency will, in many cases, match or best your most recent salary or a current and reasonable competing offer.

➤ **If you are a new college graduate,** the hiring agency will probably offer you its standard offer for recent graduates, or match or best a current and reasonable competing offer. Here are the guidelines for standard offers for new graduates under the GS pay system:

- An applicant who has a college degree without any specialized experience in their field qualifies for a GS-5 position. But an applicant who has at least a B average or other desirable college can expect to start at a GS-7 position.

- An applicant who has a masters degree qualifies for at least a GS-9 position.

- An applicant who has a Ph.D. qualifies for a GS-12 position.

The more work experience an applicant has in addition to degrees, the higher up the GS-ladder s/he will probably land.

➡ **If you are a recent high school graduate degree without any work experience,** you will qualify for jobs at the GS-2 level. Alternatively, if you have some work experience, you may start at the GS-3, 4 or 5 level.

➡ **If you applying for a Trade and Craft job,** your salary offer will be based upon your ability to measure up to your target job's Knowledge, Skills and Abilities (KSAs).

For additional general information about federal qualification requirements, visit *opm.gov*, and then click on the following sequence of links: "Career Opportunities" ... "Job FAQs" ... "Qualification Requirements."

It is important to understand that salary policies can vary widely from agency to agency. For example, the base salaries for entry-level professional staff at the Government Accountability Office, which operates under a pay banding system, currently range from around $40,000 to almost $70,000, depending on the individual's qualifications and the job location. This range is considerably higher than that for starting salaries under the GS system. To stay informed on trends in federal salaries, check agency websites and use the online resources for researching federal agencies provided in Chapter 2 and Chapter 9.

WIGGLE ROOM

Although you probably cannot raise the ceiling of your opening's salary range, you probably *can* negotiate for a higher offer within your opening's available range. Nevertheless, many job seekers accept a federal salary offer without negotiating — only to regret it within a few months of starting their federal job and discovering that:

➡ Colleagues whose credentials are comparable to theirs but who drove harder bargains than they did are earning higher salaries than they are.

➡ Even capable, diligent professionals may move up the career ladder slowly. Grade increases are not necessarily granted frequently, and their pace generally declines as employees move up the federal career ladder.

The brutal truth is that you may be locked into your starting grade and salary, or close to it, for years to come. This possibility increases the importance of negotiating the highest possible starting salary that you can.

THE POWER PLAY

The time between when you receive an offer and when you accept or reject the offer is the only time during the selection process, and perhaps the only time during your career, when the tables are turned in your direction, and you get to call the shots. Yes, until the salary negotiations began, the hiring agency ran the show, and the selection process revolved entirely around its needs.

Finally, during salary negotiations, you can assert your salary and benefits needs, and the agency — temporarily rendered powerless — twists in the wind awaiting your next move. But don't get too excited. Once you accept or reject the offer, the tables will turn again…the natural order will return….and the hiring agency will once again wield the upper hand.

SALARY-BOOSTING RESEARCH

Before you negotiate, improve your bargaining position by taking these actions.

1. Get a competing salary offer from another employer in writing. As previously mentioned, a hiring agency will usually match a current and reasonable competing offer from another employer. This is one of the best kept secrets among hiring managers!

    To get a competing offer, you might have to apply for jobs that you don't even want. Granted: Applying for jobs is work. But, you should be applying for multiple jobs at the same time anyway. Moreover, the multiple offer route could end up literally boosting your annual federal salary by thousands of dollars per year. Not a bad payback for a few extra hours or days of work.

2. Get a copy of the classification standards used by the hiring agency to determine the grade level of the position. Access these documents by typing "Classification Standards" into the search window at *opm.gov*. Alternatively, you can probably obtain a copy of the classification standards that apply to your opening from the contact person identified on the position's vacancy announcement.

3. Visit the employment section of the hiring agency's website, and familiarize yourself with the agency's benefits.

4. Find out whether the hiring agency or another hiring agency is offering any special recruitment bonuses for people in your profession. (See the following box on Special Recruitment Bonuses.) Be aware that such offers can change rapidly, and that they are not always posted on agency websites. So ask the contact person identified on you opening's vacancy announcement if your target agency offers any special incentives. Also, surf through the free online resources provided in Chapter 2 and Chapter 9 for articles about special recruitment bonuses.

5. Discuss your offer with any federal employees whom you know. Your federal contacts may be able to help you gauge the reasonableness of your offer. (Federal salaries are generally not treated with the "cone of silence" confidentiality of salaries in other sectors. So federal employees are relatively open about discussing them.)

HOT • TIP

SPECIAL RECRUITMENT BONUSES

A new hire from inside or outside the federal government may receive a recruitment or relocation bonus that is worth up to 100 percent of his/her annual salary. (Such incentives may involve a service agreement obliging the new hire to stay at the agency for a specified amount of time.)

In addition, some agencies can arrange for new hires who are experienced professionals to accrue leave at the same rate as federal employees with similar levels of experience. By contrast, experienced new hires at many agencies accrue leave at the same rate as entry-level newcomers.

To be eligible for a recruitment or relocation bonus, your opening must be designated as a hard-to-fill position or your hiring manager must be willing to have it designated as such. Hard-to-fill designations are based upon factors including current market conditions, the position's turnover rates and the success of the agency's recent recruitment efforts. For more information about recruitment bonuses, go to *opm.gov,* then click on the following sequence of links: "Employment & Benefits"..."Pay and Performance"..."Allowances & Bonuses" and finally either "Recruitment Bonuses" or "Relocation Bonuses."

Here are some leads on recruitment and relocation bonuses:

- The Central Intelligence Agency offers hiring bonuses worth up to $35,000 to some language experts.

- The National Security Agency (NSA) offers up to $7,500 in recruitment bonuses to new hires. NSA also covers college tuition for some types of major who agree to work at NSA after graduation.

- Agencies that have a history of awarding bonuses to some types of new hires include NASA, the Bureau of Labor Statistics and the Nuclear Regulatory Commission. For more information, check the employment sections of these agencies' websites.

- Some agencies, such as the NASA and the Nuclear Regulatory Commission, pay particularly high salaries to scientists and engineers.

- Some agencies that are under particular pressure to expand can hire employees under special, fast-track procedures. For example, when the Securities and Exchange Commission needed to quickly staff up in order to support its efforts to restore investor confidence, it hired accountants, economists and securities compliance examiners under streamlined procedures that enabled the agency to complete the hiring process in only a few weeks.

LET THE GAMES BEGIN: THE NEGOTIATION

When you are selected for a federal job, the selecting official or a human resources officer will probably invite you into the office to discuss an offer or give you an offer over the telephone. It is always more effective to negotiate in person than over the telephone, where facial cues are obscured. So if the hiring manager makes an offer over the telephone, express interest in the position; but don't commit. Make an appointment to discuss the position in person.

THE FACE TO FACE

Open your meeting with your hiring manager by mentioning how happy you were to receive an offer and by quickly reviewing several reasons why you and the position would make a good fit, and how you would add value to the organization.

Then go into negotiating mode. If you really do want this job, don't issue any ultimatums or outright demands. Instead, open the negotiation with a question.

ULTIMATUM OR DEMAND	NEGOTIATING QUESTION
Thanks for your offer, but it will really take at least one higher grade for me to take it.	I am so excited about the possibility of contributing my skills to this organization. But is there any flexibility or wiggle room in your offer?
I appreciate your offer. But I'm afraid that compensation might be a deal-breaker.	I'm excited about this job. I'd like to work out an agreement that would make both of us feel great. Do you have any room to negotiate?

NO FLEXIBILITY

If, by chance, your hiring manager responds by stating that there is no flexibility in the offer, you may *still* negotiate: How? First, emphasize concessions you are making. For example, mention that the job change would be a lateral transfer for you; or requires you to sacrifice vacation, sick leave or other benefits; or requires you to move to a location that has a higher cost of living than exists in your current home city.

Then, ask your hiring manager to consider evaluating you in six months if you take the job, and agreeing to give you a merit-based step increase or cash award if your performance is judged positively. (Be aware that agencies can grant an employee a cash award based upon a favorable rating. Such awards may total up to 10 percent of salary or up to 20 percent for exceptional performance.)

Even if, in the unlikely event, your hiring manager does not offer you any concessions, you've lost nothing just by asking for an opportunity to negotiate. And if nothing else, you have established yourself as an assertive, goal-oriented professional, and you have set the stage for your future requests for promotions.

YES, WE DO HAVE FLEXIBILITY!

Alternatively the hiring manager may respond to your invitation to negotiate by saying something like, "What did you have in mind?" Provided below are some possible responses that you can pick and choose from, as appropriate.

HOT • TIP

BODY LANGUAGE SPEAKS VOLUMES

When you negotiate, convey confidence with your body language and speaking style. Keep your posture slouch-free, maintain eye contact, keep your hands folded in your lap or on the table, smile, suppress nervous, jittery mannerisms, and don't speak too fast even though you probably want to get the negotiations over with as quickly as possible.

1. **Suppose you have received a competing offer:** Present documentation of your competing offer, and say, "I understand that the federal government usually matches reasonable competing offers for applicants. I am wondering whether you can match or come closer to this offer."

Alternatively, if your research has revealed that another federal agency is offering special recruitment incentives to people in your profession, ask whether the hiring manager can come closer to matching whatever the other agency is offering.

2. **Suppose you are a current government employee:** If you are currently eligible for a grade or step increase, cite the fact that you have earned eligibility for a promotion and you deserve it because of your superior performance. Support your claim by citing your achievements and objective validation of your success, as discussed in Chapter 6.

   If you are currently a government employee who is ineligible for a grade increase or step increase because you have not yet fulfilled your time-in-grade or step-in-grade requirements, ask your hiring manager if s/he can commit to giving you a grade increase, a merit-based step increase or a merit-based cash award when you do fulfill whatever time requirements are applicable to your situation.

3. **Suppose you have received bonuses on previous jobs:** Provide documentation of these awards. Cite these awards as evidence of your superior performance and evidence that your previous salary was underestimated by your previous base pay, which provided the basis for the hiring agency's salary offer.

4. **Suppose your qualifications exceed those of the grade you have been offered and match the upper end of your opening's grade range:** Show your hiring manager the position classification criteria for the higher grade that you deserve and explain how your qualifications satisfy those criteria.

One of the best kept secrets in government is that in many cases, all a hiring manager must do to increase the grade of an offer is justify the higher offer in writing to his/her senior management. By showing your hiring manager how your qualifications match the upper end of your opening's grade range, you will provide your hiring manager with grist for this pivotal written justification.

"I can only discuss salary and benefits. You'll have to analyze the babe situation yourself."

5. **Suppose you have truly superior qualifications:** The hiring agency can probably set your pay at a middle step — instead of at the lowest step — of your grade level. Present a justification of why your educational or work experience is superior and ask your hiring manager whether s/he is willing to use Superior Qualifications and Special Need Pay-Setting Authority. For more information about Superior Qualifications and Special Need Pay-Setting Authority, see *opm.gov/oca/pay/html/sqafacts. asp.*

6. **Suppose the job change would require you to move to a location that would increase your cost of living:** Document the difference between the cost of living of your current home city and that of your target job's location. Tell your hiring manager that you deserve a higher salary in order to help you offset the increased cost of living that the job transfer will impose on you.

7. **Suppose you are an experienced nongovernment employee:** Mention to your hiring manager that at some agencies, new hires who are experienced professionals accrue leave at the same rate as federal employees with similar levels of experience, instead of at the standard accrual rate for new hires. Ask if it would be possible for you to receive this same benefit. Strengthen your request by citing how much leave you will be sacrificing at your current job.

8. **Suppose you are currently a nongovernment employee who works in a high-demand profession:** Ask your hiring manager if it is possible for your position to be designated as a hard-to-fill position so that you may receive a recruitment bonus. (See box on Recruitment Bonuses on page 235.)

9. **Suppose you would like to receive scheduling flexibilities:** Ask your hiring manager whether the opening would be suitable for such arrangements.

10. **Suppose you are a new graduate:** Ask your hiring manager whether you are being given the agency's standard offer for new graduates. If so, point out, if appropriate, that your qualifications exceed those of the typical new graduate because of your exceptional academic record and significant relevant work experience. In addition, a college graduate whose major is directly related to the job may be able to negotiate a higher starting salary than one whose major is unrelated to the job. Also, the starting salary of a recent graduate with two masters degrees should exceed that of a recent graduate with only one masters degree.

11. **Suppose you are a new graduate who has outstanding student loans:** Ask your hiring manager for coverage in the agency's student loan repayment program. (See box at right on Student Loan Repayments.)

12. **Suppose you want to pursue a job-related degree:** Ask your hiring manager to reimburse you for the cost of the degree. Agencies can pay for training and education to improve an employee's performance of official duties, and may pay for education leading to an academic degree.

13. **Suppose you plan to drive to work:** Ask your hiring manager whether the agency can give you free parking. In some cities, this perk is worth several thousand dollars per year. Be creative: One new federal employee convinced her new boss to transfer to her the parking privileges of her predecessor so that she would not have to join the agency's waiting list for free parking.

> **HOT•TIP**
>
> **FOR RECENT GRADS: STUDENT LOAN REPAYMENTS**
>
> Under the Student Loan Repayment Program, agencies can repay up to $10,000 of an employee's academic debt per year, up to a total of $60,000. In return, the employee must agree to stay with the agency for at least three years.
>
> Although dozens of agencies offer student loan repayments, the most student loan repayments have traditionally been paid by the State Department, the Defense Department, the Securities and Exchange Commission, the Government Accountability Office and the Justice Department. For more information about the Student Loan Repayment Program, see *opm.gov/oca/PAY/StudentLoan/index.asp*.

SEALING THE DEAL

The hiring agency may pressure you to make a decision by emphasizing how eager everyone is to get someone into the position. Nevertheless, you are completely within your rights to ask for a day or two to consider any offer. You may also ask for a written offer letter.

HOT • TIP

ASK FOR A PROMOTION

Do you think that your boss will automatically give you a promotion when you deserve one…that it would be as rude to ask your boss for a promotion as it would be to ask a friend for a birthday gift…that promotions only come to those who don't ask for them?

Well think again. Remember that your boss's primary concern is probably not *your* well-being, but *his* or *her* own well-being. So if you have done a stellar job on a demanding project, put in a banner year or are handling increased responsibility, your boss may need a tactful reminder that you are due for some financial positive feedback.

Under the General Schedule (GS) pay plan, a supervisor can:

- Give a Quality Step Increase (QSI) to an employee who receives the highest possible rating on a performance review. A QSI moves the employee up one step within his/her grade before the required waiting period for a step increase has passed. (An employee can only receive one QSI per year.)

- Give a cash award worth up to 10 percent of annual salary to an employee who earns a favorable performance review or a cash award worth up to 20 percent of salary to an employee whose accomplishments significantly improve operations.

Under pay banding plans, supervisors generally have even more latitude for rewarding performance than under the GS pay plan.

Give your request for a performance reward extra umph by submitting a clear, cogent justification for why you deserve it. Don't assume that your boss remembers all of your successes and the positive feedback that they drew; itemize your successes in a bulleted list that incorporates the tips provided in Chapter 6 for describing achievements in impressive terms.

A particularly strategic time to remind your supervisor of your recent glories is before your annual performance review — in time for your supervisor to incorporate your list of successes into your review.

CHAPTER 13: RESPONDING TO AN AGENCY'S DECISION

If you don't hear from the hiring agency within about six weeks of submitting your resume or within a couple of weeks of interviewing for your target job, ask the opening's contact person or your interviewer about the status of your application.

YOU GOT THE JOB!

So you've received an offer! You won the jackpot…the grand slam…the ultimate prize. Give yourself a big fat slap on the back and go collect some high-fives from friends and relatives.

YOU WANT THE JOB

Sometimes, the decision over whether to accept an offer is a no-brainer. The job is a perfect fit for you, and you are chomping at the bit for it. But no matter how heavenly an offer may be, you should still consider negotiating your salary or other benefits; see Chapter 12 for tips on managing such negotiations without jeopardizing your offer.

You may also want to negotiate, within reason, other aspects of the deal, such as your start date. If, for example, you would like a few weeks before starting your new job to finish an important project on your current job or to take a well-deserved vacation, request such time from the hiring manager. (If you are currently a federal employee, your start date may also hinge upon the "release date" that your current agency agrees to.)

Here are some additional tips for what to say when you accept a job offer:

➠ Thank the hiring manager for the offer.

➠ Express excitement about the job, cite some of the factors that make it appealing and reaffirm your commitment to making first-rate contributions to the organization. You might say something like, "You made the right decision; I will make sure that you will be pleased that you selected me."

⟶ If the terms of the job are not provided to you in writing, you may: a) request such documentation; b) trust in your verbal agreement; or c) send the hiring manager a brief letter summarizing the terms of your agreement, including your start date, salary and title.

UNCERTAINTY

Although it is always flattering and ego-building to be selected for a job, do not reflexively accept a questionable job just because it was offered to you or because it represents a new opportunity. Change merely for the sake of change will not necessarily make you happier or advance your career. You should only accept a job because you *really* want it, or *really* need a source of income…now!

Yes, accumulating bills or the need "to get your foot in the door" might justifiably compel you to accept a questionable job — imperfect though it may be. But in such cases, at least be honest with yourself (but not necessarily with the hiring manager) about your needs, and extend your job-search accordingly.

But do not accept an unappealing job just to escape a current, unappealing job. By doing so, you will only go from the fire to the frying pan. After all, if a potential supervisor seriously rubs you the wrong way or the description of the job turns you off, the situation is unlikely to improve once you dive into the day-to-day drudgery of the job. Moreover, if you intend to keep looking for a better job, remember that the demands of a new job usually consume time and energy needed for job-searching.

If you feel undecided about an opening, more information about it might help you clinch your decision. If this is the case, when you talk to the hiring manager, thank him/her for the offer, express enthusiasm about the job, and then ask for a meeting during which you will be able to clarify a few points. If salary is the sticking issue, see Chapter 13 for tips on negotiating salary. Once you gather more information, ask the hiring manager for a day or two to finalize your decision, if you need it.

REJECTING AN OFFER

If the offer isn't right for you, let the hiring manager down courteously, quickly and graciously. Don't burn any bridges; you never know if you and the hiring manager's paths might cross again. Here are some tips for turning down an offer:

⟶ Thank the hiring manager for taking the time to interview you and for selecting you.
⟶ Cite something impressive about the organization.
⟶ Mention that you gave the offer much thought, and that turning it down was a tough decision for you.
⟶ Give a specific reason for turning down the offer, such as the salary, or leave your reasons vague by saying something like, "It wasn't the right fit for me right now."

IF AT FIRST YOU DON'T SUCCEED...

Success is the ability to go from failure to failure without losing your enthusiasm.
— Winston Churchill

If you are turned down for a job, do NOT take it personally; never regard your standing in a job competition as a referendum on your abilities, personality, smarts or career choices. As one recently rejected federal job applicant sensibly explained, "How can I take being turned down personally? Its not like the hiring managers *really* knew me or what I can do."

Moreover, take solace in the fact that almost everyone — no matter how successful they are — has, at one time or another, been rejected for a job that they just *knew* they were perfect for. Indeed, many of the roads to success are rutted with failures.

And even if you are rejected for a job that seemed like it was the BEST JOB IN THE WORLD, sooner or later, another equally exciting opportunity will almost certainly present itself.

KEEP ON KEEPING ON

Many job-searchers let their fear of failure derail their job search. Instead of rolling with the punches, they let rejections confirm their conviction that that they are destined to fail, and so they suspend their job search — sometimes indefinitely. They thereby succumb to a self-fulfilling prophecy: By stopping their job search, they guarantee that they will not find a job, and thereby further reinforce their poor self image.

THE POWER OF PERSISTANCE

If you recently experienced a professional disappointment, you are in good company. In fact, many of the most fabulously successful people have overcome setbacks that would have thwarted less determined people. For example:

- Screen writer Marc Cherry spent three staffing seasons without so much as an *interview*, let alone a job. He recently told *The Washington Post* that his spec script for the blockbuster hit *Desperate Housewives* had been "born of desperation" and was initially turned down by all four networks. But yesterday's desperado is today's Hollywood royalty. According to *The Washington Post*, Cherry now parks his Lexus (license plate: DSP HSWV) in his own reserved parking space.

- The Beatles were turned down by Capitol Records FOUR times before Capitol signed the group.

- *Chicken Soup for the Soul* is one of the best selling non-fiction books in US history. But the proposal for the book was rejected by more than 24 publishers before it was accepted for publication.

- It took Rowland Macy seven tries to get his department store off the ground.

- High jumper Dick Fosbury failed at conventional straddle jumping. So he pioneered the goofy-looking backwards "Fosbury Flop," and won a gold medal in the 1968 Olympics.

Remember: The quality that distinguishes many successful people from others is neither intelligence, talent nor luck, but sheer persistence. Successful, persistent professionals take setbacks in stride; instead of turning away from obstacles, they step around or over them. They incorporate any lessons that might be gleaned from setbacks into their strategies without losing their resolve, their determination, their self-confidence.

MAXIMIZING YOUR ODDS

Keep in mind that every federal agency, and even every office within every federal agency, is run by different people and follows different philosophies. Moreover, most job competitions are evaluated by different hiring mangers. So your rejection from one federal office will not affect your standing in a job competition in another federal office; it probably won't even affect your standing in another job competition within the same federal office.

But the raw reality is that no matter how impressive your application is, there will always be factors beyond your control that can nix your application. For example:

➠ Another applicant may have pivotal connections.

➠ Another applicant may have more experience or more relevant experience than you.

➠ A hiring manager may fail to review your application carefully.

➠ A hiring manager may have a quirky, personal bias against some aspect of your background.

➠ A hiring manager may have poor judgment, and be a bad judge of applicants' professional potential.

➠ Your target job may be cancelled because of budgetary or other reasons.

To a certain extent, hiring decisions are based on chance. You can always increase your odds by submitting an A+ application and giving an impressive interview. But no matter how hard you work on your application, you can never guarantee your success.

The best way to improve your odds in the job-searching numbers game is to apply to as many jobs as are appropriate for you. Moreover, the more logs you keep in the fire, the less disappointed you will be if any one of them burns out.

REEVALUATE YOUR APPROACH

If you are having trouble hitting employment paydirt, you would be wise to calmly and objectively reevaluate your strategy, and to — if possible — seek a fresh, objective perspective from a trusted source.

A case in point: A career expert at the Office of Personnel Management (OPM) recently explained to me that a job applicant had sought her advice because he had been rejected for over 200 federal jobs. The hapless applicant had no idea why he kept hitting dead ends. But when the OPM expert showed me his resume and KSAs — which were printed in tiny type and covered over 20 pages of unbroken text without so much as a paragraph break — the hopelessness

"I'm not against public service. I just think I can do more damage in the private sector."

of his application became painfully apparent. "It is normal for any professional to have to apply to a number of jobs in order to get hired by the federal government," the OPM expert commented. "But if someone has been rejected by hundreds of jobs, then they definitely need to take another look at their strategy."

Here are some ways to get fresh perspectives on your application:

➡ Call your interviewer and ask for candid suggestions on how you can improve your performance in future interviews.

➡ Check that you are qualified for your target jobs and not setting your sights too high.

➡ Ask friends, relatives and colleagues to give you honest feedback on your resumes and essays, and to practice interviewing with you. Incorporate any reasonable advice that you receive into your job searching strategy.

➡ Review the guidance on writing resumes, KSAs and cover letters and on interviewing provided in this book and on job-searching websites. Make sure that your job-searching documents and interviewing strategies measure up.

➡ Seek advice from a professional career counselor. Yes, such counseling will involve fees. But the real question is, can you afford NOT to pursue options that could advance your career?

Remember: Perseverance is a critical component of success. If you keep improving your application…keep plugging…and keep applying, you will eventually land a career-boosting job.

APPENDICES:

fpmi

APPENDIX 1:
TIP SHEET FOR VETERANS AND THEIR FAMILIES

APPENDIX 2:
TIP SHEET FOR APPLICANTS WITH DISABILITIES

APPENDIX 3: FORMATTIING TIPS

APPENDIX 4: GLOSSARY

APPENDIX 1: TIP SHEET FOR VETERANS AND THEIR FAMILIES

Veterans represent a highly qualified and motivated skill pool that must be tapped into if we are to maintain a high quality work force in the future...Our veterans have put their lives on the line for the freedom we enjoy in America. It is our responsibility to ensure they are given every opportunity to join the federal civil service when their military service concludes.

— Kay Coles James, previous Director of the Office of Personnel Management, which is the federal government's human resources agency (from the Office of Personnel Management website *www.opm.gov*)

The federal government is a very veteran-friendly employer:

☆ More than 450,100 veterans currently work for the federal government.

☆ Veterans account for about 20 percent of the federal work force, which is about double the rate in the private sector.

☆ The federal government is hiring increasing numbers of veterans. New veteran hires increased by more than 19 percent in 2002 alone, the last year for which figures are available. Such increases are partly due to programs that give veterans an edge in landing federal jobs. Federal agencies are currently particularly eager to hire women veterans.

COMPETITIVE APPPONTMENTS

These programs give veterans and some relatives of veterans an edge in landing jobs that are open for competition:

☆ **Veterans Preference:** Gives points to veterans on their ratings in merit-based competitions for federal jobs. These additional points often serve as the deciding factor in who gets hired.

- **Ten point veterans preference:** Typically given to a disabled veteran, a purple heart recipient, the mother of a veteran who died in active duty, the mother of a disabled veteran, and the spouse of certain disabled or deceased veterans.

- **Five point veterans preference:** Typically given to veterans who served on active duty for at least 2 years during a period of war or in a campaign or expedition for which a campaign badge was authorized.

Veterans preference is considered in competitions for most Competitive Service and Excepted Service jobs. But veterans preference is not considered in competitions for Senior Executive Service jobs or jobs that are only open to applicants who have Status. For more information about veterans preference, go to *opm.gov*, and then click on the following sequence of links: "Career Opportunities"…"Veterans"…"Veterans Preference." Alternatively, click on the Department of Labor's online advisor gizmo to compute your veterans preference points at *dol.gov/elaws/vetspref.htm*.

☆ **Reinstatement Eligibility:** Enables former federal employees to apply for jobs that are otherwise limited to current federal employees. For veterans and former career employees, reinstatement eligibility has no deadline; for others it lasts for three years after end of federal employment.

☆ **Veterans' Employment Opportunities Act of 1998 (VEOA):** Enables veterans to apply for some openings that are otherwise limited to current federal employees. (Veterans who are current federal employees or who have reinstatement eligibility are not eligible for VEOA jobs.)

NONCOMPETITIVE APPPONTMENTS

These programs enable qualified veterans to be appointed into federal jobs without competing against other applicants:

☆ **Reinstatement Eligibility:** Enables veterans to be appointed into positions at grades that are equal or lower than those previously held. For veterans and former career employees, reinstatement eligibility never expires; for others it expires three years after end of federal employment.

☆ **Veterans' Recruitment Appointment (VRA):** Enables veterans to be appointed into two-year temporary positions that are up to GS-11 or equivalent. (A GS-11 job is a mid-level position.) VRA appointments may be converted into permanent positions.

☆ **30 Percent or More Disabled Program:** Enables veterans to be appointed into temporary jobs that may be converted at any time into permanent positions. More positions are open under this program than under VRA.

If you are interested in landing a job under reinstatement eligibility, VEOA, VRA or the 30 Percent or More Disabled Program, contact the Human Resources Office where you are interested in working. You may also find openings that can be filled through these programs by conducting keyword searches using the program name as keywords on USAJOBS at *usajobs.opm.gov*, and by participating in job fairs.

Note that veterans are never guaranteed a job by any of these programs. To be hired, all applicants must meet, and usually exceed, the minimum requirements for the job.

MILITARY SPOUSE PREFERNCE

The spouses of active duty military members who move with their spouse to a new active duty station receive priority consideration for many types of federal jobs. For more information about military spouse preference, *see dod.mil/mapsite/spousepref.html.*

MORE RESOURCES

More information about employment opportunities for veterans is available from the following resources:

☆ The US Department of Labor's Veterans Employment and Training Service (VETS) site. This site broadcasts information about jobs and on-the-job rights for veterans. See *dol.gov/vets/welcome.html.* Among the site's features is the e-law advisor, which helps veterans identify the veterans preferences to which they are entitled. See *dol.gov/elaws/vetspref.htm.*

☆ Facts sheets on veterans and federal employment. To access these fact sheets, go to *opm.gov*, and click on the following sequence of links: "Career Opportunities" ... "Veterans."

☆ The Department of Veterans Affairs, Vocational Rehabilitation & Employment Service. The Department offers help in finding employment as well as various training programs and can direct you to employers who want to hire veterans. Also be aware that some federal agencies recruit veterans from lists of veteran job seekers provided by the Department of Veterans Affairs. For more information, contact your state Veterans Affairs office or see *vba.va.gov/bln/vre.*

☆ The Army Materiel Command (AMC) "Always a Soldier" website. This site helps match disabled veterans from all branches of the service with jobs throughout the US. See *amccareers.com/ww1/wwhome.php*.

☆ The website of Transition Assistance Online. See *taonline.com*. This site provides free career guidance to separating military service members, retirees, veterans, spouses and dependents, Department of Defense employees and others. The site boasts 12,000 jobs announcements from federal and private sector employers who want to hire members of the military community.

ON YOUR APPLICATION...

☆ Some vacancy announcements invite applications under more than one veterans program, such as veterans preference and the Veterans Recruitment Appointment. To maximize your chances, be sure to state on your application all of the relevant programs for which you qualify.

☆ Are you a current or former federal employee with veterans preference who is applying for a federal job that is open to the public? If so, you can apply for the job under competitive procedures or merit promotion procedures. Which option is better? While competitive procedures would allow you to use your veterans preference, merit promotion procedures would not. (See Glossary for definitions of competitive procedures and merit promotion procedures.) But beware that if you are hired under competitive procedures, you must undergo a one-year probationary period that you would otherwise avoid under merit promotion procedures. If you can and want to be covered by competitive procedures, specifically say so on your application; otherwise the hiring agency may assume that you want to be covered by merit promotion procedures.

☆ According to a recent report on veterans in the federal work force, veterans can improve their hiring prospects by: 1) Avoiding or defining acronyms and other descriptive terms that are commonly used in the military but are unfamiliar to civilians. 2) Specifically explaining what skills they gained in the military — rather than just identifying their rank. A platoon sergeant, for example, should explain how his or her military training and assignments improved his or her leadership skills, ability to make decisions quickly, or skill in communicating with people of diverse backgrounds. 3) Submitting all documents required for receiving veterans preference, such as a DD-214 form providing proof of military service and a certificate of disability rating from the Veterans Affairs Department, if appropriate. CAUTION: Applicants using automated application systems often forget to submit these documents or don't offer enough information when submitting them to ensure that they are matched to their electronic applications.

APPENDIX 2: TIP SHEET FOR APPLICANTS WITH DISABILITIES

I have been employed at the U.S. Department of Education since 1987.... I am blind and use a computer equipped with a screen reader with speech output to enable me to review and edit the work of my staff... With the advent of accessible computer technology, I now find that I am as efficient and productive as any employee with sight ... I do not believe my disability is a barrier to my success on the job.

— Roseann Ashby, Chief, Basic State Grants Branch Rehabilitation Services Administration
(from the Office of Personnel Management website *www.opm.gov*)

The federal government currently employs more than 120,000 disabled workers and almost 20,000 severely disabled workers. These numbers are steadily growing.

Disabled applicants may be hired for federal jobs through the same competitive procedures as nondisabled applicants. But disabled applicants may also be hired through noncompetitive Schedule A Appointments. Under a noncompetitive Schedule A Appointment, a federal agency simply appoints an eligible disabled person to any position for which they are qualified without considering other qualified candidates. This approach involves minimal red tape for the agency and the applicant, and helps the federal government fulfill its obligation to hire thousands of disabled people in the coming years.

GET CERTIFIED

To be considered for a noncompetitive Schedule A Appointment, you must have a severe physical disability, psychiatric disability and/or be mentally retarded. You must also have a certification statement that identifies you as a person with a disability and that describes your ability to perform the essential duties of the position in which you are interested. To get this certification, contact a state vocational rehabilitation agency or Gallaudet University's placement office in Washington DC; or if you are veteran, contact a Department of Veteran's Affairs Vocational Rehabilitation Counselor.

Good news! A regulatory change that is currently in the works will permit agencies to self-certify that an applicant has a mental or physical handicap and is employable, without requiring the applicant to be certified by vocational agencies, the Veterans Administration or Gallaudet.

FIND OPENINGS

Some federal agencies do not advertise some openings that they want to fill with disabled applicants. Instead, they may recruit for these openings via methods that target disabled applicants. Once you get certified, you may find these openings by contacting the Selective Placement Coordinator or the equivalent at a federal agency where you wish to work. These Coordinators stay current on job openings for disabled job seekers, including unadvertised openings. To access a list of Coordinators, click on the following sequence of links on USAJOBS at *usajobs.opm.gov:* "Federal Employment of People with Disabilities"…"Applicants and Employees"…"Selective Placement Coordinators."

Some federal agencies recruit applicants with disabilities from state vocational rehabilitation agencies. Therefore, you may find some unadvertised federal openings by contacting your state agency. To access a list of vocational rehabilitation agencies, go to the Social Security Administration's Work Site at *ssa.gov/work,* and then click on "Service Providers" and then "List of State Rehabilitation Providers."

Some agencies also recruit people with disabilities by advertising openings through organizations such as the American Association for People with Disabilities, Easter Seals and The Arc.

You may also apply to vacancy announcements posted on the USAJOBS website at *usajobs.opm.gov.* USAJOBS works with screen reading software like JAWS (Job Access with Speech). And if you are using Internet Explorer, you can increase the font size of USAJOBS screens.

You may also obtain vacancy announcements posted on USAJOBS by telephone on the federal government's jobs hotline at 703-724-1850 or TDD at 978-461-8404.

REASONABLE ACCOMMODATION

The law requires the federal government to make reasonable accommodations for a worker's disabilities. Examples of reasonable accommodation including providing interpreters, readers or other personal assistance, modifying job duties, restructuring work sites, and providing alternative work schedules and/or work-at-home options. Hiring agencies will also provide special accommodations to help disabled applicants take tests or be interviewed for openings if they are asked to do so.

IF YOU ARE A VETERAN

If you are a veteran, see Appendix 1 to determine if you are also eligible for any veterans programs.

ON YOUR APPLICATION...

☆ If you want to be considered for a job opening under a noncompetitive Schedule A Appointment, be sure to say so in the cover letter of a paper application, and in an electronic application. Although you are not required to do so, you may provide assurance in your cover letter that you could get the job done with reasonable accommodation.

You will probably want to begin your cover letter just like any other applicant for a competitive appointment. See Chapter 9 for more instruction on writing cover letters. But after you identify your target job, and review your credentials, you could say something like this:

Please consider me for the [name of the position goes here] opening under a noncompetitive Schedule A Appointment because I am deaf. I assure you that I am a top-notch producer, and I could perform the job effectively; my certification letter is attached. I can communicate articulately as long as I have an interpreter for meetings and telephone calls.

I have a solid record as a team-player. My contributions to group projects are reflected in my successful completion of [cite specific types of projects you completed and objective validation of your success, as discussed in Chapter 6].

I would be happy to show you my portfolio of work and discuss my communication abilities in person. My references can verify my skills, positive attitude and reputation as a team player, as well.

☆ In job interviews, employers are technically restricted by law to asking if the applicant can do the job, and in some cases, to asking the applicant for an illustration of how s/he does so. Nevertheless, you are certainly permitted to answer the unspoken questions that may loom large in the interviewer's mind. For an excellent article on how to address disabilities in interviews, see *quintcareers.com/disabled_job_strategies.html*.

☆ You may also ask your references to specifically discuss your disability with potential employers and provide additional validation of your on-the-job effectiveness.

MORE RESOURCES

☆ For internship programs for disabled college and graduate students and recent graduates, see Chapter 3.

☆ For the federal government's fact sheets on people with disabilities and federal employment, see *opm.gov/disability/appempl. asp.*

☆ See *Job Hunting for the So-Called Handicapped or People Who Have Disabilities* by Richard Nelson Bolles and Dale Susan Brown. This book will guide you through rights guaranteed by the Americans with Disabilities Act and provides insightful job-hunting tips. (Bolles also wrote the blockbuster job-hunting book, *What Color is Your Parachute?*)

☆ The websites of some agencies have special sections devoted to people with disabilities. To find them, conduct searches on Internet search engines using the name of the agency that interests you, along with other keywords such as *employment* and *people with disabilities.*

HOT • TIP

AGENCIES THAT HAVE GOOD TRACK RECORDS

• **The Department of Defense (DOD) — which has won accolades from *Careers and the Disabled* magazine for its commitment to recruiting, hiring and promoting people with disabilities — aims to increase the percentage of disabled employees in its work force from 1 percent to 2 percent. With more than 600,000 employees working at more than 6,000 locations, DOD offers a wealth of opportunities.**

• **In 2004, the Homeland Security Department launched an initiative to hire more people with disabilities.**

• **The Treasury, Agriculture and Veterans Affairs Departments have particularly good track records in disability hiring.**

☆ For the US Labor Department's comprehensive federal website that provides one-stop access to governmental disability information, see *disabilityinfo.gov.*

☆ The federal government's Computer/Electronic Accommodations Program (CAP), provides assistive technology and services free of charge for employees at more than 50 federal agencies. See *tricare.osd.mil/cap.* The CAP website also posts updates on federal disability hiring, and provides links to other sites addressing federal opportunities for people with disabilities.

☆ *Careers and the Disabled* magazine, which provides insightful job-searching articles. See *eop.com/ cd.html.*

APPENDIX 3: FORMATTING TIPS

As discussed in Chapter 8, WHAT STANDS OUT ON THE PAGE IS WHAT STANDS WILL STAND OUT IN THE READER'S mind. In order to make your most important credentials leap off the page and into the reader's mind, you must use effective formatting techniques. This appendix provides tips for attractively formatting your documents in Microsoft WORD and in automated applications systems. Note that all of the formatting features incorporated into the resumes included in the CD accompanying this book are explained here.

FORMATTING TEXT IN AUTOMATED APPLICATION SYSTEMS

As discussed in Chapter 5, most automated application systems do not accommodate formatting options such as bold, bullets, various font types and sizes, and shading. Although you can write your unformatted document in an automated application system, it is better to create and edit it in another program and then copy it into the automated application system. That way you can revise your document until you are satisfied with it, and keep a copy of it for future use.

The best way to create unformatted text that will be accepted by an automated application system is to create the text in an ASCII file. (ASCII is short for American Standard Code for Information Exchange.) You can create an ASCII document by saving a Microsoft WORD document in a "Text Only" format under the "Save As" option.

Make your document as readable as possible by:

☆ Creating horizontal lines before or after headings, and between document sections by repeating a keyboard character, such as a tilde (~), plus sign (+), minus sign (-), equal sign (=), period (.), or a lower case "o".

☆ Creating bullets using asterisks or another keyboard character. Follow each bullet with two or three spaces; do not use tabs because they are not accommodated by most automated application systems.

☆ Aligning each heading next to the left margin. Do not try to center text.

☆ Emphasizing headings and important information by using capital letters.

☆ Emphasizing headings by skipping a line before and after each heading.

☆ Creating spaces by using the space bar — not tabs.

☆ Using white space liberally.

☆ Limiting each line to a maximum of 60 characters. Note that characters include spaces and punctuation marks. It is important to limit your line to 60 characters because most automated application systems limit lines to between 60 to 70 characters, depending upon the system. Use the character counter function in WORD to help you limit each line to 60 characters. If you exceed the maximum number of characters per line, your document will incorporate line breaks in odd places. As a result, some lines will inevitably have only a few words followed by large empty spaces. This will obscure your bullets, and make your document generally hard to read.

☆ Using a hard return by hitting the "Enter" key before you reach 60 characters at the end of each line. Do not use word wrap.

☆ Writing in short paragraphs.

☆ Proofreading your document.

☆ Testing the appearance of your document by pasting it into an e-mail, and e-mailing it to yourself.

These formatting techniques are incorporated into the sample ASCII resume provided on the next page. By incorporating these formatting techniques into resumes and KSAs that you submit via automated application systems, you can help emphasize your most important credentials as well as break up the monotony and relieve the density of your text. You will thereby improve the allure and readability of your text.

When you are satisfied with the text of your ASCII resume or KSAs, copy and paste your text into the automated application system. Be sure to save a copy for yourself! Note that if you do write your document directly into an automated application system, you should cut and paste it into a Word document or another type of word processing document, spell check it in WORD, and then cut and paste it back into the automated application.

```
============================================================

JANE SMITH

============================================================

1234 Yellow Brick Road; City, State, ZIP Code
Work: (123) 123-567
Home: (123) 123-4567
E-Mail: Jsmith@Email.com
Social Security Number:  000-00-0000
U.S. Citizen


++++++++++++++++++++++++++++++
SUMMARY OF QUALIFICATIONS
++++++++++++++++++++++++++++++

   *  AWARD-WINNING CONTRACT MANAGER:  Seven years of
experience in managing multi-year, multi-million dollar
contracts for large federal agencies.

   *  REGULATORY EXPERT

   *  POLISHED COMMUNICATOR

   *  B.A. in ECONOMICS


++++++++++++++++++++++++++++++
PROFESSIONAL EXPERIENCE
++++++++++++++++++++++++++++++

SENIOR CONTRACT SPECIALIST:  May 2000 to Present
ENVIRONMENTAL PROTECTION AGENCY (EPA)
Office of the Chief Information Officer
1200 Pennsylvania Avenue, NW Washington DC  20460
Salary:  $66,229 (GS-13/Step 1) (1102 Series)
40 hours per week
Supervisor: Mike Jones (You may contact at 101-111-1111)

   *  Authorized to award contracts for goods and services
worth up to $5 million without additional approvals.

   *  Serve as technical advisor to senior EPA officials,
including the Chief Financial Officer, on developing
streamlined procedures for conducting pre-award cost
analyses; planning, negotiating and soliciting contracts;
and managing and closing out contracts.

   *  Advise program managers on cradle-to-grave
acquisition planning, including preparing Statement of
Works (SOW); conducting market research of vendors;
and researching contractors' capabilities for
handling government contracts.

   *  Lead team of six EPA Contract Specialists who
procure Information Technology (IT) support and services
worth approximately $6 million annually.
```

TO ADD SPECIAL CHARACTERS

The diamonds in the resume header below are an example of a special character.

Jane Doe

Apt 723 ✦ 2001 Veazey Terrace NW ✦ Washington DC 20008
(123) 123-4567 (W) ✦ (012) 123-4567 (H) ✦ E-Mail: JaneDoe@email.com

STEPS TO ADD SPECIAL CHARACTERS:

1. Access the "Insert" pull-down menu.
2. Select "Symbol."
3. Click on the symbol you would like to select.
4. Click "Insert."
5. Click "Close."

TO CREATE SMALL CAPS

Small caps provide an excellent device for setting off the name of an employer in a resume. For example, the words "SIECOR OEPRATIONS LLC" in the line below appear in small caps.

Inquiry Resource Coordinator; SIECOR OPERATIONS LLC — Hickory, NC 1996-1998

STEPS TO CREATE SMALL CAPS:

1. Select the text that you want to appear in small caps.
2. Access the "Format" menu.
3. Select "Fonts."
4. Click on "Small caps" under "Effects.".
5. Click "OK."

TO CREATE BULLETED AND NUMBERED LISTS

Capitalize each item in a bulleted list. If each item in a list consists of a word or just a few words, don't punctuate listed items with periods. If each listed item is a sentence, end each item with a period. Use numbers when rank or sequence is important. Use bullets when rank or sequence is not important.

STEPS TO FORMAT AND POSITION BULLETS:

1. Select text to be bulleted.
2. In your toolbar, access the "Format" pull-down menu.
3. In the pull-down menu, select "Bullets and Numbering."
4. At the top of the menu box, select "Bulleted."
5. Select the desired symbol for bullets from menu box options.
6. At the bottom right of the menu box, select "Customize."
7. At the left side of the customized bulleted list menu box, fill in numbers for "Bullet Position" and "Text Position." To position bullets flush with the left margin, select "0" for "Bullet Position," and a higher number, such as .3 for "Text Position." The higher the numbers selected for "Bullet Position" and "Text Position," the further bullets and accompanying text will be indented from the left margin.
8. Select "Font" in the middle of the Customized Bulleted List menu box if you want to adjust the font or size of bullets or bold bullets. Bullets should usually be about the same sized fonts as the text they accompany.
9. Select "OK."

STEPS TO CREATE A BULLETED LIST INSIDE OF ANOTHER BULLETED LIST:

1. Complete steps 1- 5.
2. Select a different symbol for sub-bullets than bullets.
3. Specify higher numbers for "Bullet Position" and "Text Position" for sub-bullets than selected for bullets, such as .3 and .6 respectively.
4. Select "OK."

STEPS TO FORMAT NUMBERED LISTS:

Follow the same steps as those for formatting and positioning bullets — except at step #4, select "Numbered" in the "Bullets and Numbering" pull-down menu.

TO CREATE AND MANIPULATE TABLES

You may want to include a Your Needs/My Skills table in your cover letter.

STEPS TO CREATE A TABLE:

1. On the toolbar, access the "Table" menu.
2. In the pull-down menu, click "Insert Table."
3. Enter the number of columns and rows that you want your table to have.

4. Adjust the sizes of the table's columns and rows by clicking on gridlines and moving them.
5. Bullet items in the table's cells.
6. Bold the table's headings.

STEPS TO DELETE A TABLE AND ITS CONTENTS:

1. Click inside the table.
2. On the toolbar, click on the "Table" menu.
3. Point to "Delete."
4. Click "Table."

STEPS TO DELETE A ROW OR COLUMN OF A TABLE:

1. Click inside the table.
2. On the toolbar, click on the "Table" menu.
3. Point to "Delete."
4. Click "Row" or "Column," as appropriate.

STEPS TO REMOVE A BORDER FROM A TABLE:

1. On the toolbar, click the "Table" menu.
2. On the pull-down menu, click Table Autoformat.
3. Click "None" in the "Formats" Box.

TO ADJUST A DOCUMENT'S MARGINS

STEPS TO ADJUST A DOCUMENT'S MARGINS:

1. From your toolbar, select the "File" pull-down menu.
2. In the pull-down menu, select "Page Setup."
3. In the lower, right side of your menu box, click "Margins."
4. To create ample white-space with your margins, set the top, bottom, right and left margins to one inch.
5. At the bottom of your menu box, click "OK."

TO CREATE HORIZONTAL LINES ACROSS THE PAGE

You can sandwich text, such as a heading in a resume or KSA, between various types of lines — some of which are showcased below.

CREATING DOUBLE HORIZONTAL LINES

CREATING DOUBLE HORIZONTAL LINES

CREATING DOUBLE HORIZONTAL LINES

CREATING DOUBLE HORIZONTAL LINES

STEPS TO SANDWICH TEXT BETWEEN LINES:

1. Select the text that you want lined. If you want the sandwich lines to extend across the entire page, make the selected area extend beyond the last letter in the text that you want lined. Alternatively, if you want the lines to end where the text ends, end the selected area where the text ends.
2. In your toolbar, access the "Format" pull-down menu.
3. In the pull-down menu, select "Borders and Shading."
4. On the top of your menu box, select "Borders."
5. Under "Setting" in your menu box, select "Custom."
6. Under "Style" in your menu box, specify a style.
7. On the right side of your menu box under "Preview," select the icon representing a line positioned above your selected text, and the icon representing a line positioned below your selected text.
8. At the bottom of your menu box, click "OK."
9. Justify or center the text between the lines just as you would justify or center text that is not sandwiched between lines.

STEPS TO CREATE A SINGLE HORIZONTAL LINE UNDER TEXT:

1. Complete Steps #1 through #6 from "Steps to Sandwich Text Between Lines" as explained above.
2. On the right side of your menu box under "Preview," select the icon representing a line positioned below your selected text.
3. At the bottom of your menu box, click "OK."
4. Justify or center the text.

STEPS TO CREATE A SINGLE HORIZONTAL LINE WITHOUT TEXT:

1. Hit the "Shift" key.
2. While keeping down the "Shift" key, hit the dash key (the key next to the zero key) at least three times.
3. Release the "Shift" key.
4. Hit the "Enter" key.

TO SHADE TEXT

You can emphasize text, such as a heading in a resume or KSA, by shading it.

STEPS TO SHADE TEXT:

1. Select the text on the line that you want shaded. If you want the shading to extend across the entire line, extend the selected area beyond the last letter of the text. Alternatively, if you want the shading to end where the text ends, end the selected area where the text ends.
2. In your toolbar, access the "Format" pull-down menu.
3. In the pull-down, select "Borders and Shading."
4. On the top of your menu box, select "Borders."
5. At the top part of your menu box, select "Shading."
6. On the left side of your menu box under "Fill", select the "fill" box representing the desired darkness of your shading.
7. At the bottom of your menu box, click "OK."
8. Justify or center shaded text just as you would justify or center text that is not shaded.

TO SHADE AND SANDWICH TEXT BETWEEN LINES

You can shade text, and sandwich the shaded text between various types of lines — some of which are showcased below.

SHADED AND SANDWICHED TEXT BETWEEN LINES

SHADED AND SANDWICHED TEXT BETWEEN LINES

SHADED AND SANDWICHED TEXT BETWEEN LINES

SHADED AND SANDWICHED TEXT BETWEEN LINES

STEPS TO SHADE AND SANDWICH TEXT:

1. Select the text that you want shaded and sandwiched. If you want the shading and sandwiching to extend across the entire line, extend the selected area beyond the last letter of the text. Alternatively, if you want the shading and sandwiching to end where the text ends, end the selected area where the text ends.
2. In your toolbar, access the "Format" pull-down menu.
3. In the pull-down menu, select "Borders and Shading."
4. On the top of your menu box, select "Borders."
5. At the top of your menu box, select "Shading."
6. On the left side of your menu box under "Fill," select the "fill" box representing the desired darkness of your shading.
7. At the bottom of your menu box, click "OK."

TO ERASE LINES AND SHADING

There are several ways to erase lines and shading. Use the steps below to erase lines and/or shading that you have just created:

1. Select the box, shading or line to be erased.
2. In your toolbar, access the "Edit" pull-down menu.
3. In the pull-down menu, select undo "borders and shading."

Alternatively, you can erase lines and/or shading by accessing the Borders and Shading menu and selecting the "No Fill" option for shading and the "None" option for borders.

TO EXPAND THE SPACING BETWEEN LETTERS IN A HEADING

You can emphasize a heading by expanding the spaces between its letters. Here are the steps for doing so:

1. Select the text that you would like to expand.
2. From your toolbar, select the "Format" pull-down menu.
3. In the pull-down menu, select "Font."
4. In the pull-down menu next to "Spacing," select "Expanded."
5. In the adjacent box next to the word "by," insert a number.
6. Click "OK."

TO CREATE BORDERS AROUND EACH PAGE

STEPS TO CREATE BORDERS AROUND EACH PAGE:

1. From your toolbar, select the "Format" pull-down menu.
2. In the pull-down menu, select "Borders and Shading."
3. On the top of the menu box, click on the "Page Border" tab.
4. In the "Style" box, select the desired style of your borders.
5. If you do not want your pages bordered by four lines, click on the lines in the picture in the preview box that would like to remove.

STEPS TO ERASE BORDERS AROUND EACH PAGE:

1. From your toolbar, select the "Format" pull-down menu.
2. In the pull-down menu, select "Borders and Shading."
3. On the top of the menu box, click on the "Page Border" tab.
4. In the "Setting" box, select "none."
5. At the bottom of your menu box, click "OK."

SPACE-SAVING TIP

You can save space by changing the size of lines between items in bulleted or numbered lists, and by changing the size of lines before or after headings to an 8-point font.

STEPS TO SHRINK THE SIZE OF A LINE:

1. Select each line that you would like to condense.
2. Acess the "Format" pull-down menu from the toolbar.
3. Click on "Font."
4. Change the font size to "8."
5. Click "OK."

MAKE LONG LISTS READABLE

Short lists are always easier to skim and remember than long lists. So by using headings to break up long lists of training courses or other credentials that are included in your KSAs or resumes, you will make them easier to skim and remember.

The power of this principle is demonstrated by the two lists of training courses provided below. These lists contain the exact same titles of training courses. Isn't List #2, which is segemented into sublists with headings, easier to skim and remember than List #1, which is long and unbroken?

LIST #1: LONG, UNBROKEN LIST

TRAINING COURSES

- PowerPoint — January 2002
- Using Spreadsheets — November 2001
- Direct Marketing Math & Finance Seminar — November 2001
- High Impact Business Writing — October 2001
- Public Speaking – September 2001
- Mediation and Conflict Management Skills — January 2001
- Project Management Principles — March 2001
- Crash Course in Direct Marketing — September 2000
- Making Direct Mail Easy — August 2000
- Creative Problem Solving — August 1999
- Diversity Training — October 1997
- Dispute Resolution — October 1997
- Personal Strategies for Navigating Change — June 1997
- Windows 95 — December 1996
- Fundamentals of Writing — February 1996
- Notetaking — September 1995

LIST #2: LIST BROKEN UP WITH SUB-HEADINGS

TRAINING COURSES

Management
- Project Management Principles — March 2001
- Creative Problem Solving — August 1999
- Diversity Training — October 1997
- Personal Strategies for Navigating Change — June 1997

Marketing
- Direct Marketing Math & Finance Seminar — November 2001
- Crash Course in Direct Marketing — September 2000
- Making Direct Mail Easy — August 2000

Conflict Resolution
- Mediation and Conflict Management Skills — January 2001
- Dispute Resolution — October 1997

Communication
- High Impact Business Writing — October 2001
- Public Speaking – September 2001
- Fundamentals of Writing — February 1996

Software
- PowerPoint — January 2002
- Using Spreadsheets — November 2001
- Windows 95 — December 1996
- Note-taking — September 1995

APPENDIX 4: GLOSSARY

Appointment: A federal job. Each federal job is filled either through a competitive appointment or noncompetitive appointment.

Basic Qualifications or Minimum Qualifications: The criteria that applicants must meet in order to be seriously considered for the job. Applications that don't meet these qualifications are summarily rejected.

Best Qualified Applicant: An applicant who has made the certification list in a job competition.

Career Appointment: Permanent federal position earned by completing a career-conditional appointment. It usually takes three years to progress from a career-conditional appointment to a career appointment. Career status confers lifetime reinstatement eligibility if the employee leaves the government. In addition, it is harder to fire or lay off career employees than career-conditional employees.

Career-Conditional Appointment: Given to most new employees in the Competitive Service. The first year of service in a career conditional appointment in the Competitive Service is a probationary period. Usually after serving three continuous years in a career conditional appointment, an employee automatically receives a career appointment.

Career Transition Assistance and Special Selection Priority (CTAP): Program that gives selection priority to displaced federal employees for some job openings in their own agencies before their federal employment ends.

Certification List: A list of most qualified or best qualified candidates that is developed either by a peer review panel or an automated hiring system during a competitive examination for a federal job. The certification is given to the selecting official who makes a final selection. In government lingo, people who are listed on the certification, "made the cert."

Civil Service: Includes the Competitive Service, the Excepted Service and the Senior Executive Service.

Civil Service Laws: Laws designed to ensure that hiring is strictly merit-based. Civil Service laws apply to all jobs in the Competitive Service. The Office of Personnel Management establishes regulations for implementing Civil Service laws. Jobs in the Excepted Service are specifically exempted from Civil Service laws.

Closing Date: The non-negotiable deadline for applications for federal jobs. Late applications are almost always summarily rejected. But note that some applications must be received by the closing date, and some applications must only be postmarked by the closing date. In addition, agencies sometimes extend the closing date if a sufficient number of applications are not submitted by the original closing date.

Competitive Appointment: A federal job that is filled through a merit-based competition, also known as a competitive examination.

Competitive Examination: A merit-based competition that is used to screen applications for federal jobs that are open for competition. In a competitive examination, applications are rated with a numerical score based upon merit and veterans preference and then ranked; the applicant who is judged most qualified for the position is selected. (These days, most competitive examinations do not involve tests.) Most jobs posted on USAJOBS are screened through competitive examinations. The traditional method for entering the federal government is by an appointment through the competitive examining process. For more information about federal screening methods used in competitive examinations, see Chapter 5.

Competitive Procedures: Procedures used to process applications of applicants who do not have civil service status. Under competitive procedures, applicants may use their veterans preference. But applicants hired under competitive procedures must undergo a one-year probationary period that is not required under merit promotion procedures. (For more information, see Merit Promotion Procedures.)

Competitive Service: Includes all jobs covered by federal Civil Service law. (Civil Service laws are designed to keep hiring procedures strictly merit-based.) Competitive Service jobs are filled through competitive examining procedures. All federal jobs that are not in the Competitive Service have been specifically exempted from civil service laws and are in the Excepted Service. Personnel regulations for Competitive Service jobs are set by the Office of Personnel Management.

Competitive Status: See "Status."

Contact Person: Person identified on a vacancy announcement who answers questions about the job opening.

Direct Hire Authority: Special streamlined procedures used to quickly fill openings when there is a severe shortage of candidates or when there is a critical mission need.

Excepted Service: Includes all jobs exempted from Civil Service laws. Excepted Service jobs can be filled via more flexible procedures than jobs in the Competitive Service. Agencies set their own qualification requirements and salary rules for Excepted Service jobs, but some Exempted Service agencies do follow some Office of Personnel Management regulations. Excepted Service jobs include:

- All political positions in the federal government.

- All jobs in federal agencies that are filled through special appointments instead of through competitive examining procedures.

- Some categories of jobs in all federal agencies, such as attorneys, chaplains, doctors, dentists and nurses.

- All jobs in some federal agencies, including the Central Intelligence Agency, Foreign Service, Federal Bureau of Investigation, State Department and Postal Service. To access a list of Excepted Service agencies, go to *opm.gov*, and then click on the following sequence of links: "Career Opportunities" ... "Job FAQs" ... "Exempted Agencies."

- Some jobs in the Department of Veterans Affairs and Department of Defense.

- Most jobs on Congressional staffs and in the Judiciary.

The classification of some federal jobs can change. For example, when a competitive job is filled through a noncompetitive appointment under a special hiring authority, it becomes an excepted job. If this excepted job is then filled again through a competitive appointment, it converts back into a competitive job.

Executive Core Qualifications (ECQs): Qualifications required for obtaining a Senior Executive Service (SES) job. Essays addressing ECQs are required in applications for SES jobs. Note that ECQs are very similar to KSAs.

Federal Wage System: The personnel and salary scale for blue-collar federal employees. This scale is based upon prevailing local rates for similar work in private industry.

Federal Resume: Type of resume required for applying for jobs in federal agencies. Federal resumes are required to contain more information than standard resumes. For more information about federal resumes, see Chapter 8.

Foreign Service: Helps design and support US foreign policy from Washington DC and about 265 international posts. The Foreign Service runs all US embassies, consulates and other diplomatic missions.

The Foreign Service's admissions process incorporates some of the most rigorous testing in federal hiring. (Think Uncle Sam's version of *Survivor*.) This process involves a written exam, a day of interviews and oral exams, as well as medical and security screenings. The entire process takes about one year.

More information about the Foreign Service is posted on the employment section of *state.gov*, and is available from various unofficial sources, such as Yahoo's Foreign Service Written Exam Group at *http://groups.yahoo.com/group/fswe*.

General Schedule (GS) Pay: The pay scale for most white-collar jobs in the federal government. GS positions range from GS-1 to GS-15. For more information about federal salaries, see Chapter 12.

Interagency Career Transition Assistance Plan (ICTAP): Program that gives selection priority for some federal job openings to displaced federal employees after their federal employment has ended. See *usajobs.opm.gov/ei32.asp*.

Knowledge, Skills and Abilities (KSAs): Main criteria by which your application will be judged. See Chapter 7. Most applications for federal jobs must include essays addressing KSAs.

Locality Pay: Special pay increases that apply to federal workers in cities with high costs of living, such as New York City, San Francisco and Washington DC.

Merit Promotion Procedures: Procedures used to process the job applications of most current or former federal employees — usually into higher grade positions; specifically, merit promotion procedures apply to applicants who have status or who have reinstatement eligibility.

When competition for a federal job is limited to status candidates, only merit promotion procedures operate. But when competition for a federal job is also open to members of the public, merit promotion procedures and competitive procedures operate. The main differences between merit promotion procedures and competitive procedures are listed in the table below.

	MERIT PROMOTION PROCEDURE	**COMPETITIVE PROCEDURES**
COVERAGE	• Applicants with status. • Applicants with reinstatement eligibility.	• All applicants who have no federal experience. • All applicants who have status or reinstatement eligibility and opt to be covered under competitive procedures.
VETERANS PREFERENCE	Veterans preference does not count. Applicants who are rated and ranked under merit promotion procedures do not gain points for veterans preference.	Veterans preference counts. Applicants who are rated and ranked under competitive promotion procedures may gain points for veterans preference.
PROBATION PERIOD, IF HIRED	No probation if applicant is hired.	One-year probation period if applicant is hired.

Are you a current or former federal employee with veterans preference who is applying for a federal job that is open to the public? If so, be aware that you may apply for the job under Competitive Procedures instead of merit promotion procedures.

What are the potential advantages of this approach? Under Competitive Procedures you can use your veterans preference, which is not accommodated by merit promotion procedures. But beware that if you are hired under Competitive Procedures, you must undergo a one-year probationary period that you would otherwise avoid under merit promotion procedures. If you can and want to use this option, specifically say so on your application; otherwise the hiring agency will probably automatically cover you under merit promotion procedures.

Noncompetitive Appointment: A federal job that is not filled through a merit-based competition; rather federal agencies fill noncompetitive appointments by using special hiring authorities or by using methods such as transferring, reassigning or promoting current federal employees or reassigning former federal employees. Each vacancy announcement for a noncompetitive appointment specifies what types of applicants are eligible for the appointment.

Noncompetitive Schedule A Appointment: A federal job that can be made available to disabled applicants without competition. See Tip Sheet for Disabled Job Seekers.

Office of Personnel Management (OPM): Sets hiring procedures for all federal agencies in the Competitive Service. Some Excepted Service agencies also follow some OPM procedures, but the degree to which they do so varies from agency to agency.

Optional Application for Federal Employment (OF-612): Form that can be submitted with federal job application instead of a resume.

30 Percent or More Disabled Program: Program that makes some disabled veterans eligible to be hired into some federal jobs without competing against other applicants.

Promotion Potential: The promotion potential assigned to each job defines the highest level that can be reached by a person holding that job without competing against other applicants. In order to climb higher than the ceiling of your job's promotion potential, you will either have to land another job that has a higher promotion potential or convince your supervisor to extend your job's promotion potential — a task that is frequently complicated by tight budgets.

Reinstatement Eligibility: Right of former federal employees who previously held career or career-conditional jobs to:

1. Be noncompetitively rehired by the federal government into positions that are grades equal or lower than those previously held. (Note that applicants with reinstatement eligibility may also apply through open competitions for jobs that are at higher grades than previously held.)

2. Apply for jobs that are open only to applicants with Civil Service status.

For veterans and former career employees, reinstatement eligibility never expires. For others, reinstatement eligibility expires three years after end of federal employment. For more information about reinstatement eligibility, go to *opm.gov*, and click on the following sequence of links: "Career Opportunities" ... "Job FAQs" ... "Reinstatement Eligibility."

Reduction-in-Force (RIF): The federal government's version of a lay-off.

Security Clearance: Authorization awarded by the federal government to a federal employee or federal contractor to access classified materials needed to do a job. You can only get a security clearance if you meet the following conditions: 1) You work for a government agency or a federal contactor on a job that requires access to classified materials. 2) Your employer requests a security clearance for you; you cannot get a security clearance by applying to an agency or company yourself. 3) You pass a security clearance investigation — a comprehensive probe of your personal and professional life.

The depth of the security investigation and the type of security clearance it yields depends upon the sensitivity of the materials that you need to access. A security clearance may involve some combination of the following: 1) A review of records about you, including where you have worked, gone to school and lived. 2) A credit check. 3) A check of police records. 4) Interviews with you and people who know you. 5) A polygraph test. Beware that a history of drug abuse is among the most common reasons for being denied a security clearance.

It commonly takes weeks or months or even longer to receive a security clearance. Some job offers are contingent upon receipt of a security clearance.

Selecting Official: Person who makes the final selection of who to hire from most qualified candidates in a competitive examination. The selecting official is usually — but not always — the supervisor of the new employee.

Senior Executive Service: The federal government's corps of executive managers.

Special Hiring Authorities: Authorities that enable federal agencies to hire applicants who meet specified criteria without an open competition. Special hiring authorities are commonly used to noncompetitively appoint the following types of applicants to federal jobs:

- **Veterans:** Veterans are eligible for noncompetitive appointments to federal jobs under the Veterans' Employment Opportunities Act of 1998 (VEOA), the 30 percent or More Disabled Program, or the Veterans Recruitment Appointment. See Veterans Tip Sheet.

- **People With Disabilities:** People who have severe physical, cognitive or emotional disabilities may receive noncompetitive appointments to certain positions under Schedule A appointments. To be eligible for such appointments, an applicant must have a certification letter from a state vocational rehabilitation office or the Department of Veterans Affairs. See Tip Sheet for Applicants with Disabilities.

- **Displaced Federal Employees:** Federal employees who have been RIFED (RIF is short for Reduction in Force and is the federal government's version of a lay-off) and federal employees whose jobs have moved are eligible for noncompetitive appointments to some federal jobs through the Career Transition Assistance Program (CTAP) or Interagency Career Transition Program (ITAP).

- **Returned Peace Corps Volunteers (RPCVs):** May receive noncompetitive appointments during the first year after completion of their tour of duty.

- **Applicants to Internships, Student Jobs Programs and the Bilingual/Bicultural Program:** May receive noncompetitive appointments under programs listed in Chapter 3.

- **Former Federal Employees:** May receive noncompetitive appointments if have reinstatement eligibility and if seeking reinstatement to a grade that is equal or lower than previous grade.

Note that none of the categories of applicants listed above are guaranteed jobs; agencies are not required to hire any applicant. To be hired, all applicants must meet, and usually exceed, the minimum qualifications for a position. For more information about noncompetitive appointments, see Chapter 4.

Status: Possessed by current and former permanent federal employees working in agencies covered by Civil Service laws. (Includes employes hired under noncompetitive appointments working in the Competitive Service; excludes employees of agencies in the Excepted Service.) It is advantageous to have status because some federal jobs are only open to employees who have it.

Temporary Appointment: Temporary job that lasts for one year or less; usually no benefits are provided.

Term Appointment: Temporary job that usually lasts between one year and four years. Benefits are usually provided.

USAJOBS: The federal government's official jobs website. See *usajobs.opm.gov.*

Vacancy Announcement: A document describing one or more job openings at a federal agency.

Veterans Employment Opportunities Act of 1990 (VEOA): Program that allows veterans to apply for some federal jobs that would otherwise be off-limits to them. See Veterans Tip Sheet.

Veterans Preference: Preferential treatment given to some veterans, and some spouses and mothers of veterans, in competitions for federal jobs. See Veterans Tip Sheet.

Veterans Recruitment Appointment (VRA): Program that enables veterans to be hired into temporary positions that may lead to permanent positions. See Veterans Tip Sheet.

ABOUT LILY WHITEMAN

CAREER COACHING

Lily Whiteman has participated in government job selections from every conceivable angle. She is a:

➤ **Federal Career Coach:** Lily has helped hundreds of professionals land jobs, earn promotions and enhance their communication skills. Currently based at the United States Mint, she leads popular seminars and provides one-on-one coaching on how to write resumes, application essays (KSAs) and cover letters, and how to ace interviews.

➤ **Veteran of numerous federal selection panels:** These experiences have given Lily first-hand, behind-the-scenes insights into how federal selection panels operate and how to win over these panels. Moreover, Lily has rounded out her own experiences by interviewing dozens and dozens of other federal hiring managers, whose advice is also included in *Get Hired!*

➤ **Successful applicant:** Lily practices what she preaches: Since 1991, she has used the techniques described in *Get Hired!* to land successively higher positions in four federal agencies, including the Vice-President's National Partnership for Reinventing Government.

As a Career Coach, hiring manager and federal employee, Lily has reviewed piles and piles of federal job applications. She knows what works, what doesn't and why. She is an expert in:

➤ Steering federal job-seekers through their confusion and around common application traps.

➤ Transforming forgettable, ho-hum applications into impressive, memorable applications that beat the competition.

➤ Translating her understanding of the federal selection process into accurate, practical and easy-to-follow guidance.

➤ Relating to federal job applicants with an insider's empathy and humor.

COMMUNICATIONS CONSULTING

Lily is a sought-after freelance writer and speaker; she is known for her informative, entertaining approaches. Lily has led communications seminars and provided consulting services to many prestigious organizations, including the National Science Foundation, the American Association for the Advancement of Science and the Council of Science Editors. In addition, Lily has published more than 20 articles on communications and other topics in flight magazines, law journals and other national publications. Her consulting websites are at *IGotTheJob.net* and *CrystalClearCommunication.com*.

EDUCATION

Lily earned a Masters in Public Health and a Masters in Environmental Management from Yale University, and completed graduate work in professional writing at Carnegie Mellon University. She holds a B.A. from Wesleyan University (Connecticut).

INDEX

FPMI Publications

- Advanced MSPB Practitioner's Handbook

- Building the Optimum Organization for Federal Agencies: The Guide for Developing the MEO through Functionality Assessment, A-76 or Other Strategic Sourcing Study

- The Human Resources Role in Managing Organization Change

- Desktop Guide to Unfair Labor Practices

- Understanding Employee and Family-Friendly Leave Policies

- The Federal Manager's Guide to Liability

- The Federal Manager's Guide to EEO

- Supervisor's Guide to Federal Labor Relations

- The Federal Manager's Handbook

- Face To Face: A Guide For Government Supervisors Who Counsel Problem Employees

- The Federal Manager's Guide To Discipline

- Understanding The Federal Retirement Systems

- Federal Manager's Guide to Improving Employee Performance

- Performance Management: Performance Standards & You

- Managing The Civilian Workforce

- The Bargaining Book

- Practical Ethics for the Federal Employee

- The Federal Employee's Guide to EEO

- Managing Leave and Attendance Problems

- Managing Effectively in the Federal Government

- A Federal Manager's Guide to Measuring Organizational Performance

For more information and to order books and libraries offered by FPMI, visit the website at www.fpmi.com.

FPMI Newsletters

• *FedNews OnLine*®
(a free daily e-newsletter covering federal issues and concerns.
Get it! www.fednews-online.com)

• *Federal Labor & Employee Relations Update*

• *EEO Update*

FPMI e-Packages

EEO Update e-Package

The *EEO Update* e-Package is an Internet-based newsletter that provides access to summaries of significant EEO case decisions as well as significant news and features on EEO events occurring in the federal government.

Federal Labor & Employee Relations Update e-Package

The *Federal Labor & Employee Relations Update* e-Package is an Internet-based service that provides articles, full-text decisions, case summaries and key points of the most significant FLRA, FSIP and MSPB cases each month.

All packages are sold through an affordable annual license that provides an agency unlimited access to this Internet service.

To learn more about FPMI newsletters and Internet e-Packages, visit www.fpmi.com.